INSPIRE / PLAN / DISCOVER / EXPERIENCE

FLORENCE
AND TUSCANY

FLORENCE AND TUSCANY

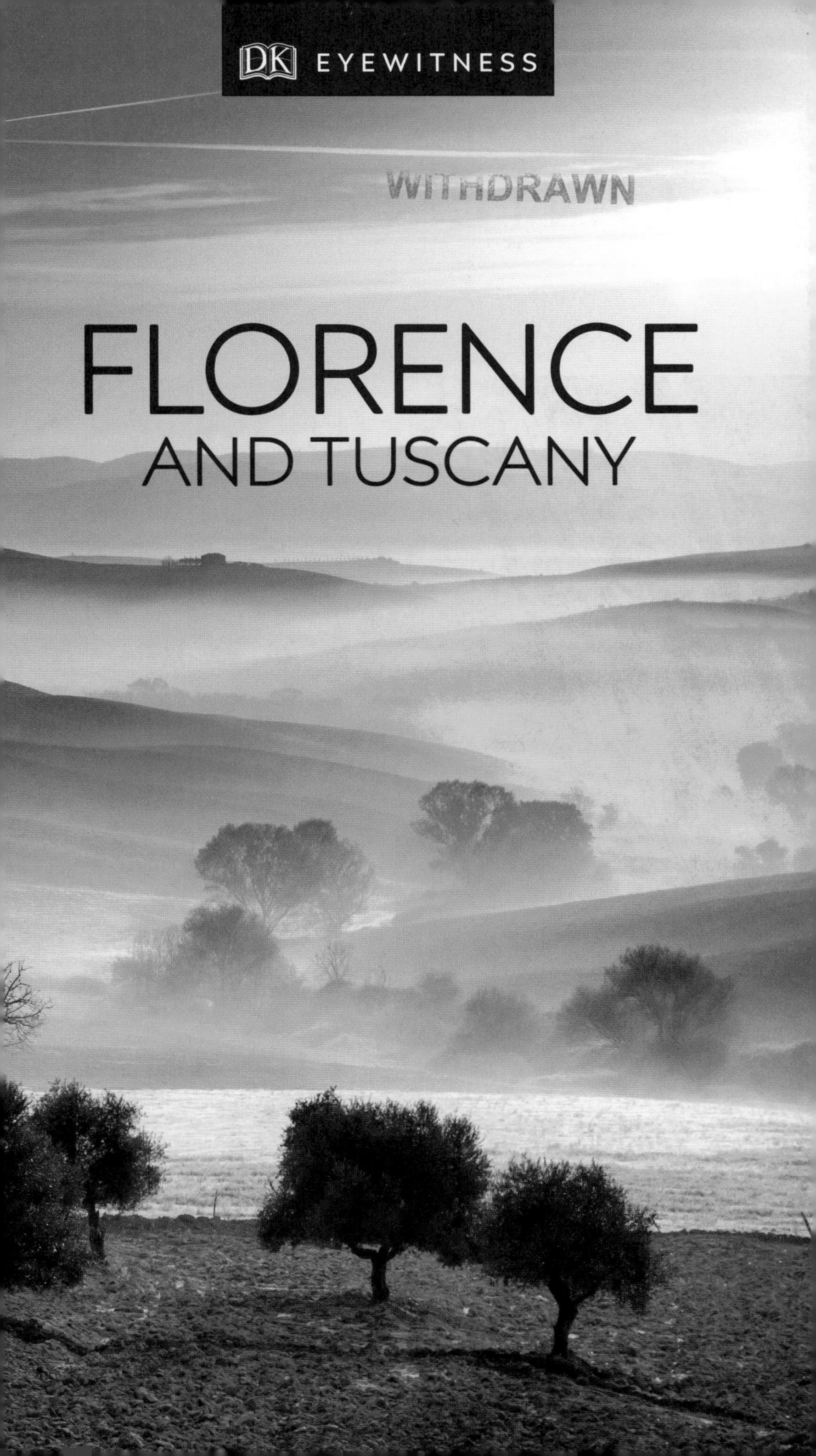

CONTENTS

DISCOVER 6

EXPERIENCE FLORENCE 56

EXPERIENCE TUSCANY 132

NEED TO KNOW 234

Left: The courtyard of Siena's Palazzo Pubblico
Previous page: Misty fields near Pienza

DISCOVER

An evening view over Florence

WELCOME TO FLORENCE AND TUSCANY

Awe-inspiring Renaissance masterpieces. Ruby-red Chianti and pungent pecorino cheese. Cypress-covered hills and maze-like medieval towns, packed with age-old tradition. Whatever your dream trip to Florence and Tuscany includes, this DK Eyewitness Travel Guide is the perfect companion.

1 Florence's Palantine Gallery in the Palazzo Pitti.

2 A rustic farmhouse and cypress trees in Tuscany.

3 The dramatic exterior of the Santa Croce in Florence.

4 The view over the Duomo and rooftops in Florence.

As the birthplace of the Renaissance, Florence and Tuscany's artistic legacy is second to none. From Michelangelo's *David* to the Leaning Tower of Pisa, the sheer concentration of world-famous icons is breathtaking. The region's culinary heritage is equally rich, with every town and village producing its own unique delicacies: try a *panino col lampredotto* in Florence, go truffle hunting in San Miniato or sup *cacciucco* in Livorno. And no trip to Tuscany would be complete without sampling the local wine. Brunello di Montalcino, Vernaccia di San Gimignano – these celebrated names are just the tip of the iceberg when it comes to the vast array of exquisite varieties on offer.

Dating back to medieval times, Tuscany's appealing towns and cities are a perfectly preserved slice of the past. Their historic streets come alive at festival time, with thrilling tournaments and vibrant costumed pageants. The countryside is calmer but no less colourful: the mesmerising landscapes include the lush green hills of Val d'Orcia, the rainbow-coloured beaches of Elba and the otherworldly white marble quarries of Carrara. Urban or rural, this is Italy at its most truly picturesque.

From the winding streets of Florence to the outer reaches of the Tuscan Archipelago, we've broken the region down into easily navigable chapters, with detailed itineraries, expert local knowledge and colourful, comprehensive maps to help you plan the perfect visit. Whether you're staying for a weekend, a week, or longer, this Eyewitness guide will ensure that you see the very best the region has to offer. Enjoy the book, and enjoy Florence and Tuscany.

REASONS TO LOVE FLORENCE AND TUSCANY

Sublime landscapes, Renaissance artworks, picturesque towns, and delectable local dishes and wines: there are so many reasons to love Florence and Tuscany. Here, we pick some of our favourites.

1 CITYSCAPES

The wide-open view of central Florence from Piazzale Michelangelo *(p94)*, taking in the famous Duomo and Ponte Vecchio, is quite simply awe-inspiring.

VAL D'ORCIA LANDSCAPES *2*

Gentle hillsides, pockets of woodland, and rows of cypresses along winding lanes and around the occasional stone chapel: picture-perfect Val d'Orcia *(p188)* is a photographer's paradise.

3 SIENA'S PIAZZA DEL CAMPO

The piazza is the centre of community life in Tuscany and the welcome upon entering the delightful shell-shaped heart of Siena *(p173)* is one of the warmest.

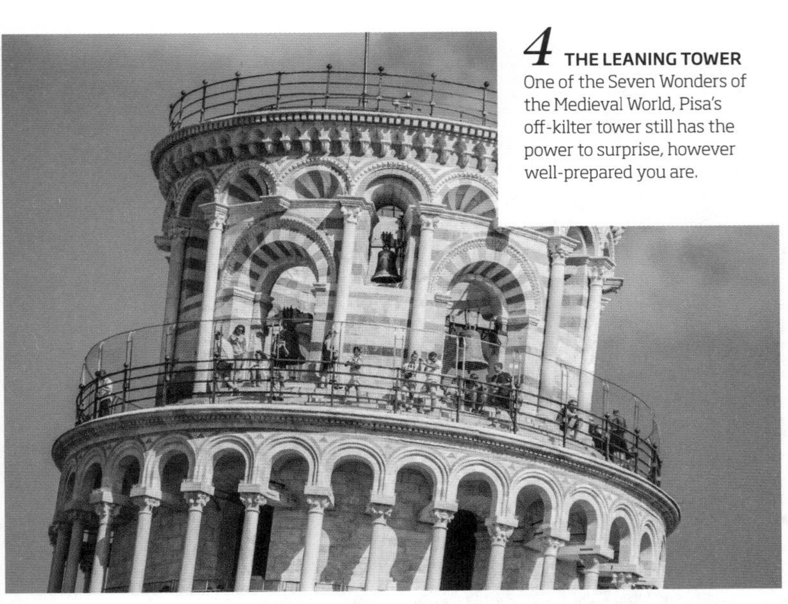

4 THE LEANING TOWER

One of the Seven Wonders of the Medieval World, Pisa's off-kilter tower still has the power to surprise, however well-prepared you are.

FLORENCE FASHION 5

Italy's original capital of fashion, Florence oozes style. Many of the world's top designers, including Gucci, hail from the city; view their eye-catching wares around Via de' Tornabuoni *(p82)*.

TUSCAN FOOD 6

Italian cuisine is a world favourite, and Tuscany's is among the tastiest. Pride of place goes to the chunky Fiorentina steak: a treat for meat lovers.

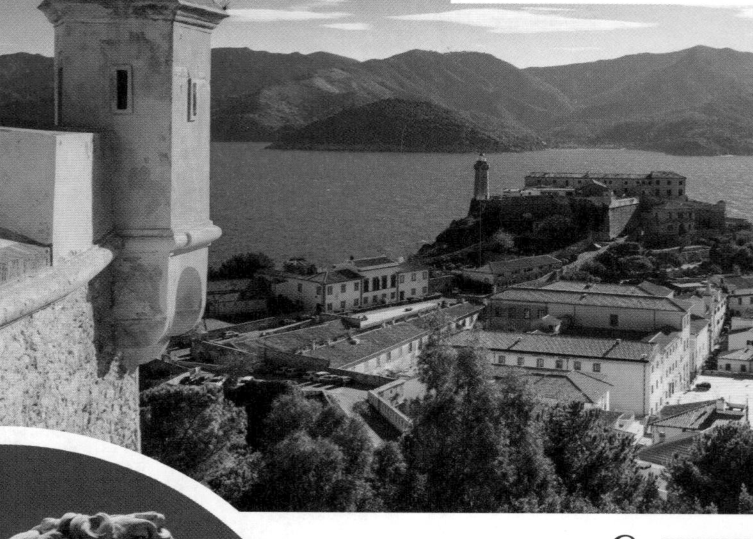

7 ELBA AND THE ISLANDS

Salty sea spray and sunbeams sparkling on the water – a boat trip around Elba and the Tuscan Archipelago *(p224)* is a joy for the senses.

SAN GIMIGNANO 8

With its forest of towers and charming medieval centre built of stone, San Gimignano *(p164)* is the quintessential Tuscan hill town. Wander at will through the pretty piazzas and alluring lanes.

9 MICHELANGELO'S MARBLE

Relive the creation of Michelangelo's *David* by touring the marble quarries of Carrara *(p213)* and then seeing the sculpture itself in the Galleria dell'Accademia *(p108)* in Florence.

ARTISTIC MASTERPIECES *10*

As the birthplace of countless Old Masters, Tuscany's artistic heritage is unparalleled. Immerse yourself in the breathtaking collections of world-class galleries such as the Uffizi *(p70)*.

ETRUSCAN TREASURES *11*

Exploring southwest Tuscany's Etruscan sites offers a fascinating insight into the ancient world. Trace the footsteps of the region's founders along the sunken roads of the Vie Cave *(p231)*.

TUSCAN WINES *12*

Brunello di Montalcino, Vino Nobile di Montepulciano and Chianti Classico – many of Italy's finest wines are Tuscan. Don't miss *cantucci* with Vin Santo as an end-of-meal treat.

EXPLORE FLORENCE AND TUSCANY

This guide divides Florence and Tuscany into six colour-coded sightseeing areas, as shown on this map. Find out more about each area on the following pages.

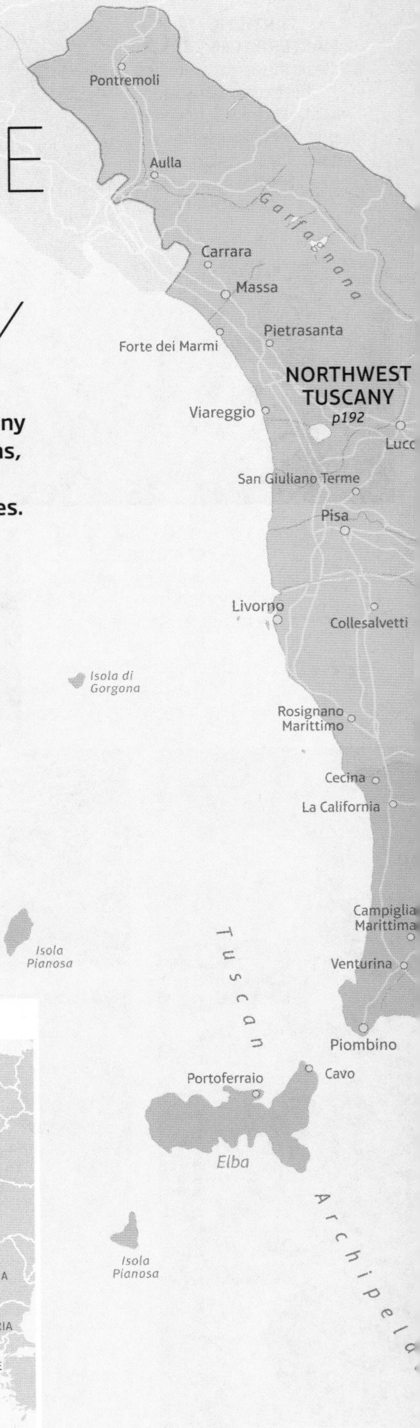

NORTHWEST TUSCANY *p192*

Pontremoli
Aulla
Garfagnana
Carrara
Massa
Pietrasanta
Forte dei Marmi
Viareggio
Lucc
San Giuliano Terme
Pisa
Livorno
Collesalvetti
Isola di Gorgona
Rosignano Marittimo
Ligurian Sea
Cecina
La California
Campiglia Marittima
Isola Pianosa
Venturina
Tuscan Archipela
Piombino
Cavo
Portoferraio
Elba
Isola Pianosa

WESTERN EUROPE

North Sea
SWEDEN
DENMARK
UNITED KINGDOM
POLAND
GERMANY
CZECH REP.
AUSTRIA
SWITZ.
HUNGARY
FRANCE
CROATIA
ROMANIA
SERBIA
BULGARIA
ITALY
SPAIN
GREECE
ALGERIA
TUNISIA
Mediterranean Sea

Bologna
EMILIA-ROMAGNA
Ravenna
Imola
Forlì
Abetone
Vernio
Mugello
Pistoia
Pescia
Agliana
Borgo San Lorenzo
Prato
Fiesole
NORTHEAST TUSCANY
p138
FLORENCE
p56
Empoli
Pontassieve
Bagno a Ripoli
ntedera
San Miniato
Poppi
Bibbiena
nsacco
Reggello
CENTRAL TUSCANY
p152
Chianti
Castelfiorentino
San Giovanni Valdarno
Certaldo
Sansepolcro
Montevarchi
Levane
San Gimignano
Poggibonsi
Bergamo
Arezzo
Monterchi
Città di Castello
Volterra
Monteriggioni
Castiglion Fiorentinó
Siena
Monteroni d'Arbia
Cortona
Umbertide
Sinalunga
Montieri
San Galgano
SOUTHEAST TUSCANY
p168
Gabekkino
Lago Trasimeno
Pienza
Massa Marittima
Roccastrada
Montepulciano
Montalcino
Perugia
Chiusi
Follonica
Paganico
SOUTHWEST TUSCANY
p220
UMBRIA
Castell' Azzara
Grosseto
Maremma
Sovana
Orvieto
Scanscano
Pitigliano
Lago di Bolsena
Montefiascone
Isola del Giglio
Orbetello
Monte Argentario
0 kilometres 25
0 miles 25
N

→

1 The Duomo dominating Florence's skyline.

2 Piazza Santo Spirito.

3 Leather goods for sale in Florence's Mercato Nuovo.

4 Interior of Palazzo Pitti.

2 DAYS
A Tour of Florence

Day 1

Morning Start the day at the magnificent Piazza Duomo *(p66)*; climb Brunelleschi's enormous dome and admire the famous bronze Baptistry doors before strolling to Piazza della Signoria *(p68)*, where a replica of Michelangelo's *David* can be seen. Just around the corner, Mercato Nuovo sells exquisite Florentine souvenirs, including leather goods and speciality paper. After crossing Ponte Vecchio *(p74)*, turn left and walk along the river for lunch at Osteria Antica Mescita San Niccolò.

Afternoon Refuelled and refreshed, you will be ready for the walk up to Piazzale Michelangelo *(p94)* for awe-inspiring views. Carry on to San Miniato al Monte before taking the shorter – but steeper – Salita al Monte back down the hill, stopping at the rose garden. Cross the Ponte alle Grazie bridge to reach Santa Croce *(p90)*. Explore the interior of this incredible church, paying your respects to the tombs of Michelangelo, Machiavelli and Galileo. Don't leave without a visit to the leather school at the rear.

Evening Have dinner at the excellent Gucci Garden *(Piazza della Signoria 10)*.

Day 2

Morning Make the San Lorenzo complex, including the startling Cappelle Medicee *(p114)*, today's first stop, and follow it with a look around the adjacent Mercato Centrale. See the frescoes at Santa Maria Novella *(p106)* nearby before making a tiny detour to the extraordinary Officina Profumo Farmaceutica SMN, a historic perfumery *(p109)*. For a tasty lunch and a glass of wine, try Cantinetta Antinori, just beyond Santa Maria Novella.

Afternoon After lunch, stroll past the designer stores of Via de' Tornabuoni, stopping just before the river at the Museo Ferragamo *(p82)* to see shoes worn by some of Hollywood's classic stars. Cross the bridge to the Oltrarno district where the shopping theme changes to antiques on the way to Palazzo Pitti *(p120)*. After visiting the rich interiors and galleries of this 15th-century palace, end the afternoon with a relaxing stroll around the Boboli Gardens *(p124)*.

Evening Reward yourself with an aperitivo in Piazza Santo Spirito *(p128)* before dining at one of the Oltrarno's authentic eateries, such as L'Brindellone *(Piazza Piattellina 10)*.

1

2

3

7 DAYS

In Tuscany

Day 1

Morning Begin your week in Pisa at the celebrated Leaning Tower and the Campo dei Miracoli *(p200)*. Climb the tower and explore the impressive Duomo and Baptistry before tucking into a traditional *cecina* (chickpea fritter) for lunch at Il Montino *(Via del Monte 1)*.

Afternoon Wander around the historic streets of central Pisa *(p196)* and then take the train to Florence.

Evening End the day with a stroll by the Arno River and a hearty Tuscan dinner at Il Latini *(Via dei Palchetti 6R)*.

Day 2

Morning Dedicate the morning to the Uffizi *(p70)* followed by a *panino* and a glass of wine at I Due Fratellini *(p83)*, just off Piazza della Signoria.

Afternoon Wander from the Duomo *(p66)* to the Ponte Vecchio *(p74)* and explore the antiques shops and quiet backstreets of the Oltrarno *(p117)*. Afterwards, visit the Brancacci Chapel to see the famous *Life of St Peter* frescoes *(p126)*.

Evening Walk to Piazzale Michelangelo *(p94)* for panoramic views of the city at sunset before dining at Enoteca Fuori Porta *(p95)* at the bottom of the hill.

Day 3

Morning Drive from Florence along the Strada Chiantigiana, through the picturesque vine-covered hills of Chianti *(p156)*. Stop at Casa del Chianti Classico in Radda, and have lunch at the bistrot.

Afternoon Drive to San Gimignano *(p164)* to see its towers, then head for Siena.

Evening En route to Siena, stop in at the walled village of Monteriggioni *(p167)* for dinner at Il Pozzo *(Piazza Roma 2)*.

Day 4

Morning Start your day at Siena's striking tiger-striped Duomo *(p176)* and, after

1 Pisa's Leaning Tower.

2 Cyclists crossing the Arno.

3 The hilltop town of San Gimignano.

4 Wheels of Pecorino cheese.

5 The centre of Pitigliano.

coffee on Piazza del Campo, climb Torre del Mangia *(p173)*. Try nearby Osteria Il Grattacielo *(Via dei Pontani 8)* for lunch.

Afternoon Explore the narrow medieval streets of central Siena, visit the serene Santuario e Casa di Santa Caterina *(p175)* and stroll in the nearby Orto de' Pecci, a green oasis in the heart of Siena.

Evening For a tasty fresh pasta dinner, head to Osteria da Cice *(Via S. Pietro 32)*.

Day 5

Morning Dedicate today to the region's best food and wine, starting at the hill town of Montalcino *(p188)*, some 40 km (25 miles) from Siena. Enjoy a tasting of Brunello at the Fattoria dei Barbi winery *(p189)* and settle down for a leisurely lunch at their bistrot.

Afternoon Nearby Pienza *(p191)* is famous for its pecorino (sheep's cheese). To buy some of the best, drop into local delicatessen Monaci Remo *(Via Tenente Niccolo' Piccolomini 2)*.

Evening End the day by visiting the ancient wine cellars and trying the Vino Nobile in Montepulciano *(p190)*.

Day 6

Morning Continue south to reach Pitigliano *(p231)*, a picturesque medieval town clamped to a tufa ridge. Explore the narrow streets and take in the dizzying views before grabbing lunch at Trattoria Il Grillo *(Via Cavour 18)*.

Afternoon From here it's a 5-km (3-mile) walk along Vie Cave to pretty Sovana *(p230)*. Walk or take the bus back to Pitigliano and drive to Saturnia *(p230)*.

Evening Spend the evening dining and using the spa at Terme di Saturnia *(p230)*.

Day 7

Spend a leisurely final day at the fishing village of Porto Ercole *(p233)*. Enjoy a meal at one of the many seafood restaurants before making the journey home.

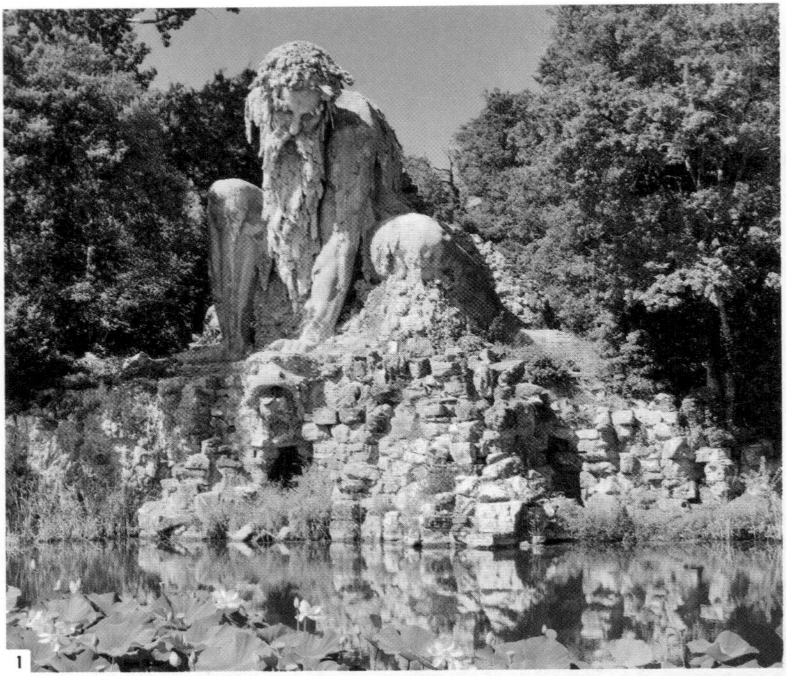

1

2

3

4

←

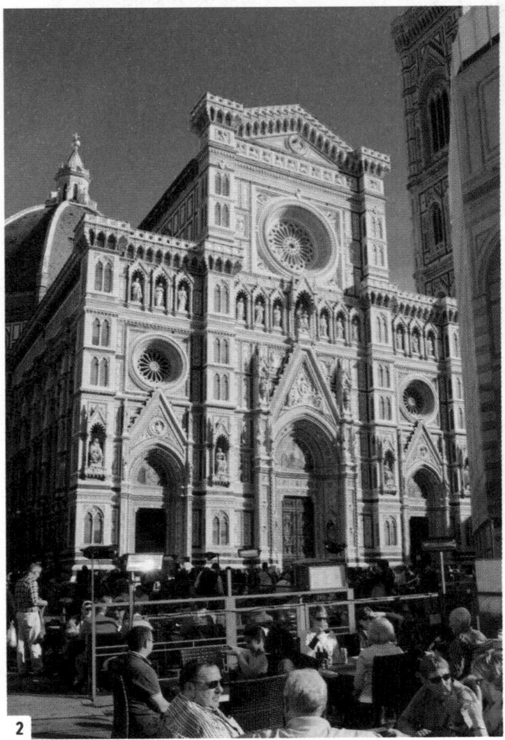

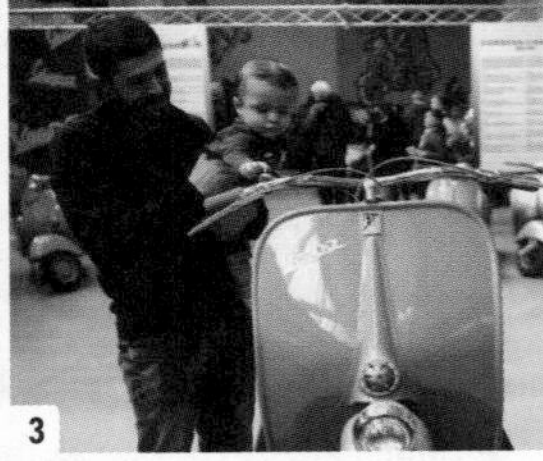

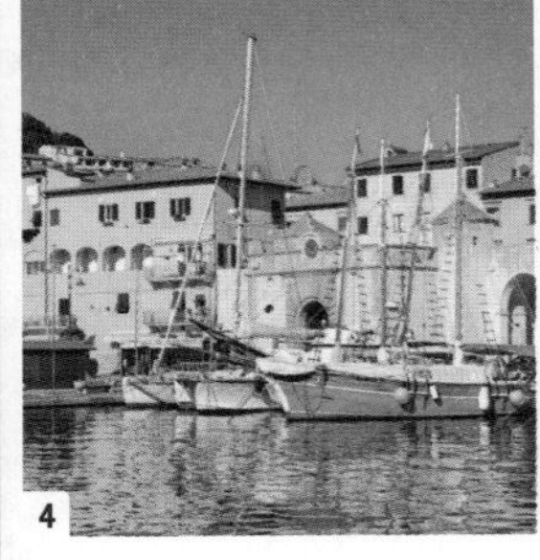

1 Parco Pratolino.

2 Florence's magnificent Duomo.

3 Piaggio Vespa museum.

4 Portoferraio.

10 DAYS

In Florence and Tuscany

Day 1

Morning Start the first day of your road trip through Tuscany by exploring the pretty town of Palazzuolo sul Senio *(p145)*. Drive on to the excellent farmhouse eatery La Selva di Frena *(Via Frena 1422)* near Firenzuola for lunch, enjoying the peace and quiet of the wooded hillsides of Mugello on the way.

Afternoon Continue past Scarperia *(p145)* to Parco di Pratolino *(p146)*, where you can stretch your legs with a stroll around the gardens. Make a quick stop in Fiesole *(p128)* before arriving in Florence.

Evening End the day with a night out in Florence's Oltrarno district, with a meal of genuine Tuscan food at Trattoria Cammillo *(57 Borgo San Jacopo)*.

Day 2

Morning Start early and go straight to see Florence's magnificent Duomo and Baptistry *(p66)*. From here it's a short walk to Piazza della Signoria *(p68)* and the Ponte Vecchio; cross the bridge and stroll along the riverside to the San Niccolò neighbourhood, where the centuries-old Osteria Antica Mescita San Niccolò *(60 Via di San Niccolò)* makes an ideal lunch stop.

Afternoon Take the short but steep walk up to Piazzale Michelangelo *(p94)* for stunning views of the city. Cross back over the Arno to Piazza Santa Croce *(p87)* and, after exploring the splendid church, visit the historic leather school *(p91)* in the former monastery at its rear.

Evening Enjoy a drink in Piazza Santo Spirito and then spend another evening among the many bars and restaurants of the Oltrarno.

Day 3

Morning Take the Fi-Pi-Li dual carriageway west from Florence towards Pisa, with a slight detour to Pontedera to see the Piaggio Vespa museum *(p199)*. Once you reach Pisa have a stroll around the centre and a coffee at one of the bars in Piazza Cairoli by the river, leaving the Leaning Tower for the afternoon. For lunch, try Pisa's speciality *cecina* (chickpea fritters) – you can find them in many informal eateries around town.

Afternoon Dedicate the afternoon to exploring the iconic Campo dei Miracoli *(p200)*: climb the Leaning Tower and visit the beautiful Romanesque Duomo and Baptistry.

Evening Take a table in the delightful garden at Osteria il Fantasma dell'Opera *(Via Palestro 20)*, which serves local dishes and excellent pizza.

Day 4

Morning Leave Pisa and drive south, enjoying the sea views en route before reaching Bolgheri *(p228)* in time for a pre-booked winery tour and tasting. Follow it with a quick swim in the sea and lunch at a beachside restaurant in Marina di Castagneto Carducci.

Afternoon Make the short drive to Piombino and catch the ferry to Elba. Spend the rest of the day exploring Portoferraio *(p226)*, making sure to have a look at Napoleon's one-time residence, Palazzina Napoleonica.

Evening Walk down to Ristorante Le Viste on the beach of the same name for dinner on the terrace while watching the sun set over the sea. →

1

5

4

Day 5

Morning Take a tour of Elba, setting off from Portoferraio *(p226)* towards Napoleon's countryside residence, Villa San Martino, then following the coast road anti-clockwise round the island. Marciana Marina has a sandy beach if you fancy a swim, or you can take the cable-car from Marciana Alta to the top of Monte Capanne *(p226)*.

Afternoon Continue on round to the hilltop village of Capoliveri *(p227)* in southern Elba and then to Porto Azzurro *(p227)* for the rest of the day. Here, relax with a swim or a stroll around the marina.

Evening There are plenty of seafront restaurants to choose from here; pick your favourite and settle in for a dinner with a view.

Day 6

Morning Return to the mainland first thing and explore the fascinating Etruscan and Roman remains at the archaeological area of Populonia *(p228)* near Piombino.

Afternoon Carry on south along the coast road to the Punta Ala promontory *(p229)*. Check in to the Golf Hotel Punta Ala and take your pick of afternoon activities from the hotel's spa, private beach and 18-hole golf course.

Evening After a restful afternoon, venture no further than the hotel's restaurant for a leisurely dinner.

Day 7

Morning Revitalized after your stay at Punta Ala, don walking boots to explore the Parco Naturale della Maremma *(p229)*. Pick up fresh produce for a picnic lunch from the Da Rita kiosk *(Via Barbicato 54, Alberese)* on your way to the entrance at the Alberese visitor centre.

Afternoon Leave the coast and drive inland, reaching the lovely hilltop village of Montalcino *(p188)* in time to visit one of the wineries in the historic centre – the wines made here are some of Italy's best.

Evening Spend the night at nearby Bagno Vignoni *(p188)*, with its unusual piazza dominated by a spa pool.

1 Hilltop town of Capoliveri.
2 Barrels of Montalcino wine.
3 *Legend of the True Cross* fresco.
4 A quaint street in Pienza.
5 Piazza Grande in Arezzo.

Day 8

Morning A camera is essential this morning as you explore the idyllic Val d'Orcia *(p188)*. You can enjoy a stunning panorama of the area over lunch at Terrazza Val d'Orcia in Pienza *(Viale Santa Caterina 1/3)*.

Afternoon Head east for more wonderful views and Renaissance palazzi at Montepulciano *(p190)*, perhaps picking up a bottle of the famous Vino Nobiledi Montepulciano from one of the town's historic cellars, before continuing on to the ancient city of Cortona *(p182)*.

Evening Spend the evening among Cortona's pretty piazzas. Trattoria La Grotta *(3 Piazza Baldelli)* is our recommendation for dinner.

Day 9

Morning Dedicate today to exploring the narrow stone alleys and churches of Cortona's historic centre. Beginning at Santa Margherita, wind your way up to the Fortezza Medicea, where you can have lunch at the bistro inside the castle.

Afternoon Visit the tranquil wooded Eremo Le Celle Franciscan complex just outside town, before getting back on the road to reach Arezzo *(p178)* for the evening.

Evening Once settled in Arezzo, head to the Piazza Grande. Here you can sit back with a drink at one of the bars overlooking the square before your evening meal.

Day 10

Morning Make sure to pre-book a visit to the Basilica of San Francesco *(p180)*, to view Piero della Francesca's stunning *Legend of the True Cross* fresco cycle. Follow this by purchasing picnic supplies at the Dal Moro deli on nearby Via Cavour, then stroll past Casa Vasari and the Duomo before choosing a spot in Il Prato park to enjoy your feast.

Afternoon End your journey through this truly delightful region with a walk around the ramparts of the Fortezza Medicea *(p175)*, with its glorious views across the Tuscan countryside.

Colourful Street Art

In between the galleries and museums, keep an eye out for art of a less classical kind. Pisa is home to the colourful *Tuttomondo* mural *(p198)* by Keith Haring, the American artist's last public work, while central Florence is dotted with Blub's reimaginings of famous portraits, in which the subjects are depicted underwater wearing a snorkel and mask. Clet, a French artist whose works adorn numerous street signs, has a studio in Florence's San Niccolò district. Explore the latest street art with the city's map of spaces available for approved open-air works *(www.firenzestreetart.com)*.

→

Street artists re-creating a Renaissance masterpiece on the pavements of Florence

Did You Know?

Copies of Michelangelo's *David* can be seen in Florence's Piazza della Signoria and Piazzale Michelangelo.

FLORENCE AND TUSCANY FOR ART LOVERS

Tuscany is a paradise for art lovers, with countless world-famous masterpieces, a multitude of stunning cities of art – including Florence, the undisputed home of the Renaissance – and a thriving contemporary art scene. With the region's inspiring landscapes, it's no wonder that so many top artists were drawn to work here.

The Uffizi

This museum *(p70)* is the ultimate Renaissance primer, with masterpieces by some of Italy's greats: Giotto, Botticelli, Leonardo da Vinci, Michelangelo, Raphael, Titian, Caravaggio and beyond. Choose your favourite from the 1,700 artworks on display – just beware overload and an attack of Stendhal, or Florence, Syndrome, a psychosomatic illness triggered by viewing lots of beautiful works of art quick succession.

→

Paintings and sculpture on display in one of the Uffizi's elegant galleries

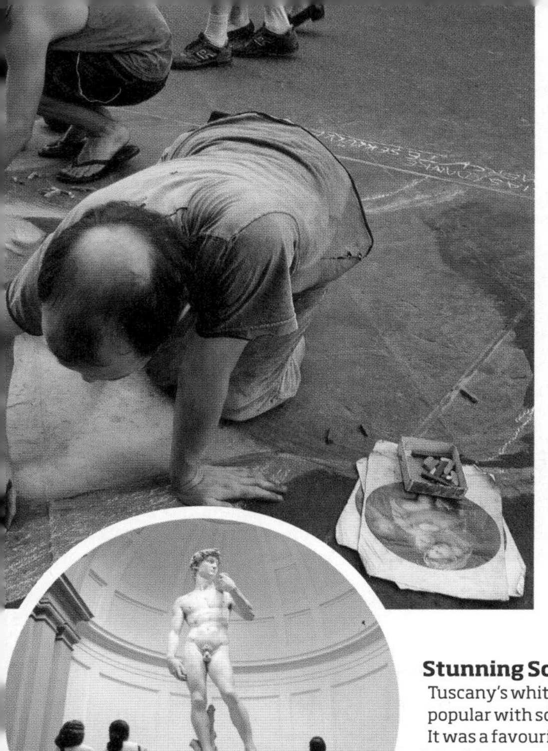

RENAISSANCE ARTISTS

Donatello (1386-1466)
The first Renaissance sculptor, who worked out perspective before the painters.

Leonardo da Vinci (1452-1519)
The ultimate Renaissance man: a painter, proto-scientist and inventor.

Michelangelo (1475-1564)
A sculptor of genius by his early 20s.

Stunning Sculptures

Tuscany's white Carrara marble has been popular with sculptors since Roman times. It was a favourite of Michelangelo, who used it for his famous *David*, and is still greatly prized by modern artists – Pietrasanta *(p212)* has numerous contemporary works on display.

←

Michelangelo's *David* in Florence's Galleria dell'Accademia

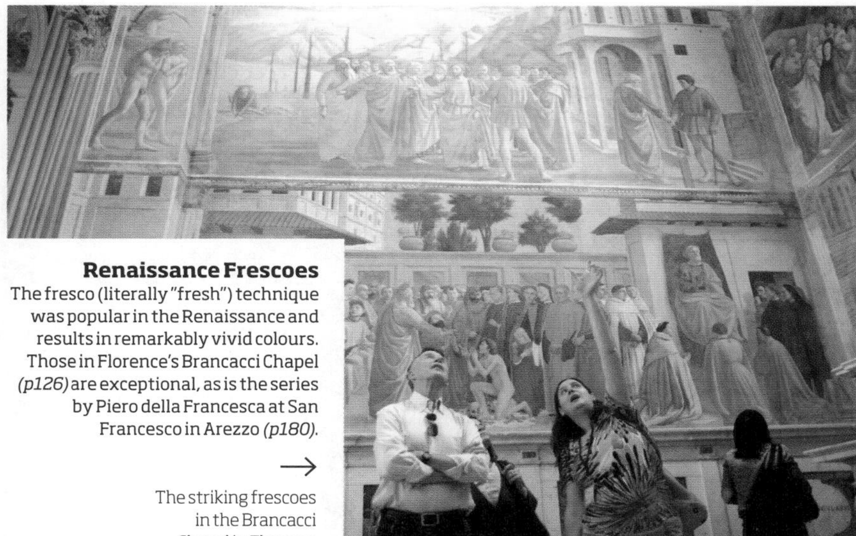

Renaissance Frescoes

The fresco (literally "fresh") technique was popular in the Renaissance and results in remarkably vivid colours. Those in Florence's Brancacci Chapel *(p126)* are exceptional, as is the series by Piero della Francesca at San Francesco in Arezzo *(p180)*.

→

The striking frescoes in the Brancacci Chapel in Florence

▽ Autumn by the Apennines

Bordering on the Apennine Mountains, the Garfagnana *(p210)*, Mugello *(p142)* and Casentino *(p148)* areas offer dramatic landscapes that alter drastically with the seasons. Visit in autumn when the colours of the trees are especially striking and local specialities such as mushrooms and chestnuts are at their best.

△ Viale dei Cipressi

The Viale dei Cipressi is a straight, 5-km- (3-mile-) long cypress-lined avenue that links the tiny San Guido oratory on the Via Aurelia to the village of Bolgheri. Elegantly grand, it owes its fame to a poem by Italy's first Nobel-winning poet, Giosuè Carducci, who lived here as a child.

FLORENCE AND TUSCANY FOR BEAUTIFUL LANDSCAPES

From the wooded mountains of the north to the wilder Maremma in the south, with the vine-covered hills of Chianti and a diverse stretch of Mediterranean coastline and islands in between, the incredible variety of landscapes in Tuscany make it one of Italy's most beautiful regions.

◁ Picture-Perfect Val d'Orcia

Landscapes don't get much more picturesque than Val d'Orcia's classic Tuscan scenes of gently undulating hills, narrow winding roads lined with cypresses, and the occasional chapel or fortress. Shaped in the Renaissance period, the area features on countless postcards and even has UNESCO World Heritage status.

△ Colourful Beaches

Thanks to the high concentration of minerals, the terrain on Elba *(p226)* displays an incredible array of colours. While the sands around Portoferraio are gleaming white, those at Terranera bay near Porto Azzurro glisten black due to the presence of hematite, and at Cala Seregola (Rio Marina) they appear reddish thanks to the iron ore once mined there. For quintessential fine golden sands, try Marina di Campo.

◁ Stunning Cityscapes

The towers that adorn many of Tuscany's piazzas are ideal for bird's-eye views of winding streets and traditional terracotta rooftops. For outstanding vistas over Florence, however, climb to Piazzale Michelangelo *(p94)*. Hilly Siena *(p172)* has startling panoramas around every corner; the rear view of Il Campo from Piazza Mercato is particularly striking.

▷ Alpi Apuane's "Snowy" Peaks

The marble-rich mountains near Carrara glisten such a brilliant white as to resemble snow from a distance, recalling the Alpine peaks of northern Italy. Get a little closer, however, and the quarry areas appear more like lunar landscapes – take a tour of the marble basins to experience their otherworldliness.

Buckets and Spades

Tuscany abounds in sandy beaches with shallow water, which are ideal for young children. Viareggio and the Versilia area *(p211)* are particularly well-off for beaches, while the resort of Marina di Bibbona is a favourite among families thanks to its relaxed atmosphere, spacious beach and entertainments such as the Bibbolandia fun park.

Building a sandcastle at the Marino di Campo beach on Elba

FLORENCE AND TUSCANY FOR FAMILIES

Families are at the centre of Italian life, so children receive a warm welcome wherever they go. An eclectic selection of family-oriented activities and attractions means that it's easy to keep kids entertained, and mealtimes are a breeze with a tempting array of child-friendly pizzas and pasta.

MUSEUMS FOR CHILDREN

Museo Leonardo da Vinci, Florence
An interactive collection of Da Vinci's weird and wonderful inventions *(p109)*.

Piccolo Museo dei Bambini, Borgo San Lorenzo
A multisensory museum specially for children, which includes a toy-swapping area *(p144)*.

Archeodromo, Poggibonsi
Medieval history is brought to life at full-sized reed and mud huts populated by costumed villagers *(p166)*.

Theme Park Fun

Exhilarating tree-top courses for all ages are on offer at adventure parks such as Il Gigante (Vaglia, opposite Parco Pratolino), while water parks like the Acqua Villages at Cecina and Follonica are perfect for cooling down in summer. Immerse yourself in a fairytale world at Collodi's Pinocchio Park *(p218)*, which also has a butterfly house and historic gardens, or spend a day thrill-seeking on the rides at Il Cavallino Matto (Castagneto Carducci).

Farm Experiences

Tuscany's Fattorie Didattiche, literally "educational farms", offer a fun, hands-on insight into traditional rural life. At Agriturismo Il Giardino *(www.agriturismoilgiardino.com)* kids can meet the animals, help with the olive harvest and take horse-riding lessons. In the Maremma *(p229)*, the *butteri* (traditional Tuscan cowboys) continue to work with the cattle at the Alberese estate *(www.alberese.com)*, where confident riders can join them on horseback.

→

Meeting the animals at Agriturismo Il Giardino

Tasty Treats

Italian food boasts some perennial favourites among children. An afternoon gelato is a delightful way to cool down, while a pizza dinner is a guaranteed hit (ask for a "pizza baby" for a smaller size).

←

Mouthwatering chocolate gelato, a treat that is guaranteed to please all the family

San Rossore Estate

Spend a day adventuring at the San Rossore Estate *(p198)*, a vast natural haven near Pisa. There are myriad ways to explore: try your hand at horse and pony-riding, hire a bicycle or pedal-powered rickshaw from the visitor centre, or, best of all, take a wagon ride through the nature reserve to the coast. Keep an eye out for the local fauna and flora, which includes white ibis and herons, wild boar, fallow deer, and the carnivorous plant *drosera*.

←

Splashing around in the pools at the Acqua Village in Follonica

→

One of the numerous deer that inhabit San Rossore Estate

Flavourful Festivals
Tuscany's countless food festivals *(sagre)* provide a fantastic opportunity to try local specialities. Highlights include the traditional steak festival held in Cortona (mid-August), the Lari cherry festival (last weekend May and first weekend June) and the *cacciucco* (hearty seafood soup) festival in Livorno (mid-June). The San Miniato truffle and Pienza cheese festivals (November and September respectively) celebrate some of the region's most prestigious produce.

→

Sampling the wares at a food festival in Livorno

FLORENCE AND TUSCANY FOR FOODIES

Traditionally hearty and flavoursome, Tuscany's largely simple specialities allow the character and taste of the region's excellent ingredients to shine through. Popular favourites include the chunky T-bone steaks, while vegetarians are well catered for with innumerable pasta and pizza options.

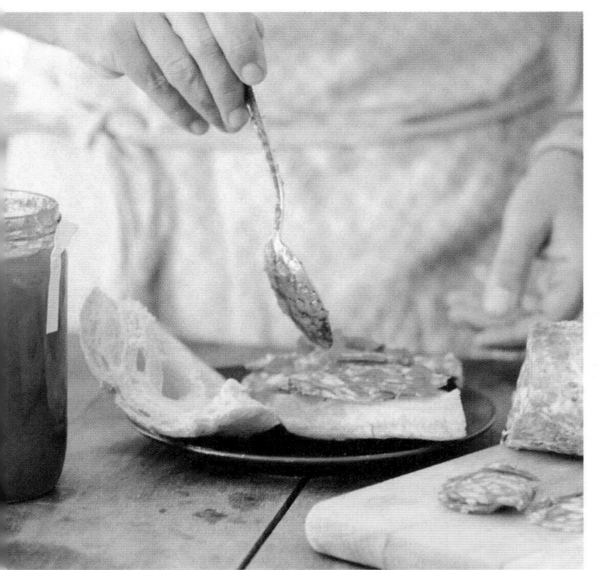

Tuscan Staples
The traditional salt-free Tuscan bread, *pane toscano* – which originated in the 12th century when Pisa placed a blockade on the trade of salt to Florence – is the perfect partner for the tasty local cold cuts and cheeses. Be sure to try *finocchiona* (the region's speciality salami flavoured with fennel seeds) and *lardo di colonnata* (pork aged with herbs and spices in marble vats), as well as the fabulous pecorino sheep's cheese from Pienza. A glass of Chianti or one of Tuscany's other red wines makes the ideal accompaniment.

Cold cuts and *pane toscano,* traditional Tuscan staples

Where to Eat

From three-star Michelin fine dining in Florence's Enoteca Pinchiorri *(www.enotecapinchiorri.it)* to street food, the choice of where to eat couldn't be more varied. For quality local produce in a relaxed environment, seek out delis like Gino Cacino (Siena) and butcher-eateries such as Macelleria Stiaccini (Castellina in Chianti) and Falorni (Greve in Chianti).

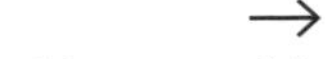

One of the gourmet dishes at Florence's Enoteca Pinchiorri

Florentine Street Food

Central Florence is peppered with kiosks laden with steaming pans of *lampredotto*, made from tripe and the city's most traditional and popular street food. The top stalls in the city include Nencioni (Piazza Mercato Nuovo), Nerbone (Mercato Centrale) and L'Antico Trippaio (Piazza de' Cimatori).

Ordering a *panino con lampredotto* from a stall in Florence

Innovative Supertuscans

While the majority of Tuscany's famous red wines (including Brunello and Chianti) must adhere to strict wine-making regulations, producers of the Supertuscans (wines made using non-traditional grapes and methods) can be much more flexible, enabling them to push for new heights with each vintage. The bottles aren't cheap, but they're worth trying for the ultimate Tuscan wine experience. Many, including Sassicaia by Tenuta San Guido (the very first Supertuscan) and Guado al Tasso by Antinori, are made in Bolgheri.

INSIDER TIP
Aleatico Passito

Try a ruby red Aleatico Passito from Elba as an alternative dessert wine to Vin Santo. It's ideal with *cantucci* biscuits or the island's traditional *schiaccia briaca* cake.

→ Vineyards at the picturesque Antinori winery

FLORENCE AND TUSCANY RAISE A GLASS

Vast and varied, Tuscany's wine scene is one of the most exciting in Italy. From punchy reds like Brunello di Montalcino to crisp whites such as Vernaccia di San Gimignano to aromatic Aleatico dessert wine, every bottle is packed with flavour. Tour the region's wineries to find your favourite.

Inviting Wine Bars

Wine is the lifeblood of Tuscany, so you are never far from an establishment where you can relax with a bottle of the latest vintage. In Florence, Fratelli Zanobini *(p111)* is traditional and easy-going, while the Chianti Classico consortium's contemporary Enoteca at Mercato Centrale *(p109)* offers guided tastings. In Chianti, enjoy a glass on the vine-canopied panoramic terrace at Il Vinaio *(Via S. Maria 22, Panzano)*, and in San Gimignano try DiVinorum *(Piazza Cisterna 30)*.

Watching the world go by with a glass of wine on an outdoor terrace in Siena

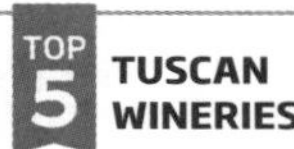

TOP 5 TUSCAN WINERIES

Il Borro
San Giustino Valdarno
A charming medieval village and estate *(p149)*.

Fattoria dei Barbi
Montalcino
Try the Brunello and visit the on-site museum.

Badia di Passignano
Tavarnelle Val di Pesa
Run by the prestigious Antinori family.

Castello di Brolio
Gaiole in Chianti
Wines have been made here since 1141.

Terre del Marchesato
Bolgheri
Tour the cellar and taste the Supertuscans.

Classic Chianti

Chiantis are made across the region, but the most prestigious varieties are produced in the designated Chianti Classico area between Florence and Siena *(p156)*. Learn about - and try - the wines at the Casa del Chianti Classico *(Circonvallazione Santa Maria 18, Radda)*. It has an excellent multisensorial display, a bistro and a delightful wine-bar.

→

The cellar of Castello di Verrazzano, a Chianti Classico producer in Greve in Chianti

Vernaccia di San Gimignano

Straw-coloured Vernaccia was Italy's first DOC certified wine, and has since been promoted to DOCG status (controlled and guaranteed designation of origin); its story is told at the multimedia La Rocca visitor centre *(Via della Rocca 1)*, in the higher part of San Gimignano. Discover the wine's fresh, almondy character with a tasting.

A glass of Vernaccia with a *cantucci* biscuit

Green Florence

For a peaceful respite from sightseeing in Florence, make your way to the city's wonderful parks and gardens. The historic gardens at Villa Bardini *(p96)* have stunning views over the city, while the elegant Boboli Gardens *(p124)* are part of the collective Medici villas and gardens World Heritage Site. There are charming rose and iris gardens off Piazzale Michelangelo *(p94)*, while Hotel AdAstra *(p129)* overlooks the lush Giardino Torrigiani, Europe's largest private urban garden.

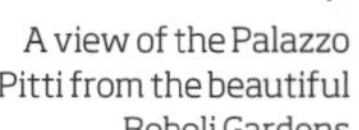

A view of the Palazzo Pitti from the beautiful Boboli Gardens

FLORENCE AND TUSCANY FOR VILLAS AND GARDENS

Tuscany is peppered with a multitude of impressively well-preserved historic villas. Built by wealthy families - including, of course, the Medici - and ranging in style from statuesque to austere to elaborate, almost all are surrounded by elegant formal gardens or beautifully landscaped parkland.

Napoleon's Elba Homes

During his exile on Elba, Napoleon enjoyed the run of two residences at Portoferraio: Villa dei Mulini, in a panoramic spot overlooking the sea, and Villa San Martino, in the countryside nearby *(p226)*. The latter is dominated by the grand mid-19th century Demidoff Gallery, housing a museum dedicated to Napoleon's memory.

→

Villa San Martino, Napoleon's country retreat while exiled on Elba

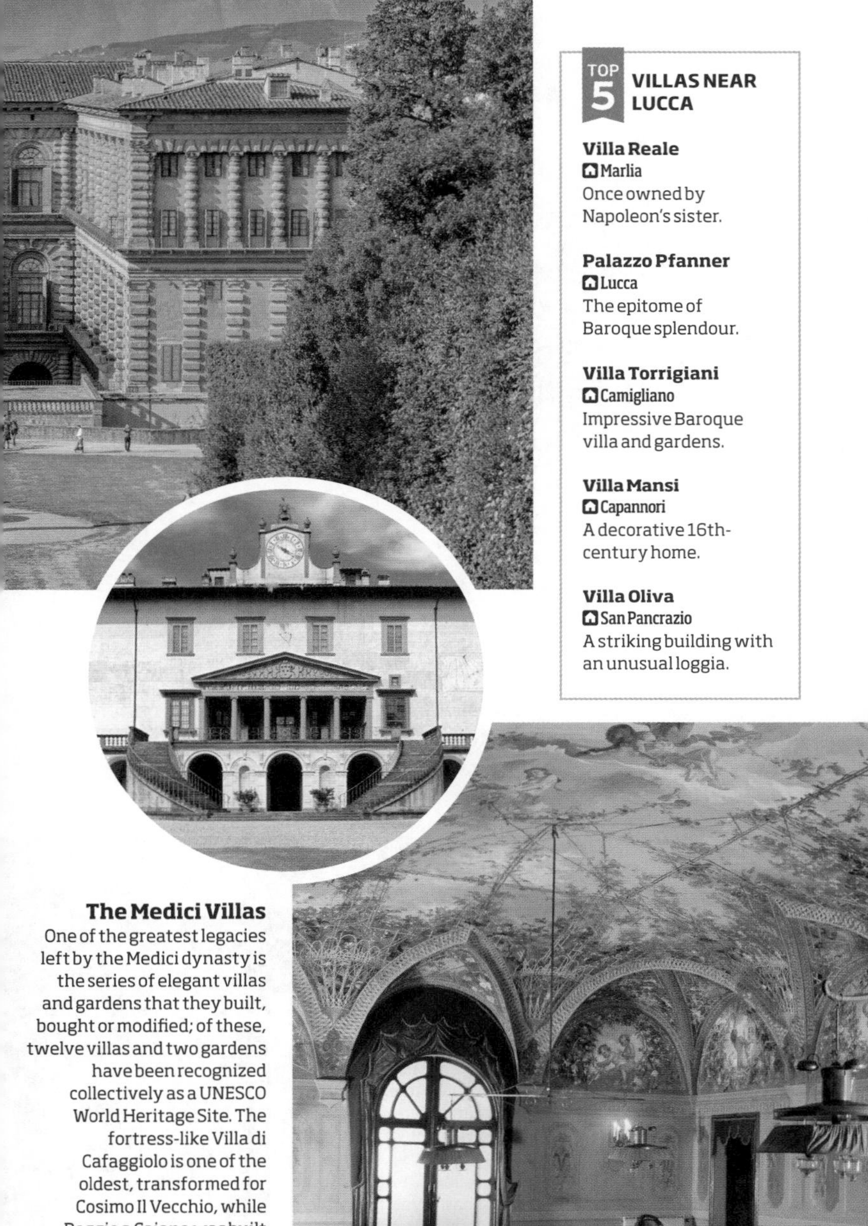

TOP 5 VILLAS NEAR LUCCA

Villa Reale
Marlia
Once owned by Napoleon's sister.

Palazzo Pfanner
Lucca
The epitome of Baroque splendour.

Villa Torrigiani
Camigliano
Impressive Baroque villa and gardens.

Villa Mansi
Capannori
A decorative 16th-century home.

Villa Oliva
San Pancrazio
A striking building with an unusual loggia.

The Medici Villas

One of the greatest legacies left by the Medici dynasty is the series of elegant villas and gardens that they built, bought or modified; of these, twelve villas and two gardens have been recognized collectively as a UNESCO World Heritage Site. The fortress-like Villa di Cafaggiolo is one of the oldest, transformed for Cosimo Il Vecchio, while Poggio a Caiano was built for Lorenzo the Magnificent. The interior, which today hosts a still-life collection, also contains some marvellous frescoes.

→ The opulent Poggio a Caiano villa, with its graceful façade *(inset)*

Boat Rides
Feel the refreshing effects of the sea air on a boat trip along the Tuscan coast; departure points include Porto Santo Stefano and Portoferraio on Elba. The Centro Ricerca Cetacei *(www.centroricerca cetacei.org)* org anizes day-trips from Elba to help monitor dolphins and whales in the International Cetacean Sanctuary, which stretches from Tuscany to France.

Departing on a cruise around Elba from Portoferraio

FLORENCE AND TUSCANY FOR RELAXATION

With so much to see in Tuscany, it can be easy to overdo things by cramming too much into a stay. Make sure to plan in some down time, and restore your energy away from the bustling tourist centres. From natural spas to sunset cruises, Tuscany has an infinite variety of ways to wind down.

TOP 5 SEASIDE SUNSETS

Orbetello
The lagoon, with its picturesque windmill, is simply stunning *(p232)*.

Terrazza Mascagni, Livorno
A popular viewpoint at sundown *(p214)*.

Elba
Unbeatable sunsets can be found at Viticcio and Marciana Marina *(p226)*.

The Versilia
Perfectly placed beach bars line the coast *(p211)*.

Monte Argentario
Ideal for a romantic sunset cruise *(p232)*.

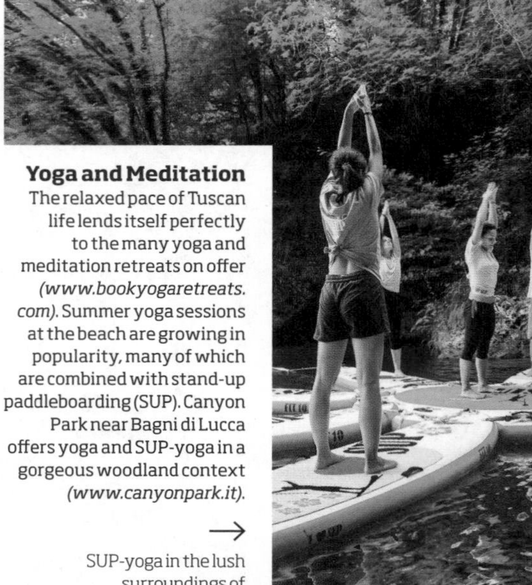

Yoga and Meditation
The relaxed pace of Tuscan life lends itself perfectly to the many yoga and meditation retreats on offer *(www.bookyogaretreats.com)*. Summer yoga sessions at the beach are growing in popularity, many of which are combined with stand-up paddleboarding (SUP). Canyon Park near Bagni di Lucca offers yoga and SUP-yoga in a gorgeous woodland context *(www.canyonpark.it)*.

→

SUP-yoga in the lush surroundings of Canyon Park

Spa Time

Follow in the footsteps of the ancient Etruscans and enjoy the revitalizing waters of Tuscany's thermal springs. In addition to high-end luxury resorts, there are also free spa-water pools at Cascate del Mulino *(p230)*. Montecatini Terme *(p218)* is the longest established spa centre, and offers numerous treatments and wellness experiences.

→

The elegant Terme Tettuccio spa in Montecatini Terme

Get Up Early

Start the day on the right foot with an early morning, crowd-free stroll through Tuscany's stunning piazzas. Dawn concerts by the sea or in the surroundings of archaeological areas are sometimes organized in summer – events vary, so look out for listings.

←

The crowd-free Piazza del Campo in Siena at sunrise

New Experiences

Detach from everyday life by trying something new. Get a fresh perspective on the Tuscan countryside from a hot-air balloon *(www.tuscanyballooning.it)*, or learn a new skill on a cookery course at Cucina Lorenzo De' Medici *(www.cucinaldm.com)* in Florence's Mercato Centrale. Many wineries offer grape harvest experiences, including Il Borro *(p149)*.

→

Floating peacefully above the vineyards in a hot-air balloon

Pedal Power

Cycling has always been a popular activity in Tuscany, but recently it has become even more accessible with the creation of clearly marked routes and web apps for road cyclists and mountain-bikers. There are plenty of hire shops throughout the region, which often stock e-bikes for those who require a little assistance with going further, higher or faster. The tracks through the attractive vineyards of Chianti are ideal for exploring by bicycle, and the major cities all have bike-sharing schemes.

A relaxing cycle through the Tuscan countryside

FLORENCE AND TUSCANY FOR OUTDOOR ADVENTURES

Wherever you are in Tuscany, there are countless reasons to venture into the great outdoors. Be it walking, cycling, horse-riding or paddling, go at your own pace and embrace the joys of exploring the region's stunning scenery.

Wonderful Walking Trails

From urban trekking to hikes through stunning natural areas, there are exceptional walking opportunities for every ability level. Long-distance routes include the Via Francigena *(p215)* and the Anello del Rinascimento, while near Pitigliano you can traverse the Etruscan Vie Cave *(p231)*, a curious network of paths carved into rock.

Hiking through the picturesque scenery of rural Tuscany

Did You Know?

Tuscany has a handful of ski resorts, including Abetone in the Apennines.

TOP 5 GOLF COURSES

Poggio dei Medici
Scarperia
An award-winning 18-hole course.

Argentario Golf Resort
Porto Ercole
A stylish spa resort with 18 panoramic holes.

Golf Club Castelfalfi
Montaione
A 27-hole course and wine estate.

Golf Ugolino
Impruneta
An 18-hole course founded in 1934.

Golf Club Punta Ala
Punta Ala
A splendid 18-hole course with sea views.

Invigorating Watersports

A top diving destination, Elba *(p226)* is also good for surface sports such as kitesurfing and windsurfing – as is Talamone near Orbetello *(p232)*. The rocky coastline of Monte Argentario *(p232)* is ideal for kayakers and boats of all kinds are easily hired. Inland, Lake Bilancino *(p146)* also offers an array of watersports.

→

A kitesurfer riding the waves along the coastline

Horse-Riding Experiences

Tuscany has a good network of bridle paths and farms offering accommodation and stable facilities. The region's many stables – including those at San Rossore Park *(p198)* and Il Borro *(p149)* – offer tuition and guided excursions, ranging from an hour to several days. In Maremma you can saddle up and join the *butteri* (Tuscan cowboys) for a morning on the Alberese estate *(www.alberese.com)*.

→

Riding through farmland on a summer's day in Val d'Orcia

Make Your Money go Further

At the seaside, opt for a free beach *(spiaggia libera)* to avoid costly lounger and umbrella hire at lidos; you can still use the lido bar. For a totally free spa experience, seek out natural spa-water pools, such as Cascate del Mulino near Saturnia *(p230)*, which is accessible to the public all year round. Apart from the glamorous coastal resorts, costs are generally lower in the southern half of Tuscany – Siena is usually cheaper than Florence, for example – and in more remote areas, such as Mugello, where tourists are rarer. Churches across the region – except the most famous monumental ones – often house artistic treasures that can be viewed without an admission charge.

→

Bathing in the balmy spa waters at the rock pools of Cascate del Mulino

FLORENCE AND TUSCANY ON A BUDGET

Although there are many luxurious options on offer, a holiday in Tuscany need not break the bank. Beautiful beaches, majestic churches and relaxing spa pools can all be enjoyed for free, and with a bit of inside knowledge you can make the most of a limited budget when drinking and dining out.

Discount Drinks

Cafés – particularly those in prime positions – often charge for table service, so stand at the bar like the locals. Drinking fountains are a free source of fresh water for filling bottles; just round the corner from Siena's Baptistry you can fill bottles for free at the Morandi grocery. The house wines served at Tuscan trattorias are usually local, inexpensive and good, and while many wineries charge for tours, some offer free tastings with no obligation to buy.

→

Enjoying a morning coffee at the bar with the locals

Did You Know?

Hotel owners favour direct reservations and will match or better prices quoted by booking agencies.

GETTING AROUND

Public transport can be surprisingly cheap - particularly buses, which are often the most convenient option for reaching hill towns (including Siena) where the railway station may be located far from the centre. Local *(regionale)* trains are inexpensive, but advance booking is essential for discounts on fast trains. Bike-sharing schemes are widely available - including in Florence, Pisa and Siena - sometimes for free.

Cheap Eats

Street food and picnics with supplies from markets or delis are good ways to enjoy local specialities at accessible prices. At restaurants, check menus for hidden costs: a cover charge *(coperto)* of €1–3 is normal, but avoid places adding a service charge. Look out for bars offering *aperi-cena*, or happy hour, when drinks include a generous buffet.

← A bargainous sandwich being made at Florence's Mercato Centrale

Open-Air Sights

The streets and piazzas of Tuscany's towns and cities resemble vast open-air galleries, full of stunning examples of sculpture and architecture. This is especially true in Pietrasanta *(p212)*, where the Parco Internazionale delle Sculture displays 70 contemporary sculptures in public places. A fun and free way to see more of Siena is by seeking out the colourful *contrada* symbols in each of the 17 city districts.

→ A sculpture by Igor Mitoraj, one of many on open-air display in Pietrasanta

INSIDER TIP
Sienese Jazz
Siena's Fortezza Medicea houses a high level jazz academy - enjoy the music wafting through the windows as you stroll past.

FLORENCE AND TUSCANY FOR MUSIC LOVERS

Summer is a special time for music lovers, as Tuscany comes alive with the strains of open-air festivals. Held in a variety of enchanting locations and ranging from large-scale events to small one-off concerts, there's a plethora of shows and genres to choose from.

Estate Fiesolana

Two months of open-air concerts and other arts performances make up the programme of this summer festival (June-July), which has been held since 1947 in the historic hill town of Fiesole. The concerts range widely in terms of genre, from classical music to jazz - and a number of them can be enjoyed free of charge. Events take place at a variety of venues; the best of all are those held under the stars in the atmospheric surroundings of the ancient Roman theatre high above town. Tickets include admission to the archaeological museum and there are extra post-show buses (number 7) back to Florence.

↑ A concert in the Roman theatre during the Estate Fiesolana

Rock, Blues and Jazz

Pistoia Blues is a major international festival held in mid-July, with top rock, soul, jazz and blues artists on stage in Piazza Duomo. In Florence, the Firenze Rocks festival (mid-June) hosts some of the world's most famous rock bands at the Parco delle Cascine arena, and there are more big-name bands at the long-standing Lucca Summer Festival (June–July). The Barga Jazz Festival brings music to the town's streets and piazzas during August.

← Musicians at the Lucca Summer Festival *(and inset)*

TOP 3 PUCCINI OPERAS

La Bohème
The tragic love story of poet Rodolfo and seamstress Mimi, who face the difficulties of poverty and ill health.

Tosca
Filled with passion and jealousy, this opera is set in Rome at the time of Napoleon's invasion of Italy.

Madama Butterfly
The heartbreaking tale of a young Japanese girl who falls in love with an American naval officer.

Opera and Classical

The work of Giacomo Puccini is celebrated every July and August with captivating lakeside performances at his home at Torre del Lago *(p211)*. In Florence, the Maggio Musicale festival (May and June) features performances of old and new classical works, while the Incontri in Terra di Siena chamber music festival (July–August) holds concerts in historic locations around Siena, including the magnificent La Foce estate.

→ A performance of *Turandot* at the Festival Puccini at Torre del Lago

Arts and Crafts

Skilled craftsmanship is a fundamental part of the local character in Tuscany's towns and villages, and centuries-old traditions are proudly upheld throughout the region. Colourfully decorated ceramics are made in many places, including Montelupo Fiorentino (near Empoli), where an international ceramics festival is held each June. Colle Val d'Elsa *(p166)* is famous for its crystal glass, Volterra *(p160)* specializes in artistic alabaster items and Arezzo *(p178)* is Italy's leading centre for goldsmiths. Florentines are masters of the craft of marbled paper, creating beautifully intricate designs.

→
A selection of colourful Tuscan ceramics

FLORENCE AND TUSCANY FOR SHOPPERS

With a rich tradition of local crafts and delicacies – from luxury fashion to tasty truffles – the range of goods is broad and the quality is high. There are few more pleasurable experiences than browsing the boutiques of Florence's medieval streets or buying artisanal produce directly from a rural farm estate.

Handmade Leather Goods

Tuscany's leather goods are famous throughout the world and Florence is a major centre for the industry. The Santa Croce leather school, Scuola del Cuoio *(p90)*, is a great place to see leather-crafters at work, and has a wonderful selection of unique, handmade items for sale. Housed in the monastery to the rear of the church, it was founded in 1950 by the friars and two family leather firms to teach skills to war orphans.

A leather craftsman at work at the Scuola del Cuoio

↑ Delicious local produce for sale at a traditional grocer in Florence

Food and Wine

Take home a taste of Tuscany with one - or several - of the numerous tempting specialities found in every town and village. Many places provide vacuum-packing, and farms and wineries often have direct sales. Buy cheese in Pienza *(p191)* and truffles in San Miniato *(p214)*, and don't miss the Saturday morning Slow Food market in Montecatini Terme *(p218)*, which promotes high-quality traditional produce.

INSIDER TIP
Personal Shopping

If time is short, hire a personal shopping service such as Exclusive Fashion Tours to help navigate your way through Tuscany's shopping opportunities *(www.exclusivefashiontours.com)*.

Florence Fashion

Many top designers hail from Florence - Italy's original fashion capital - including Salvatore Ferragamo and Gucci. Peruse their glamorous wares in the high-fashion hub around Via de' Tornabuoni *(p82)* and uncover the brands' histories at the Museo Ferragamo *(p82)* and the striking Gucci Garden *(p68)*.

→ Browsing the elegant items on display at the Gucci Garden

Gorgeous Garfagnana

This astonishing area of natural beauty hosts some striking sights, including the Eremo di Calomini hermitage built into a sheer rock face. Picturesque Vagli lake, meanwhile, hides an underwater village only in view on the rare occasions when the lake is dredged.

→

The peaceful waters of Vagli lake, particularly enchanting at sunset

FLORENCE AND TUSCANY

OFF THE BEATEN TRACK

Tuscany's cities can get rather busy, but it's easy to escape the masses: turn into a quiet side-street, stop in a village you've never heard of or explore one of the beautiful natural parks. Plan your visit outside of the busy Easter to October period, and interact with the locals away from the tourist crowds.

Wild Maremma

You can walk all day in solitude on the quiet footpaths of the vast and wild Parco Naturale della Maremma *(p229)*, which range greatly in terms of difficulty and length; guided tours of the park are available, including night walks in summer. The tranquil beaches and roads of the area are also ideal for a secluded excursion.

→

Strolling along the wild beach of the Parco Naturale della Maremma

Etruscan Tuscany

Explore the fascinating Vie Cave and ancient Etruscan archaeological areas near Pitigliano, Sorano and Sovana, in the southernmost part of the region *(p230)*, for an immersive insight into Tuscany's past. A multitude of burial chambers are hidden among the trees and the atmosphere is usually calm and peaceful.

↑ Remains of the ancient Etruscan civilization in southern Tuscany

The Hidden Side of the Cities

It's possible to find quiet areas even in Tuscany's most celebrated cities. In Florence, explore the side-streets around Santa Croce and Oltrarno, and in Siena, head towards the Porta Romana and Porta San Marco city gates to visit the characterful *contradas* (districts).

← A quiet street in Florence's Santa Croce neighbourhood

Magnificent Mugello

The towns and villages of Mugello *(p142)* don't feature on the main tourist routes, so are ideal for an authentic Tuscan experience. They house an assortment of interesting museums and excellent eateries – drivers in the know often stop at Barberino for a good meal.

→ Dicomano, one of many picturesque small towns in the Mugello region

Religious Masterpieces

The sumptuous façades of Tuscany's many magnificent cathedrals are fitting preludes to the artistic treasures contained within. It's hard to miss the voluminous dome of Florence's vast and decorative cathedral *(p66)*, which can be glimpsed from numerous side-streets around the centre. A world-famous landmark designed by Brunelleschi, its construction marked a major breakthrough in architectural techniques. Siena's black-and-white striped cathedral *(p176)* also has an intricate façade, while the tiered colonnades of Pisa's striking Duomo *(p200)* are often unjustly ignored in favour of the Leaning Tower behind. And don't forget Lucca, Pistoia and Massa Marittima, all of which have similarly impressive cathedrals.

→

The beautiful façade of Florence's Duomo, topped by Brunelleschi's famous dome

FLORENCE AND TUSCANY FOR ARCHITECTURE

Medieval castles, decorative Romanesque cathedrals and elegant Renaissance palazzi: the region's monuments represent the whole spectrum of architectural styles. Marvel at the façades, walk the walls and scale the towers to get under the skin of historic Tuscany.

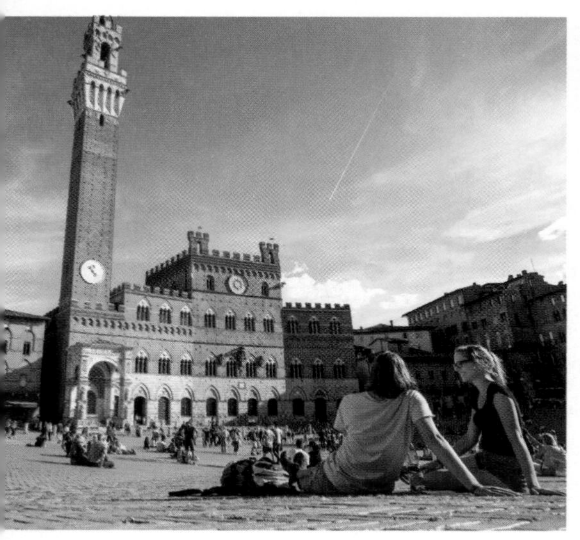

Priceless Piazzas

The life of any Italian community centres on the piazza. Tuscany's most celebrated examples include Siena's shell-shaped Piazza del Campo *(p173)* and Pisa's stunning Piazza dei Miracoli *(p200)*, but don't overlook lesser-known gems such as the perfectly oval Piazza dell'Anfiteatro in Lucca, the triangular Piazza Matteotti in Greve in Chianti and central Cortona's curious succession of squares. Florence's Piazza Santa Croce is the site of an annual Christmas market that begins in late November.

Relaxing in Siena's Piazza del Campo, in front of the impressive bell tower

4 million

The number of bricks used to construct Brunelleschi's dome.

TOP 5 TUSCAN CASTLES

Castello di Meleto
Gaiole in Chianti
A striking 13th century structure.

Castello di Poppi
Poppi
Features a curious internal courtyard.

Castello Malaspina
Fosdinovo
An imposing castle with panoramic views.

Castello di Poggio alle Mura
Montalcino
Houses a glass museum.

Castello di Brolio
Gaiole in Chianti
At the heart of the Ricasoli wine estate.

Tall Towers

Tuscany has an abundance of tall, narrow buildings – climb to the top for incredible panoramic views. Pisa's Leaning Tower *(p202)* is the most famous, but the tower of the Palazzo Vecchio in Florence *(p68)* is the highest. San Gimignano, meanwhile, has over a dozen striking tower houses.

→

The many towers of San Gimignano, built as status symbols in the Middle Ages

Imposing Ramparts

A walk around the ramparts of Tuscany's towns and villages makes an alternative stroll and provides intriguing glimpses of otherwise hidden corners. Monteriggioni *(p167)* is the most striking walled village, while Lucca's wide Renaissance walls are nowadays a popular elevated park *(p207)*.

→

Monteriggioni, with its remarkably well-preserved walls

A YEAR IN FLORENCE AND TUSCANY

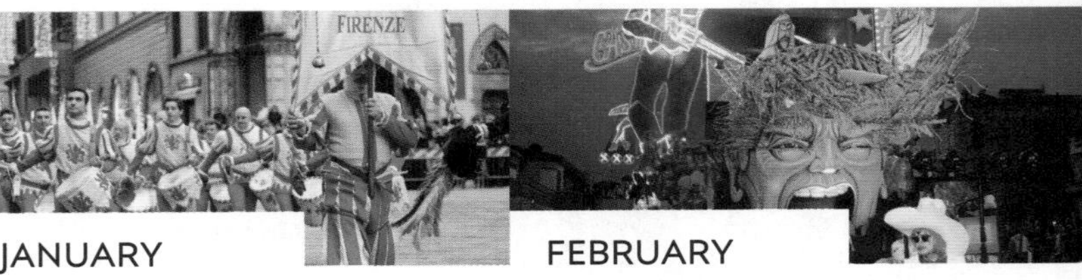

JANUARY

La Befana *(6 Jan)*. Throughout Italy children receive stockings containing sweets and gifts from La Befana, the Epiphany witch.

△ **La Cavalcata dei Magi** *(6 Jan)*. A parade through Florence in Renaissance dress.

FEBRUARY

△ **Carnevale** *(Shrove Tuesday and preceding weekends)*. Viareggio's carnival is one of Italy's most famous, renowned for its sharply satirical floats; smaller carnival celebrations are also held elsewhere.

MAY

Maggio Musicale *(May–Jun)*. Arts festival in Florence, including music, drama and dance.

△ **La Notte dei Pirati** *(first weekend)*. The night festival in Porto Ercole includes pirate raids, games, cannon fire and a treasure hunt.

JUNE

△ **Calcio Storico** *(24 Jun)*. Florence's authentically violent football match in Renaissance costume.

Gioco del Ponte *(last Sat)*. A ritual battle played out on the Ponte di Mezzo bridge in Pisa.

SEPTEMBER

Fiera del Cacio *(first week)*. A week of cheese-tasting and market stalls in Pienza, culminating with a Sunday afternoon bowls-like competition using Pienza cheeses.

△ **Palio della Balestra** *(second Sun)*. Renaissance costume parade and flag-throwing in Sansepolcro.

OCTOBER

Sagra della Castagna *(every Sun)*. Food stands in Marradi serve specialities made with local chestnuts; there are also market stalls.

△ **L'Eroica** *(first Sun)*. A non-competitive cycle race in Gaiole, for which participants wear historical dress and ride vintage bicycles.

MARCH

△ **Scoppio del Carro** *(Easter Sun)*. A celebration in Florence of the Resurrection, the "Explosion of the Carriage" involves a gilded cart and fireworks in Piazza Duomo.

Traditional New Year *(25 Mar)*. Pisa celebrates the traditional new year (abolished 1749) with several days of festivities, including Renaissance costume parades and fireworks; Florence puts on a simpler historical procession.

APRIL

△ **Mostra Mercato Internazionale dell'Artigianato** *(last week)* An important European exhibition of the work of artists and artisans held in Florence's Fortezza da Basso.

Festa degli Aquiloni *(first Sun after Easter)*. Traditional handmade kites are flown in San Miniato, and there's a parade with historical costumes.

Liberation Day *(25 Apr)* A national holiday to commemorate the end of the Fascist regime.

JULY

Palio di Siena *(2 Jul & 16 Aug)* . A medieval bareback horse race between 10 of Siena's 17 *contradas* (districts).

△ **Pistoia Blues Festival** *(mid July)*. Famous international festival in Pistoia, with five days of blues and rock concerts.

Estate Fiesolana *(late Jun–mid Aug)*. A long-standing arts festival in Fiesole, with events held in the ancient Roman theatre.

AUGUST

Puccini Festival *(late Jul–all Aug)*. Performances of the composer's operas in an open-air theatre by his home at Torre del Lago.

Fish and Chips Festival *(first-half Aug)*. An event with food and dancing in celebration of the historical links between Barga and Scotland.

△ **Bravio delle Botti** *(last Sun)*. A race between representatives of Montepulciano's eight districts, who roll 80 kg (175 lb) barrels uphill.

Calici di Stelle *(10 Aug)*. Open-air wine-tasting and star-gazing in various locations.

NOVEMBER

△ **Mostra Mercato Nazionale del Tartufo Bianco** *(last three weekends)*. Market stalls, displays and speciality food stands dedicated largely to San Miniato's local white truffle, one of Italy's most prestigious delicacies.

DECEMBER

△ **Mercatino di Natale** *(first three weeks)*. A Christmas market held in Piazza Santa Croce in Florence, selling decorations, gifts and festive specialities, and featuring Santa's grotto and an area dedicated to quality crafts.

A BRIEF HISTORY

Tuscans are renowned for their strong character, and feuds and fighting have been common throughout the region's history. But it's also a centre of arts and culture; Florence led artistic development during the Renaissance.

Ancient Tuscany

The ancient Etruscan civilization – from which the name Tuscany derives – was already established by the 8th century BC. It covered an area known as Etruria, which spanned Tuscany as well as the regions of Lazio and Umbria. The Etruscans founded a number of towns including Cortona, Arezzo, Fiesole and Volterra (the latter of which is home to an Etruscan acropolis). After multiple wars with Rome in the 4th and 3rd centuries BC, Etruria was conquered and renamed Tuscia. With the rise of Roman culture came the construction of new roads, including the panoramic Via Aurelia coastal road from Pisa to Rome, and new towns such as Florence and Siena.

Did You Know?

Tuscany's unusual salt-free bread was born out of a 12th-century dispute between Pisa and Florence.

Timeline of events

9th century BC

Etruscan civilization flourishes on Elba.

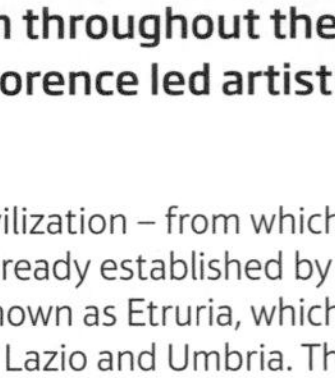

294 BC

The Romans defeat the Etruscans and conquer Roselle.

20 BC

Siena is founded as a military colony.

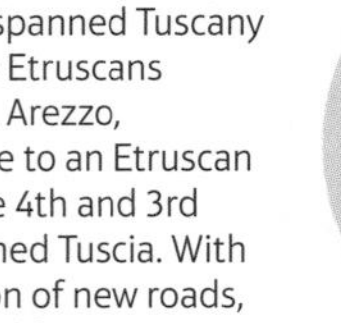

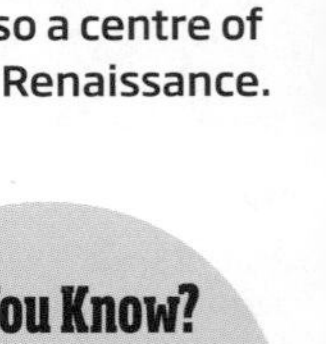

59 BC

Florence is founded to house veterans of the Roman army.

Medieval Tuscany

Tuscany was attacked multiple times in early medieval times by northern tribes such as the Goths and the Lombards. The Frankish king, Charlemagne, in response to a request from Pope Leo II, drove the Lombards out of Tuscany and was rewarded by being crowned the first Holy Roman Emperor in 800 AD. The Church played a significant role in the area during this period and numerous religious buildings were constructed. The region underwent considerable urbanization until the advent of the Black Death in 1348. Gothic and Romanesque architectural styles became popular, including the particularly decorative Pisan Romanesque style, and Tuscany's many complex medieval town and village centres were built, with their narrow alleys, robust surrounding walls, and castles and towers.

Merchants' guilds gained increasing influence throughout the region. The wool merchants were particularly powerful in Florence, which led to the Tuscan city becoming Italy's foremost centre for textiles and fashion; it is still a leader in those industries today.

1 A map of Tuscany from 1814. ↑

2 An engraving showing the Romans conquering Etruria.

3 The ancient Roman amphitheatre in Volterra.

4 Charlemagne, the Holy Roman Emperor, in a 19th-century portrait.

c 1025

Guido d'Arezzo invents the first system of musical notation.

1265

Poet Dante Alighieri is born in Florence.

1301

Dante is exiled from Florence, never to return.

1350

The Leaning Tower of Pisa is completed, already leaning.

Renaissance Tuscany and the Medici Family

The Renaissance was the most glorious period of Tuscany's history, with the region leading the world in artistic and intellectual development. This was due largely to the patronage of the Medici family, who governed Florence (and later Tuscany) from 1434 to 1743. The Medici wealth was the legacy of astute merchant banker Giovanni di Bicci, father of the first Medici ruler, Cosimo il Vecchio. The long period of relatively peaceful Medici governance had a brief interruption from 1494 to 1530 when the city of Florence was run as a republic, before the family dynasty was restored by the Medici Pope Clement VII.

The Grand Duchy and Florence as Capital

By 1570 the Medici rulers of Florence had added the rest of Tuscany to their territories, and Cosimo I was officially declared the first Grand Duke of Tuscany. A lengthy period of prosperity and political unity followed, and the region became a popular destination for wealthy aristocrats conducting a Grand Tour of Europe. When the Medici line eventually came to an end with the death of Gian Gastone in 1737, the Grand Duchy was

NEW YEAR

Although Tuscans mark 1 January with characteristic gusto, both Florence and Pisa continue to celebrate their own New Year on 25 March, coinciding with the Feast of the Annunciation.

Timeline of events

1472

Monte dei Paschi di Siena, the world's oldest operational bank, is founded.

c 1485

Leonardo da Vinci designs his first flying machine.

1504

Michelangelo completes his *David* statue.

1633

The first Siena Palio is held.

1749

Florence and Pisa are obliged to adopt the Gregorian calendar.

inherited by the Austrian Dukes of Lorraine, which continued until Italian unification in 1860. Florence played an important role in the new kingdom of Italy, even serving as the nation's capital from 1865 to 1871, before Rome joined the unified nation and took the helm.

Challenging Times

The 20th century was a turbulent time for Tuscany, with the interwar period bringing social unrest, the rise of Fascism and economic recession. The region suffered heavy bomb damage during World War II, including the destruction of all but one of Florence's historic bridges, and severe floods in 1966 damaged many of Florence's art treasures. Nonetheless, Tuscany flourished as a major cultural centre and its textiles and agricultural industries continued to thrive.

Florence and Tuscany Today

Tourism plays a fundamental role in the local economy, and Tuscany leads the way in Italy for protecting its historic centres from pollution by restricting traffic.

1 Statue of Giovanni di Bicci. ↑

2 Cosimo I being crowned Grand Duke of Tuscany.

3 Bombed houses along the Arno in World War II.

4 View across the Duomo and Arno River.

Did You Know?

The young Michelangelo lived with the Medicis for several years.

1786

Tuscany becomes the first state in the world to abolish the death penalty.

1814–15

Napoleon is exiled on Elba.

1865–71

Florence has a short spell as capital of Italy.

1951

Italy's first fashion show is held in Florence.

2013

Twelve Medici villas and two gardens are declared Tuscany's seventh UNESCO World Heritage Site.

EXPERIENCE FLORENCE

The Ponte Vecchio at sunset

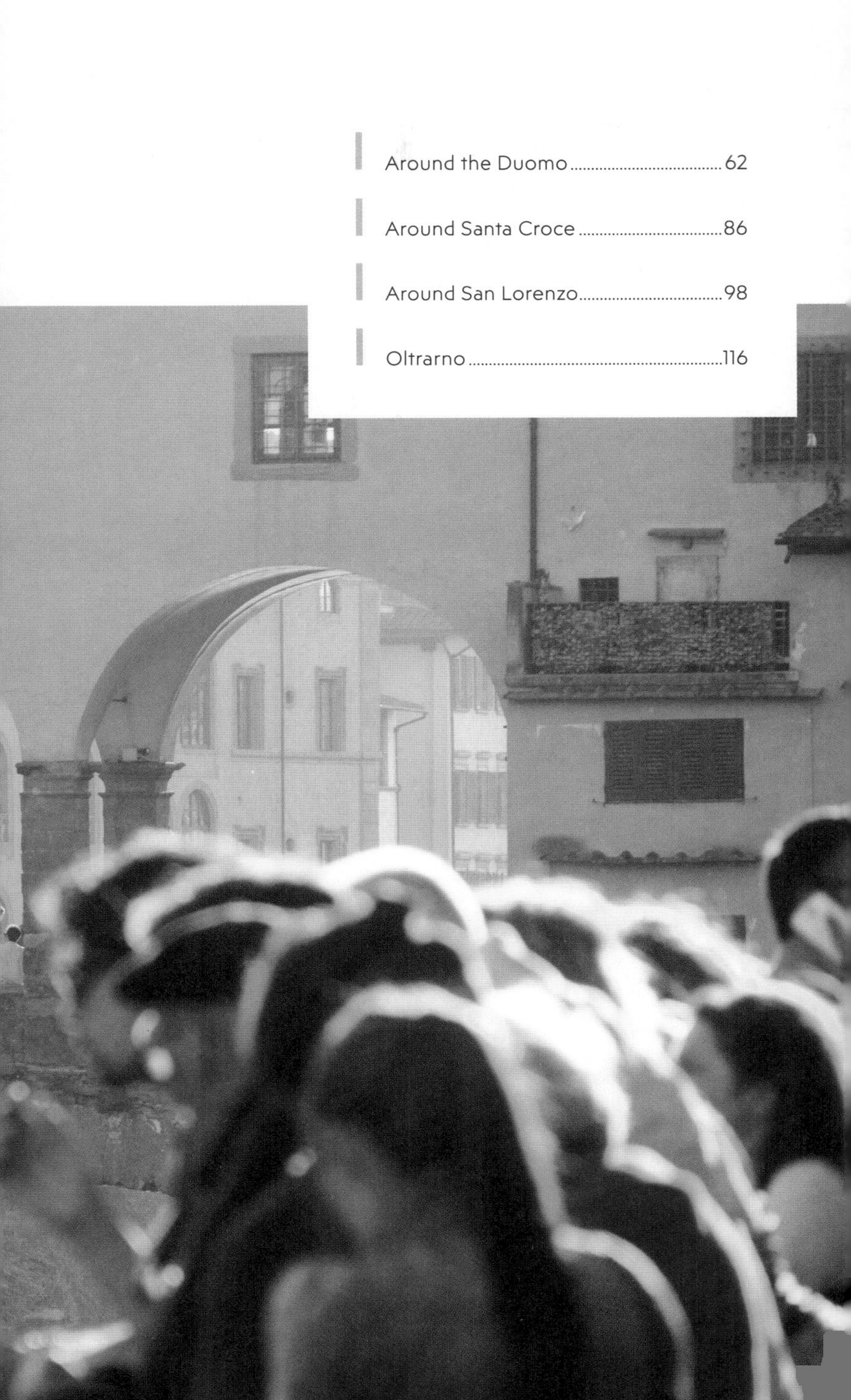

EXPLORE FLORENCE

This guide divides Florence into four areas, as shown on this map. Find out more about each area on the following pages.

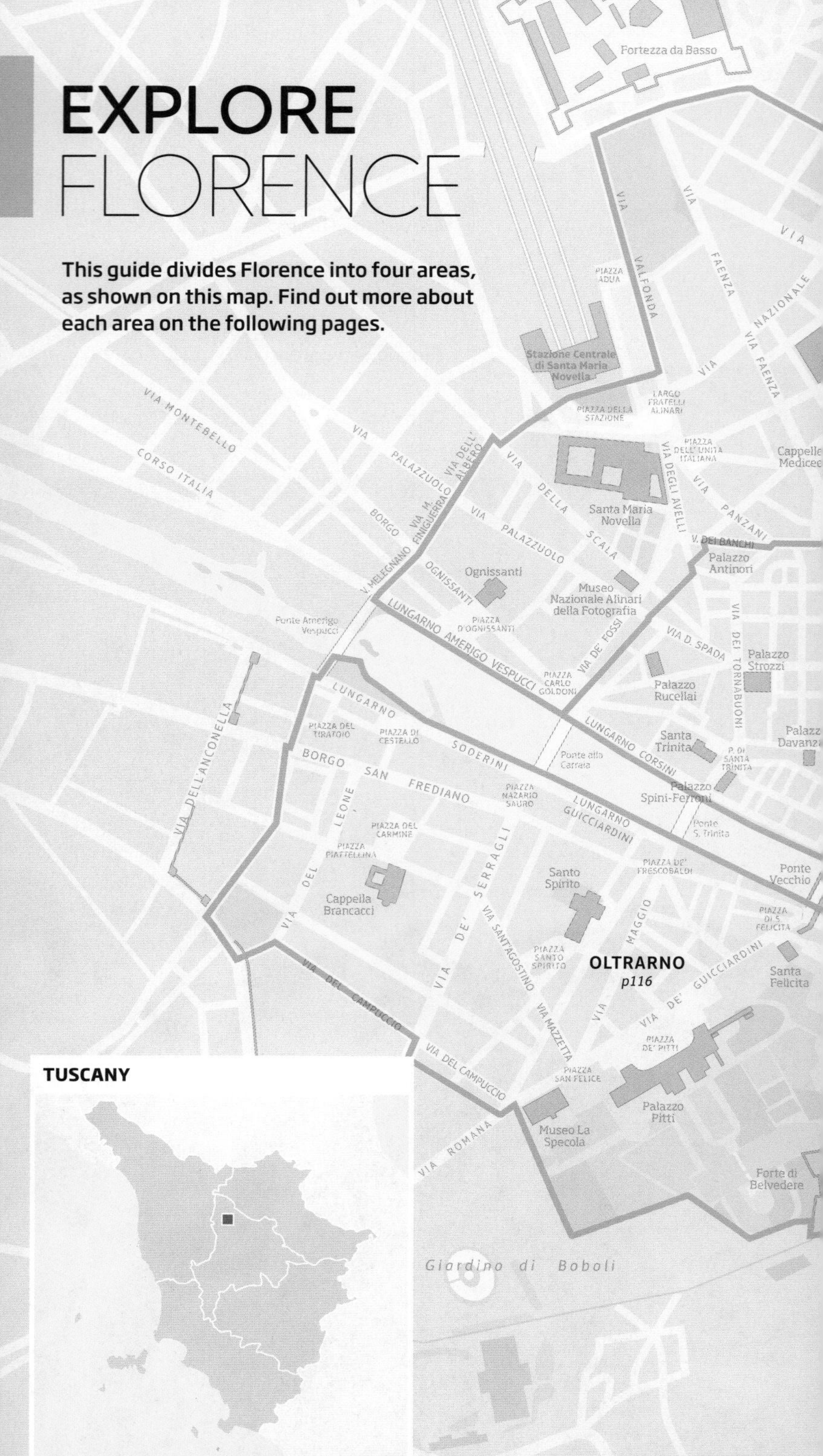

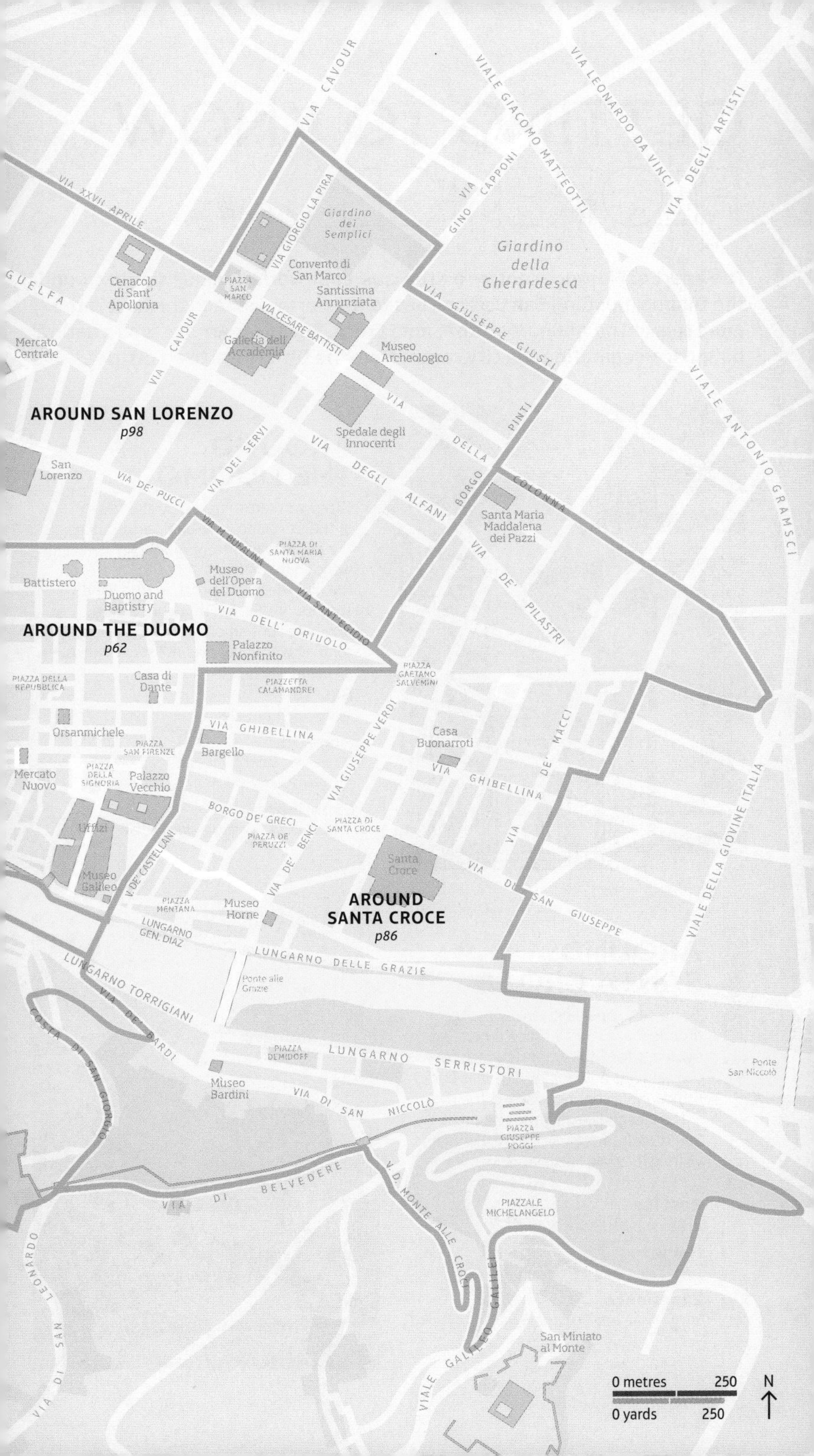

AROUND SAN LORENZO
p98
AROUND THE DUOMO
p62
AROUND SANTA CROCE
p86
Giardino dei Semplici
Convento di San Marco
Santissima Annunziata
Giardino della Gherardesca
Cenacolo di Sant' Apollonia
Mercato Centrale
Galleria dell' Accademia
Museo Archeologico
Spedale degli Innocenti
San Lorenzo
Santa Maria Maddalena dei Pazzi
Battistero
Duomo and Baptistry
Museo dell'Opera del Duomo
Palazzo Nonfinito
Casa di Dante
Orsanmichele
Bargello
Casa Buonarroti
Mercato Nuovo
Palazzo Vecchio
Uffizi
Museo Galileo
Santa Croce
Museo Horne
Ponte alle Grazie
Museo Bardini
Ponte San Niccolò
Piazzale Michelangelo
San Miniato al Monte
Piazza San Marco
Piazza di Santa Maria Nuova
Piazza della Repubblica
Piazzetta Calamandrei
Piazza Gaetano Salvemini
Piazza San Firenze
Piazza della Signoria
Piazza di Santa Croce
Piazza de' Peruzzi
Piazza Mentana
Piazza Demidoff
Piazza Giuseppe Poggi
Via Cavour
Viale Giacomo Matteotti
Via Leonardo da Vinci
Via degli Artisti
Via XXVII Aprile
Via Giorgio la Pira
Via Gino Capponi
Guelfa
Via Cesare Battisti
Via Giuseppe Giusti
Via della Colonna
Viale Antonio Gramsci
Via dei Servi
Via degli Alfani
Borgo Pinti
Via de' Pucci
Via M. Bufalina
Via Sant'Egidio
Via de' Pilastri
Via dell' Oriuolo
Via Ghibellina
Via Giuseppe Verdi
Via de' Macci
Viale della Giovine Italia
Borgo de' Greci
Via de' Benci
V. de' Castellani
Via di San Giuseppe
Lungarno Gen. Diaz
Lungarno delle Grazie
Lungarno Torrigiani
Via de' Bardi
Costa di San Giorgio
Lungarno Serristori
Via di San Niccolò
Via di Belvedere
V. d. Monte alle Croci
Viale Galileo Galilei
Via di San Leonardo
0 metres 250
0 yards 250
N

GETTING TO KNOW FLORENCE

The heart of Florence centres on the cluster of world-famous sights around the Duomo. Bustling San Lorenzo lies to the north, while to the east is the more relaxed neighbourhood of Santa Croce. The River Arno acts as a natural boundary, separating the city centre from the Oltrarno artisan district.

PAGE 62

AROUND THE DUOMO

Office workers mingle with sightseers at the cafés and wine bars surrounding the area's magnificent monuments, while sharp dressers strut through the high-fashion district around Via de' Tornabuoni. Santa Trinita bridge is a favourite spot among romantic young couples, who linger over the sunset views.

Best for

Masterpieces of art and architecture

Home to

Duomo and Baptistry, the Uffizi, Piazza della Signoria, Ponte Vecchio

Experience

A climb up the Duomo for stunning city views

PAGE 86

AROUND SANTA CROCE

There's an appealing sense of space around Piazza Santa Croce, where bar owners and leisurely locals watch over the comings and goings. The laid-back atmosphere continues across the river in the village-like neighbourhood of San Niccolò, a popular stop for walkers visiting Piazzale Michelangelo.

Best for

Iconic views of the city

Home to

Santa Croce, Bargello, Piazzale Michelangelo

Experience

Shopping for leather goods at Scuola del Cuoio

PAGE 98

AROUND SAN LORENZO

Close to the city's transport hub, Piazza Santa Maria Novella is the realm of suitcase-pulling travellers, either hurrying towards the station or gazing in wonder at the stunning church façade that greets them on arrival. The austere buildings and busy bus routes around San Marco and the Accademia are less conducive to lingering, while the frenetic life of the Mercato Centrale brings housewives and restaurant chefs shoulder to shoulder in search of the freshest produce.

Best for
Market-fresh food at the Mercato Centrale

Home to
San Lorenzo, San Marco, Santa Maria Novella

Experience
A cookery lesson at the Mercato Centrale

PAGE 116

OLTRARNO

As soon as you cross the river to the Oltrarno (literally "beyond the river") the atmosphere changes. Modest buildings housing age-old craftsmen's workshops, where aproned experts work with wood, glass or silver, are interspersed with bohemian student bars, contemporary literary cafés and experimental eateries designed to stimulate the appetites of Florence's young professionals. The bars on Piazza Santo Spirito overflow at aperitivo time, with locals gathering before a meal of home-cooked food like nonna used to make at one of the area's simple, old-fashioned trattorias.

Best for
Artisan workshops, offbeat bars and traditional trattorias

Home to
Palazzo Pitti, Boboli Gardens, Brancacci Chapel

Experience
Sipping an aperitivo in Piazza Santo Spirito

The striking colours of the Duomo

AROUND THE DUOMO

The heart of Florence, this area has been the home of religious and political life – the Duomo and the Palazzo Vecchio respectively – since the 14th century. Previously known as Palazzo della Signoria, the Palazzo Vecchio was the residence of the Medici family until their mid-16th century move to Palazzo Pitti. They retained a close connection to the area, however, via an impressive covered corridor that passed through the Uffizi and over the Ponte Vecchio to link the two palaces. The Palazzo Vecchio later housed the Italian parliament for the brief period that Florence was Italy's capital (1865–71) and still functions as the town hall today.

Piazza della Repubblica and the surrounding streets are the result of 19th-century redevelopment; the piazza housed the city's main market in medieval times and before that the Roman forum. As Florence's reputation as a fashion capital became established in the 20th century, Via de' Tornabuoni – the most elegant of the city's streets since the Renaissance – became a hub for top couturiers. It is still lined with designer boutiques today, and forms the heart of the city's main shopping district.

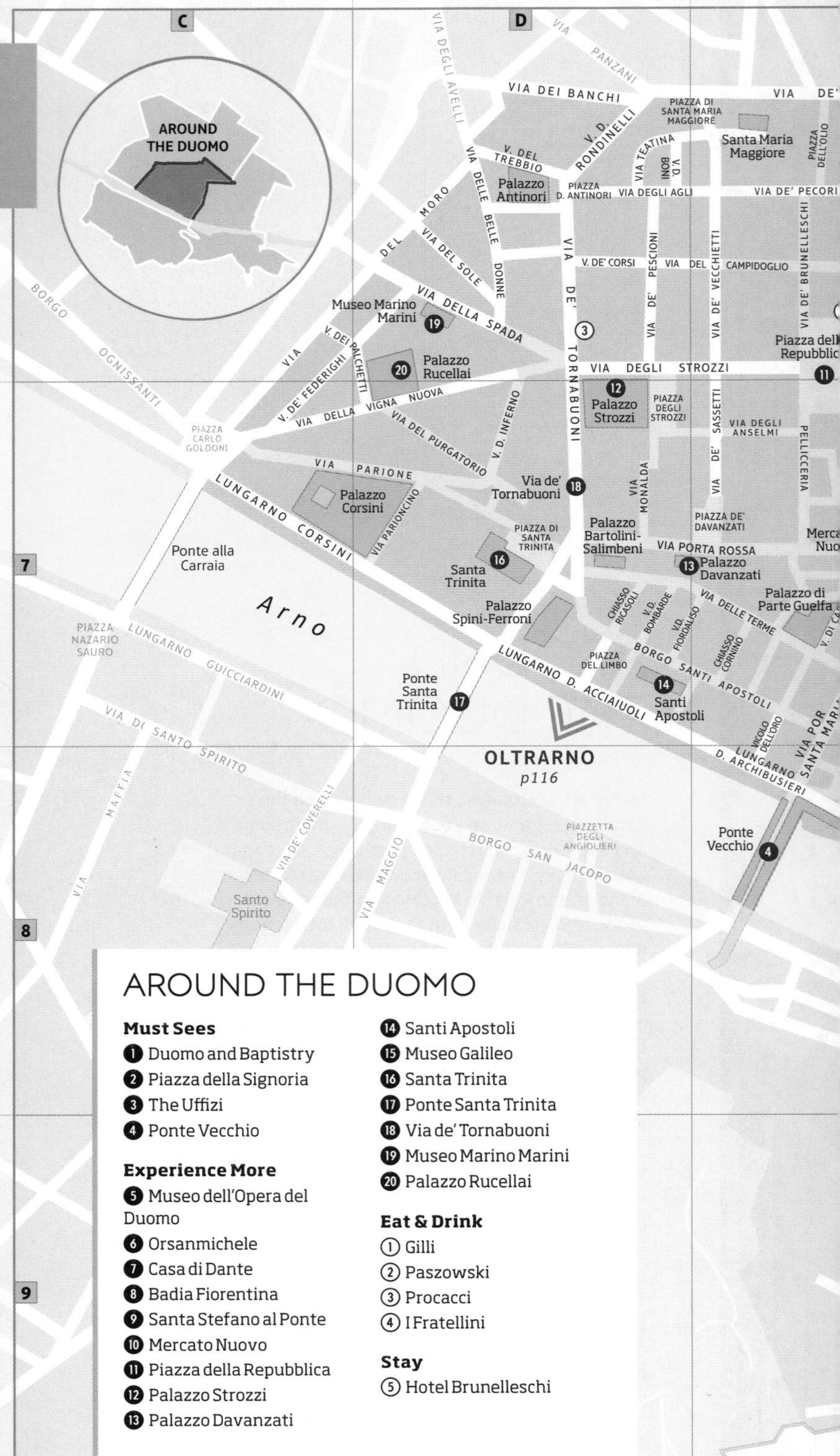
C
D
7
8
9
AROUND THE DUOMO
VIA DEGLI AVELLI
VIA PANZANI
VIA DEI BANCHI
PIAZZA DI SANTA MARIA MAGGIORE
VIA DE'
V. D. RONDINELLI
V. DEL TREBBIO
VIA TEATINA
V. D. BONI
Santa Maria Maggiore
PIAZZA DELL'OLIO
VIA DELLE BELLE DONNE
Palazzo Antinori
PIAZZA D. ANTINORI
VIA DEGLI AGLI
VIA DE' PECORI
VIA DEL MORO
VIA DEL SOLE
V. DE' CORSI
VIA DE' PESCIONI
VIA DEL CAMPIDOGLIO
VIA DE' VECCHIETTI
VIA DE' BRUNELLESCHI
BORGO OGNISSANTI
Museo Marino Marini
19
VIA DELLA SPADA
VIA DE' TORNABUONI
3
Piazza della Repubblica
V. DEI PALCHETTI
VIA DE' FEDERIGHI
20
Palazzo Rucellai
VIA DEGLI STROZZI
11
12
Palazzo Strozzi
PIAZZA DEGLI STROZZI
VIA DELLA VIGNA NUOVA
VIA DEL PURGATORIO
V. D. INFERNO
VIA DEGLI ANSELMI
VIA DE' SASSETTI
PIAZZA CARLO GOLDONI
VIA PARIONE
PELLICCERIA
Via de' Tornabuoni
18
VIA MONALDA
LUNGARNO CORSINI
Palazzo Corsini
VIA PARIONCINO
PIAZZA DI SANTA TRINITA
Palazzo Bartolini-Salimbeni
PIAZZA DE' DAVANZATI
Mercato Nuovo
Ponte alla Carraia
16
Santa Trinita
VIA PORTA ROSSA
13
Palazzo Davanzati
Arno
Palazzo Spini-Ferroni
CHIASSO RICASOLI
V. D. BOMBARDE
V. D. FIORDALISO
VIA DELLE TERME
Palazzo di Parte Guelfa
PIAZZA NAZARIO SAURO
LUNGARNO GUICCIARDINI
LUNGARNO D. ACCIAIUOLI
PIAZZA DEL LIMBO
BORGO SANTI APOSTOLI
CHIASSO CORNINO
14
Santi Apostoli
Ponte Santa Trinita
17
VIA DI SANTO SPIRITO
VICOLO DELL'ORO
VIA POR SANTA MARIA
OLTRARNO
p116
LUNGARNO D. ARCHIBUSIERI
VIA MAFFIA
VIA DE' COVERELLI
VIA MAGGIO
PIAZZETTA DEGLI ANGIOLIERI
BORGO SAN JACOPO
Ponte Vecchio
4
Santo Spirito
AROUND THE DUOMO
Must Sees
1 Duomo and Baptistry
2 Piazza della Signoria
3 The Uffizi
4 Ponte Vecchio
Experience More
5 Museo dell'Opera del Duomo
6 Orsanmichele
7 Casa di Dante
8 Badia Fiorentina
9 Santa Stefano al Ponte
10 Mercato Nuovo
11 Piazza della Repubblica
12 Palazzo Strozzi
13 Palazzo Davanzati
14 Santi Apostoli
15 Museo Galileo
16 Santa Trinita
17 Ponte Santa Trinita
18 Via de' Tornabuoni
19 Museo Marino Marini
20 Palazzo Rucellai
Eat & Drink
① Gilli
② Paszowski
③ Procacci
④ I Fratellini
Stay
⑤ Hotel Brunelleschi

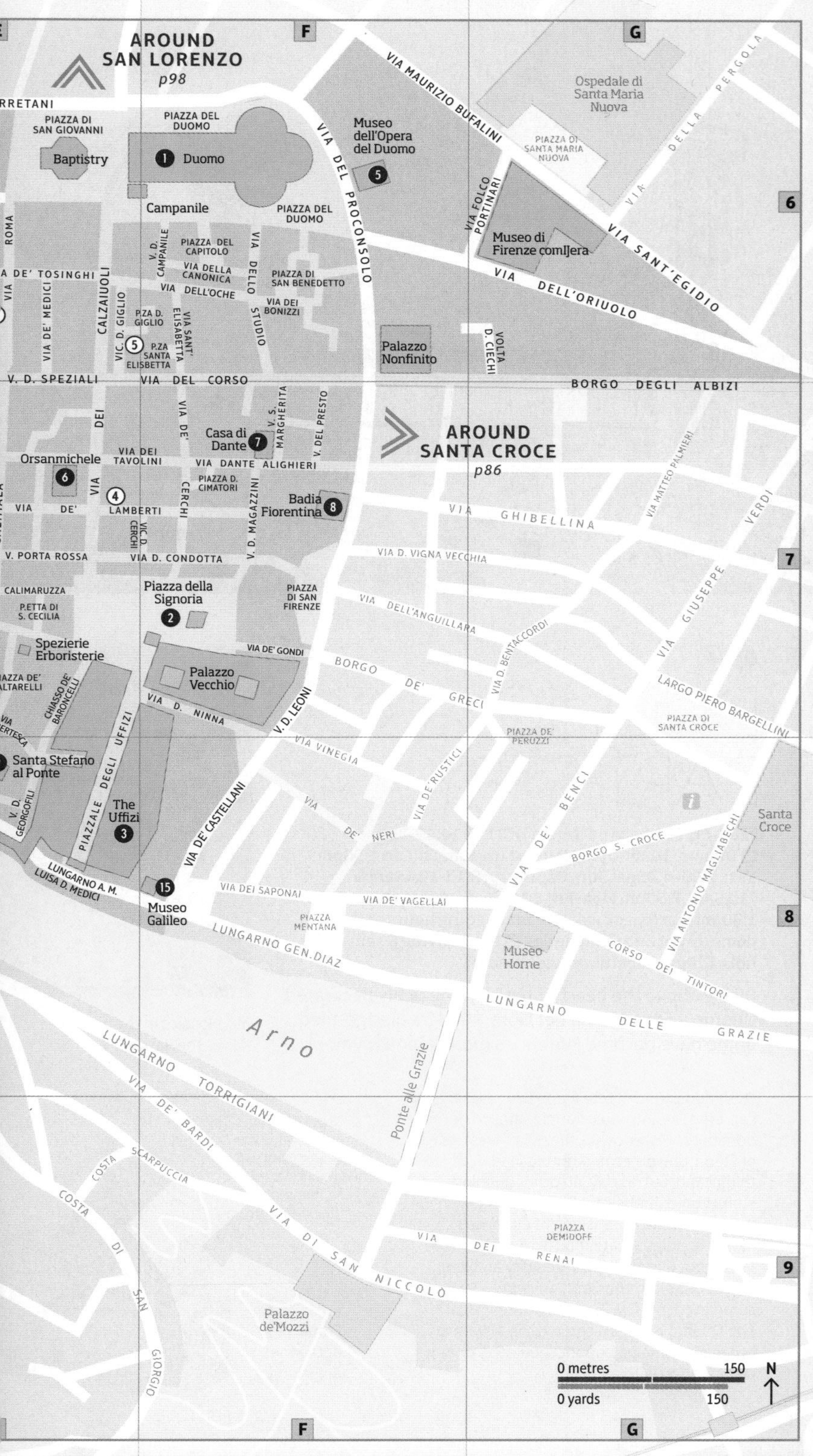

AROUND SAN LORENZO
p98
AROUND SANTA CROCE
p86
F
G
6
7
8
9
RRETANI
PIAZZA DI SAN GIOVANNI
PIAZZA DEL DUOMO
Baptistry
1 Duomo
Campanile
PIAZZA DEL DUOMO
Museo dell'Opera del Duomo
5
VIA MAURIZIO BUFALINI
Ospedale di Santa Maria Nuova
PIAZZA DI SANTA MARIA NUOVA
VIA DELLA PERGOLA
VIA DEL PROCONSOLO
VIA FOLCO PORTINARI
Museo di Firenze com'era
VIA SANT'EGIDIO
VIA DELL'ORIUOLO
ROMA
VIA DE' TOSINGHI
VIA DE' MEDICI
CALZAIUOLI
V. D. CAMPANILE
PIAZZA DEL CAPITOLO
VIA DELLA CANONICA
VIA DELL'OCHE
VIA DELLO STUDIO
PIAZZA DI SAN BENEDETTO
VIA DEI BONIZZI
VIC. D. GIGLIO
P.ZA D. GIGLIO
VIA SANT' ELISABETTA
5
P.ZA SANTA ELISABETTA
Palazzo Nonfinito
VOLTA D. CIECHI
V. D. SPEZIALI
VIA DEL CORSO
BORGO DEGLI ALBIZI
DEI
VIA DE' CERCHI
V. S. MARGHERITA
V. DEL PRESTO
Casa di Dante
7
Orsanmichele
6
VIA DEI TAVOLINI
VIA DANTE ALIGHIERI
PIAZZA D. CIMATORI
VIA
4
VIA DE' LAMBERTI
VIC. D. CERCHI
V. D. MAGAZZINI
Badia Fiorentina
8
VIA GHIBELLINA
VIA MATTEO PALMIERI
VIA GIUSEPPE VERDI
V. PORTA ROSSA
VIA D. CONDOTTA
VIA D. VIGNA VECCHIA
CALIMARUZZA
P.ETTA DI S. CECILIA
Piazza della Signoria
2
PIAZZA DI SAN FIRENZE
VIA DELL'ANGUILLARA
Spezierie Erboristerie
VIA DE' GONDI
AZZA DE' ALTARELLI
CHIASSO DE' BARONCELLI
Palazzo Vecchio
BORGO DE' GRECI
VIA D. BENTACCORDI
LARGO PIERO BARGELLINI
PIAZZA DI SANTA CROCE
VIA D. NINNA
V. D. LEONI
PIAZZA DE' PERUZZI
PIAZZALE DEGLI UFFIZI
VIA VINEGIA
Santa Stefano al Ponte
VIA DE' RUSTICI
VIA DE' BENCI
The Uffizi
3
V. D. GEORGOFILI
VIA DE' CASTELLANI
VIA DE' NERI
BORGO S. CROCE
VIA ANTONIO MAGLIABECHI
Santa Croce
LUNGARNO A. M. LUISA D. MEDICI
15
Museo Galileo
VIA DEI SAPONAI
VIA DE' VAGELLAI
PIAZZA MENTANA
Museo Horne
LUNGARNO GEN. DIAZ
CORSO DEI TINTORI
LUNGARNO DELLE GRAZIE
Arno
Ponte alle Grazie
LUNGARNO TORRIGIANI
VIA DE' BARDI
COSTA SCARPUCCIA
COSTA DI SAN GIORGIO
VIA DI SAN NICCOLÒ
VIA DEI RENAI
PIAZZA DEMIDOFF
Palazzo de'Mozzi
0 metres
150
0 yards
150
N

1

DUOMO AND BAPTISTRY

E6–F6 Piazza del Duomo 1, 6, 14, 17, 23 Duomo: 10am–5pm Mon–Sat (to 4pm Thu, to 4:30pm Sat), 1:30–4:45pm Sun; Baptistry: 8:15–10:15am & 11:15am–7:30pm Mon–Fri, 8:15am–6:30pm Sat, 8:15am–1:30pm Sun (check website for opening hours of the dome, crypt and Campanile) 1 Jan, 15 Aug & religious hols ilgrandemuseodelduomo.it

Rising above the heart of the city, the richly decorated Duomo – Santa Maria del Fiore – and its orange-tiled dome have become Florence's most famous symbol.

↑ Mosaics in the interior of the Baptistry

Designed by architect Filippo Brunelleschi, the cathedral's enormous, double-shelled dome dominates Florence. Its sheer size was typical of Florentine determination to lead in all things and, to this day, no other building stands taller in the city. The Baptistry, with its celebrated doors, is one of Florence's oldest buildings, dating back to perhaps the 4th century. In his capacity as city architect, Giotto designed the Campanile in 1334; it was completed in 1359, 22 years after his death. The Duomo is free to enter, while tickets to other areas can be bought separately or in combination with each other.

Colourful 13th-century mosaics illustrating the Last Judgment *decorate the ceiling of the Baptistry.*

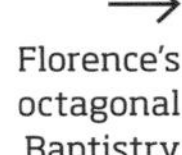

Florence's octagonal Baptistry

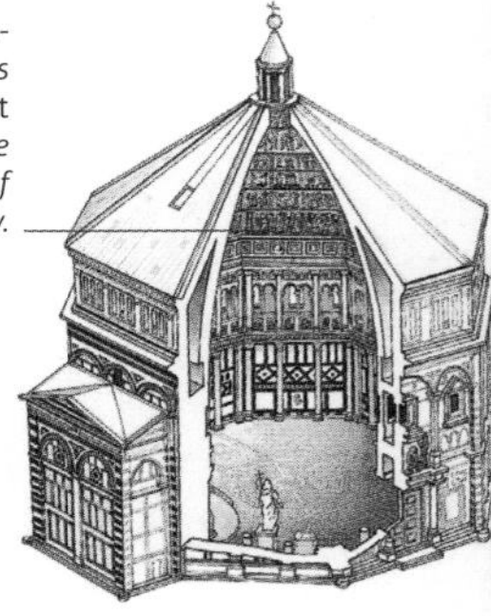

BAPTISTRY DOORS

Lorenzo Ghiberti won a competition in 1401 to design the north doors of the Baptistry. In 1425–52 he designed the east doors, which Michelangelo dubbed the "Gate of Paradise". The original ten relief panels are in the Museo dell'Opera del Duomo *(p76)*; those on the Baptistry are copies.

↑ Frescoed interior of Brunelleschi's dome

← The Duomo's enormous dome and Campanile towering over Florence's skyline

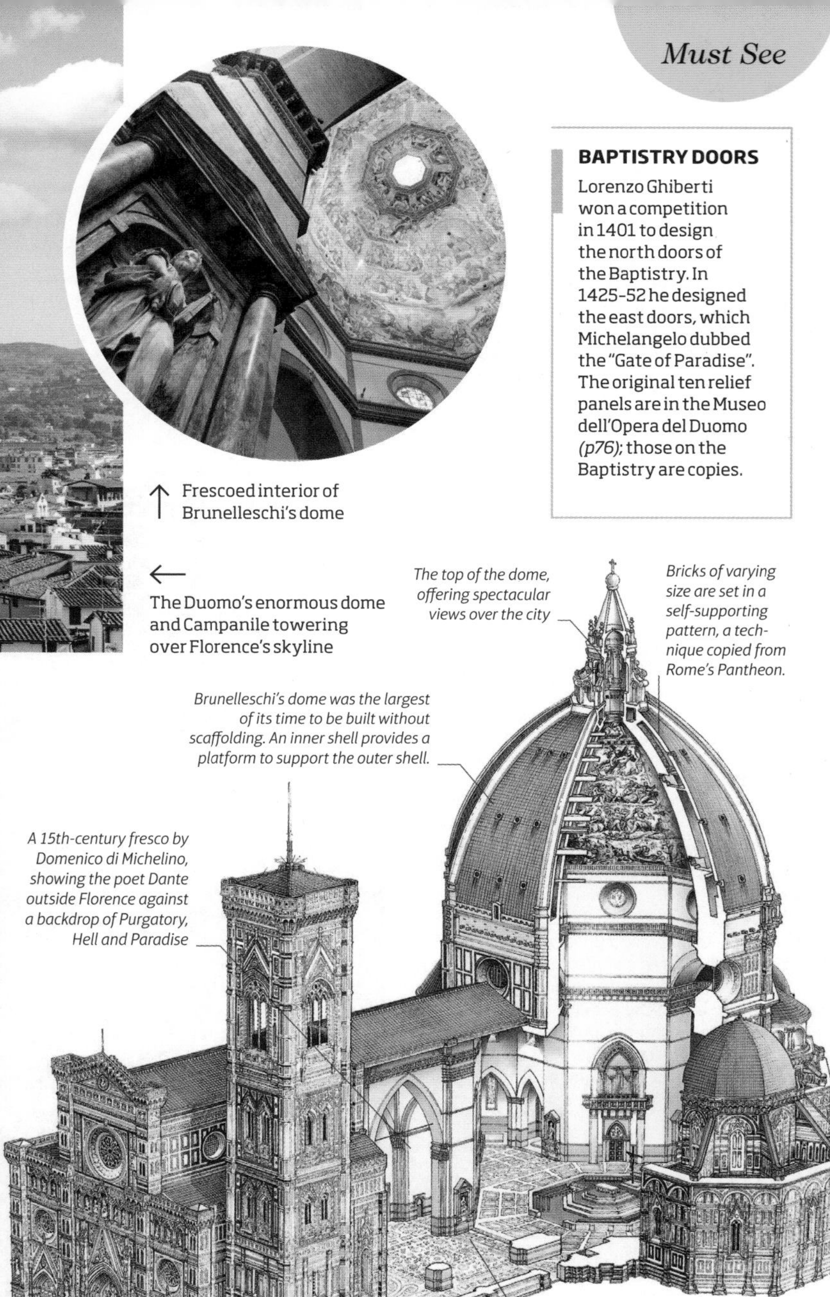

The Duomo, seen from the Piazza del Duomo ↑

2

PIAZZA DELLA SIGNORIA

F7 A, B Palazzo Vecchio: Apr-Sep: 9am-11pm Fri-Wed (tower to 9pm), 9am-2pm Thu; Oct-Mar: 9am-7pm Fri-Wed (tower 10am-5pm), 9am-2pm Thu 1 Jan, Easter, 1 May, 15 Aug, 25 Dec Palazzo Vecchio: museicivicifiorentini.comune.fi.it

This L-shaped square sits in the heart of the city, and is overlooked by some of Florence's most famous buildings. Most significant of all is the imposing Palazzo Vecchio, which has stood for centuries as the site of the town hall.

The piazza is a unique outdoor sculpture gallery and, with the Palazzo Vecchio, has been the hub of Florentine politics since the 14th century. Citizens gathered here when called to a *parlamento* (a public meeting) by the Palazzo's great bell. The statues, some copies, commemorate major events in the city's history. Many are linked to the rise and fall of the Florentine Republic *(p54)*, during which the religious leader Girolamo Savonarola was executed here.

Palazzo Vecchio

The Palazzo Vecchio ("Old Palace") still fulfils its original role as Florence's town hall. It was completed in 1322 when a huge bell – used to call citizens to meetings or warn of fire, flood or enemy attack – was hauled to the top of the 95-m- (311-ft-) high bell tower. The palazzo has retained its medieval appearance, but much of the interior was remodelled for Duke Cosimo I when he moved into the palace in 1540. Leonardo and Michelangelo were asked to redecorate the interior, but it was Vasari who finally undertook the work. His many frescoes (1563–5) glorify Cosimo and his creation of the Grand Duchy of Tuscany.

GUCCI GARDEN

Housed in the imposing Palazzo della Mercanzia, the Florentine design giant's recently refurbished premises has a boutique stocking quirky one-offs and a stylish, contemporary eatery run by triple-Michelin-starred chef Massimo Bottura. There is also a museum on-site, the galleries of which are lined with multimedia exhibitions dedicated to the history of the brand, including vintage advertising posters, garments and other items.

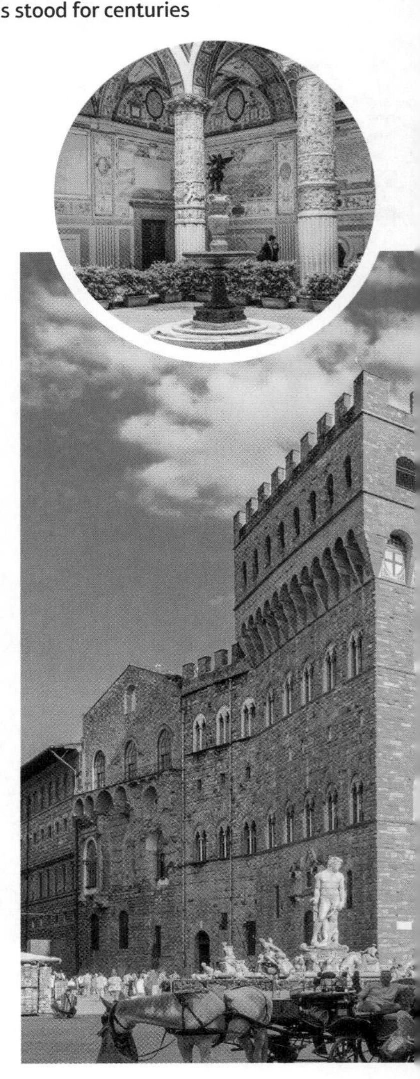

1 Giambologna's *Rape of a Sabine Woman* is located in the Loggia dei Lanzi just outside the Palazzo Vecchio.

2 This leonine sculpture also stands in the *loggia*, one of a pair of imposing marble "Medici lions" that guard the square.

3 The Gucci Garden galleria exhibits some of the fashion brand's most significant pieces.

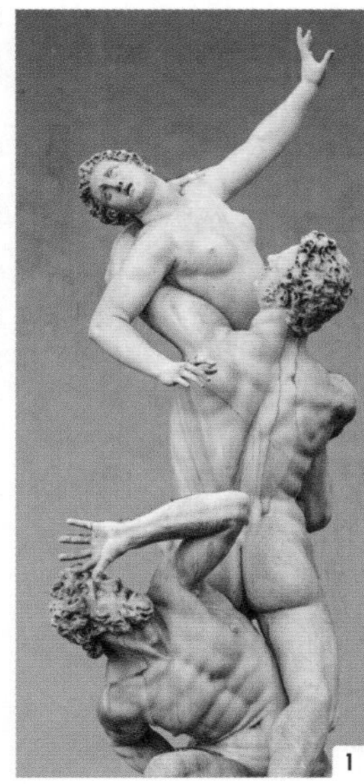

Did You Know?

Members of Florence's medieval government were chosen randomly every two months.

←

The entrance courtyard *(inset)* and façade of the Palazzo Vecchio, in the Piazza della Signoria

THE UFFIZI

E8 Piazzale degli Uffizi 6 B, 23 8:15am-6:50pm Tue-Sun (occasional extended hours in summer) 1 Jan, 1 May, 25 Dec uffizi.it

Florence's best-known gallery draws larger crowds than any other art museum in Italy. The Uffizi's notorious queues are almost unavoidable, but once inside you'll forgive the wait.

The Uffizi was built in 1560–80 as a suite of offices (*uffici*) for Duke Cosimo I's new administration. The architect Vasari used iron reinforcement to create an almost continuous wall of glass on the upper storey. From 1581, Cosimo's heirs used this well-lit space to display the Medici family art treasures, creating what is now the oldest gallery in the world packed with some of the greatest works of the Renaissance.

The collection was born from the immense wealth of the Medici family who commissioned pieces from many great Florentine masters. Francesco I was the first to house the family collection at the Uffizi, and his descendants added to it until 1737, when Anna Maria Ludovica, the last of the Medici, bequeathed it to the people of Florence (on the condition that it never leave the city). Though the Renaissance collection is undoubtedly the highlight, the works on display reach into the 20th century.

GALLERY GUIDE

The paintings are hung in a series of rooms to show the development of Florentine art from Gothic to Renaissance and beyond. The earliest works are on the second floor; start here to explore the collection in a broadly chronological order. Some familiar High Renaissance masterpieces, by artists such as Titian and Raphael, are hung on the first floor, and masters from other European countries are in rooms 44-55. To minimize queuing, book your ticket in advance.

The museum's galleries line either side of the narrow Piazzale degli Uffizi ↑

1 A detail of Botticelli's *Birth of Venus,* which is one of the museum's most famous artworks.

2 Visitors wandering a gallery filled with sculptures and vast paintings.

3 Various pieces by Contini Bonacossi are on display in the museum.

Artworks on display in one of the Uffizi's elegant galleries

Exploring the Uffizi

The Renaissance galleries are undoubtedly the jewel in the Uffizi's crown, comprising the world's largest and most complete collection from this period. A growing understanding of geometry and perspective allowed artists of the time to create an illusion of space and depth in their works.

In room 8, two panels by Piero della Francesca (1410–92) depict the Duke and Duchess of Urbino on one side with representations of their virtues on the other. These were two of the first Renaissance portraits. In the same room, Fra Filippo Lippi's *Madonna and Child with Angels* (1455–66) is a masterpiece of warmth and humanity. Like so many Renaissance artists, Lippi uses a religious subject to celebrate earthly delights. The Botticelli paintings in rooms 10–14, meanwhile, are unmatched, and include *The Birth of Venus*, which still captivates viewers 600 years after it was painted. His brilliant colours and crisp draughtsmanship are a reminder that Renaissance artists often experimented with new pigments to achieve striking effects. The museum also contains works attributed to the young Leonardo da Vinci, such as the unfinished *Adoration of the Magi* (1481), while works by Michelangelo, Raphael and Titian are featured in the High Renaissance and Mannerist galleries.

A visitor admiring Botticelli's *Annunciation* (c 1489-90)

Botticelli's *Primavera*, illustrating a pagan rite of spring

Other Highlights

Gothic Art

▶ Rooms 2 to 6 of the gallery are devoted to Tuscan Gothic art from the 12th to the 14th century. Giotto (1266-1337) introduced a degree of naturalism that was new in Tuscan art. The angels and saints in his *Ognissanti Madonna* (1310) express a broad range of human emotions *(right)*. The throne in this painting and the temple in Lorenzetti's *Presentation in the Temple* (1342), in room 3, show a concern for three-dimensional depth quite at odds with the flatness of much Gothic art.

Giotto's naturalist influence extends throughout the works in room 4. One key example is the *Pietà* (1360-65) attributed to Giottino: look at the difference between the characters' expressions, their medieval - rather than biblical - style of dress and the blood, still fresh on the cross.

Did You Know?

Botticelli was buried at the feet of the model for *Venus*, though her grave has since been moved.

European Art

The works in room 45 show how the naturalism pursued by Northern European masters, such as Dürer (1471-1528) and Cranach (1472-1553), had a profound influence on Renaissance painters. Later Flemish paintings, including those by Rubens (1577-1640) and Van Dyck (1599-1641), are in room 55. Dutch paintings of the 17th and 18th centuries, including a number of Rembrandt self-portraits, are in room 49, while paintings by Spanish masters El Greco (1541-1624), Velázquez (1599-1660) and Goya (1746-1828) are exhibited in room 46.

Later Italian Paintings

Rooms 90 to 93 are dedicated to Caravaggio (1571-1610) and his legacy in the early 17th century. There are works by several of his followers, including Gerard van Honthorst (1592-1656), a Dutch artist renowned for his depictions of artificially lit scenes, and Artemisia Gentileschi (1593-1656), a celebrated female painter perhaps best known for her brutal masterpiece *Judith Slaying Holofernes* (1611-12).

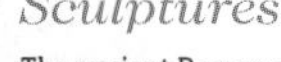

Sculptures

The ancient Roman sculptures displayed along the corridors and in room 56 were mainly collected by the Medici during the 15th century. Their anatomical precision and faithful portraiture were much imitated by Renaissance artists, who saw themselves as giving rebirth to Classical perfection in art.

The Tribune

◀ The octagonal tribune was designed in 1584 by Buontalenti so that Francesco I could display all his favourite works in one room. Notable paintings include Bronzino's portrait (1545) of Eleonora di Toledo with her son, and the same artist's portrait of Bia de'Medici, Cosimo I's illegitimate daughter *(left)*. It was painted just before her early death in 1542.

4

PONTE VECCHIO

E8 B, D

This iconic medieval bridge spans the Arno at its narrowest point. Having withstood floods and wars since the 14th century, it remains a popular spot for visitors keen to sample its famous *botteghe* (workshops) and take in the breathtaking views along the river.

The Ponte Vecchio, or "Old Bridge" – indeed, the oldest bridge in Florence – was built in 1345. It was the only bridge in the city to escape destruction at the hands of retreating Germans during World War II. There have always been workshops on the bridge, but the butchers, tanners and blacksmiths who originally plied their trades here (and who used the river as a convenient rubbish tip) were evicted by Duke Ferdinando I in 1593 because of the noise and stench they created. The workshops were rebuilt and led to the more decorous – and sweet-smelling – goldsmiths. To this day, the shops lining and overhanging the bridge continue to specialize in new and antique jewellery.

GREAT VIEW
On Ponte

One of Italy's most romantic spots, there are few better places than the Ponte Vecchio viewpoint for enjoying Florence's river vistas. Buskers, portrait painters and street traders all congregate on the bridge, creating a lively, colourful scene.

Did You Know?

The Ponte Vecchio escaped Nazi destruction, allegedly because Hitler himself ordered its survival.

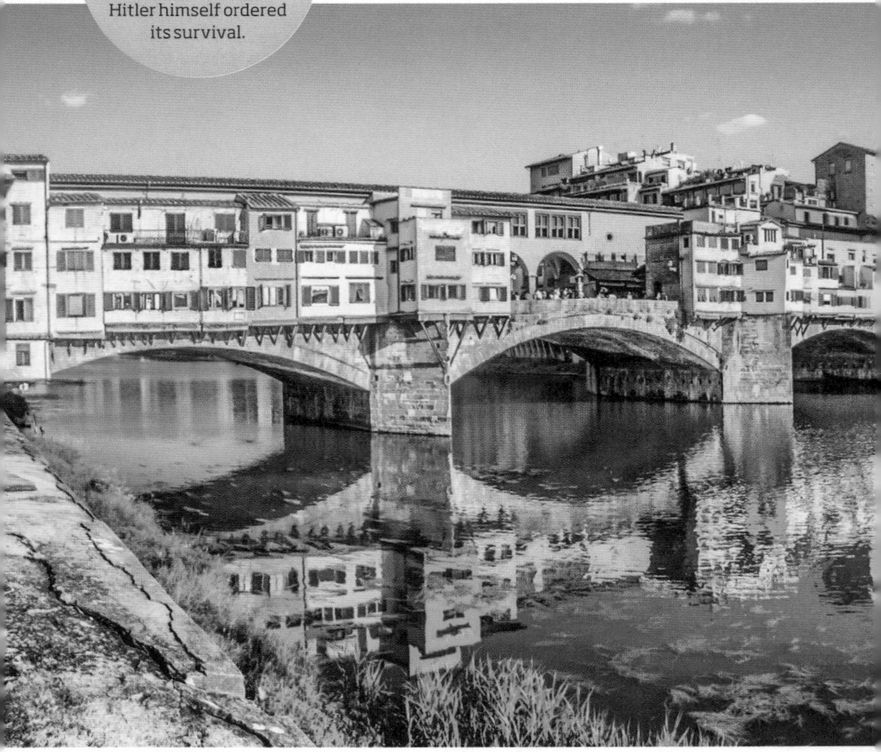

1 Shuttered workshops line the bridge, the oldest of which have rear extensions overhanging the river supported by timber brackets called *sporti*.

2 The bridge is usually packed with people, both tourists and locals alike, plus street perfomers who liven up the popular site.

3 Shops along the Ponte Vecchio sell everything from affordable modern earrings to precious antique rings.

↑ The striking Ponte Vecchio, with its stone arches reflected in the Arno River

THE VASARI CORRIDOR

The Corridoio Vasariano was built in 1565 by Giorgio Vasari and links the Palazzo Vecchio with the Palazzo Pitti, via the Uffizi. This private elevated walkway, also known as Percorso del Principe ("Prince's Route"), allowed the Medici family to move between their residences without having to mix with the crowds on the street below. The corridor is open only to organized tours, which can be booked online *(www.florencetown.com)*.

EXPERIENCE MORE

5 Museo dell'Opera del Duomo

F6 Piazza del Duomo 9 9am-7pm daily (Jun-Aug: to 9pm Fri, Sat & Mon) 1 Jan, Easter Sun, 25 Dec museumflorence.com/museum

This museum, spread across three floors and 25 rooms, offers an extraordinary experience for visitors. It chronicles the building of the Duomo, with an innovative layout and multimedia presentations that bring the sheer scale and ambition of the original project alive. The exhibits are given settings that imitate their original environments; relics from the Duomo and the Baptistry, for example, are displayed in a reconstructed octagonal chapel. There are some dazzling sculptural pieces on show. Donatello's striking *La Maddalena* (1455) stands at the centre of one room, its starkness in marked contrast to the colourful artworks on the walls. Michelangelo's next-to-last work of art, *Pietà* (1555), is here too; a remarkably personal masterpiece, it was abandoned and mutilated by Michelangelo when he found flaws in the marble. It was later acquired and pieced together by the Medici family.

The main attraction on the ground floor is the ancient façade of the Duomo, which was originally unfinished and dismantled in 1587. It has been re-created with the help of a 16th-century drawing. Many of the statues are placed in their original positions opposite the Baptistry doors. On the first floor, a similar reconstruction has been carried out with the sculptures of the bell tower. These statues are life-sized, built to be seen from a distance, and illustrate Renaissance ideals about secular art. The mechanical obstacles faced by Brunelleschi when building the dome are explained in the Cupola hall. The room displays tools specifically invented for the dome's construction. The last stop is the third-floor terrace, with its magnificent view of the Duomo.

It chronicles the building of the Duomo, with an innovative layout and multimedia presentations that bring the sheer scale and ambition of the original project alive.

STAY

Hotel Brunelleschi

This unique hotel, part 15th-century tower, is furnished in opulent boutique style. Some rooms have views of Brunelleschi's dome.

F6 Piazza Santa Elisabetta brunelleschihotelflorence.com

↑ Admiring the statuary at the Museo dell'Opera del Duomo

Orsanmichele

E7 Via dell'Arte della Lana 055 238 86 06 10am-4:50pm daily Aug, 1 Jan, 1 May, 25 Dec

Orsanmichele was built in 1337 as a grain market, but was soon turned into a church. The open arcades became windows and, though these are now bricked in, the original Gothic tracery can still be seen. Niches on the outer walls each hold a statue of the patron saint of one of Florence's major *Arti* (guilds). The interior has two parallel naves. To the right is an extraordinary 1350s altar by Andrea Orcagna, covered in cherubs and carved reliefs and encrusted with coloured marble and glass. Within is Bernardo Daddi's *Virgin and Child* (1348), its frame beautifully carved with angels.

Casa di Dante

F7 Via Santa Margherita 1 055 21 94 16 10am-5pm Tue-Fri, 10am-6pm Sat & Sun

It is uncertain whether the poet Dante Alighieri (1265–1321) was actually born here, but at least the house looks the part. In 1911, the remains of a 13th-century tower house were restored to give the building its rambling appearance. Just a short stroll away is the 11th-century church of Santa Margherita de' Cerch, where Dante is said to have first caught sight of Beatrice Portinari, whom he idolized in his poetry.

Badia Fiorentina

F7 Via del Proconsolo 055 234 45 45 8am-6pm Tue-Sat

This abbey, one of Florence's oldest churches, was founded in 978 by Willa, the widow of Count Uberto of Tuscany. Their son, Count Ugo, was buried inside the church in 1001. His splendid tomb was carved by Mino da Fiesole and dates from 1469–81. Filippino Lippi's *The Virgin Appearing to St Bernard* (1485) also enlivens an otherwise drab and solemn interior. The peaceful Chiostro degli Aranci ("cloister of the orange trees") is worth a visit, even though it is open only on Monday afternoons and is a little hard to find. Look for a door to the right of the altar. Sadly, the orange trees that the monks used to cultivate here are gone, but there are some lovely early frescoes and views of the hexagonal campanile, mentioned by Dante in the *Paradiso* section of *The Divine Comedy*.

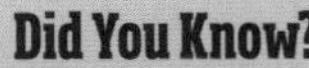

Did You Know?

"Orsanmichele" is a corruption of Orto San Michele, the monastic kitchen garden once on this site.

Santo Stefano al Ponte

E8 Piazza Santo Stefano al Ponte 055 012 46 45 2-6pm Mon-Fri

St Stephen "by the bridge", dating from 969, is so called because of its close proximity to the Ponte Vecchio. The Romanesque façade, dating from 1233, is its most important architectural feature. Now deconsecrated, the church today hosts orchestral concerts and international art exhibitions.

The elaborate 14th-century altar in Orsanmichele, a masterpiece of Gothic style

A view towards the Badia Fiorentina

Mercato Nuovo

E7 Apr-Oct: 9am-7pm daily; Nov-Mar: 9am-7pm Tue-Sat mercatodelporcellino.it

The New Market is often referred to as the Mercato del Porcellino, after its little fountain featuring a bronze boar (*porcellino* means "piggy"). It is also sometimes called the "Straw Market" because goods woven out of straw, such as hats and baskets, were sold here from the end of the 19th century until the 1960s. The market was originally built in 1547–51 as a central market for silk and other luxury goods. Today's stallholders sell leather goods and souvenirs, and on summer evenings buskers gather to entertain visitors.

INSIDER TIP
Lucky Pig

Head to the Il Porcellino fountain to perform a popular good luck ritual: stroke the shiny snout of the bronze wild boar while dropping a coin into the fountain. If it passes through the grating, your wish will come true!

Piazza della Repubblica

E6

Until 1890, when the present square was laid out, this was the site of the Mercato Vecchio (Old Market) and before that, of the ancient Roman forum. A single column from the old market remains, topped by an 18th-century statue of Abundance. Dominating the western side is a triumphal arch, built in 1895 to celebrate the fact that Florence was then the capital of Italy.

The square, popular with both tourists and locals, is lined with cafés. In the early part of the 20th century, the Giubbe Rosse – so called because of the red jackets of the waiters – was the haunt of writers and artists, including those of Italy's avant-garde Futurist movement.

Palazzo Strozzi

D7 Piazza degli Strozzi 10am-8pm daily (to 11pm Thu) palazzostrozzi.org

Awesome for its sheer size, the Strozzi Palace was commissioned in the 15th century by the banker Filippo Strozzi who, having made a fortune in Naples, returned to Florence with one aim: to build a palace that was bigger and more magnificent than that of his great rivals, the Medicis. To this end he bought up and demolished 15 buildings around his existing home, and in 1489 the first stone was laid. Two years later Strozzi was dead, leaving his heirs struggling with the massive costs necessary to complete his grandiose vision.

Completed, eventually, in 1536, the palace is massive. While it is only three storeys high, each floor is as tall as a normal palazzo. The exterior is built of huge rusticated masonry blocks; look out for the original Renaissance torch-holders, lamps and rings for tethering horses which adorn the corners and façades.

Did You Know?

Filippo Strozzi called in astrologers to divine the best day on which to lay the foundation stone of his palazzo.

Antique carousel in the Piazza della Repubblica ↓

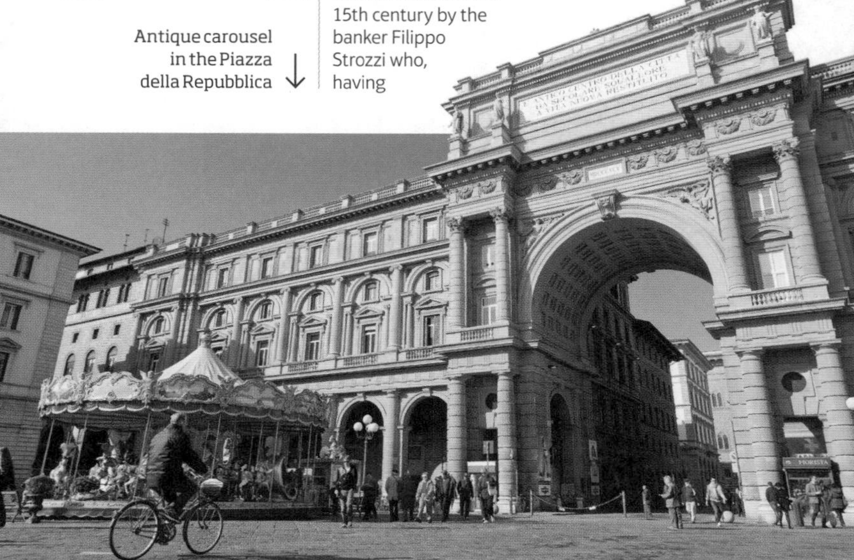

↑ Visitors inside the incredibly vast Palazzo Strozzi

The palace is now a major cultural venue, hosting world-class exhibitions of art and antiquities. When there are no exhibitions in progress, only the courtyard is open.

Palazzo Davanzati

D7 Via Porta Rossa 13 8:15am-1:50pm Mon-Fri, 1:15-6:50pm Sat-Sun 1st, 3rd & 5th Mon and 2nd & 4th Sun of the month; 1 Jan, 1 May, 25 Dec

The Palazzo Davanzati is preserved as a typical house of wealthy Florentines of the 14th century. The entrance courtyard was designed to repel intruders; holes in the vaulted ceiling were used for dropping missiles. In the more peaceful inner courtyard, a staircase links all the floors. In one corner is a well and an ingenious pulley system to raise buckets of water to each floor – quite a luxury when most households of the time had to fetch all their water from a public fountain. The Salone Madornale, where large gatherings would have been held, and the Sala dei Pappagalli (Parrots Room), with its frescoes and rich tapestries, are impressive.

Santi Apostoli

D7 Piazza del Limbo 055 29 06 42 10am-noon, 4-7pm daily

The little church of the Holy Apostles is, with the Baptistry, among the oldest surviving churches in Florence. Florentines like to think that the church was founded in AD 800 by the first Holy Roman Emperor, Charlemagne, but it more likely dates to 1059–1100. The church has a simple Romanesque façade and the basilican plan typical of early Christian churches, but with 16th-century side aisles.

Museo Galileo

F8 Piazza de'Giudici 1 055 265 3311 9:30am-6pm daily (to 1pm Tue) 1 Jan, 25 Apr, 1 May, 24 Jun, 15 Aug, 8, 25 & 26 Dec

This small museum is something of a shrine to the Pisa-born scientist Galileo Galilei (1564–1642). Exhibits include his telescopes and the lens he used to discover the largest moons of Jupiter. There are large-scale reconstructions of his experiments into motion, weight, velocity and acceleration, sometimes demonstrated by the attendants.

In 1657, in memory of Galileo, Florence founded the world's first ever scientific institution, the Accademia del Cimento (Academy for Experimentation). Some of the academy's inventions, such as early thermometers, hygrometers and barometers, are on show here.

Also look out for the 1554 map of the world created by Portuguese cartographer Lopo Homem, and the nautical instruments invented by Sir Robert Dudley, the Elizabethan marine engineer employed by Medici dukes to build the harbour at Livorno.

→ Sixteenth-century armillary sphere at the Museo Galileo

Frescoes in the Sassetti Chapel, within the church of Santa Trinita

Santa Trinita

D7 Piazza di Santa Trinita 055 21 69 12 7am-noon, 4-7pm daily

The original church here, built in the second half of the 11th century by the Vallombrosan monastic order, was very plain – a reflection of the austerity of an order that was founded in Florence in 1092 to restore the simplicity of monastic rule. Gradually, the building became more ornate, with a Baroque façade added in 1593.

Ghirlandaio's frescoes in the Sassetti Chapel (right of the High Altar) show what the church looked like in 1483–6. In one scene, St Francis of Assisi performs a miracle in the Piazza di Santa Trinita, with the church and the Palazzo Spini-Ferroni in the background. The donors of the chapel, Francesco Sassetti and his wife Nera Corsi, are portrayed on either side of the altar. Sassetti, who was general manager of the Medici bank, is shown with his son, Teodoro, and with Lorenzo de'Medici to his right, along with Antonio Pucci. Lorenzo's sons are climbing steps with their tutors. The altar painting, *The Adoration of the Shepherds* (1485), is also by Ghirlandaio; he is the first, dark-haired shepherd. The black sarcophagi of Sassetti and his wife are by Giuliano da Sangallo.

Ponte Santa Trinita

D7 Piazza di Santa Trinita

Just south of Piazza Santa Trinita is what is considered to be Florence's most beautiful bridge, the Ponte Santa Trinita. It affords fine views of the surrounding hills and especially of the Ponte Vecchio *(p74)*. Originally built in wood in 1252, it was rebuilt by Ammannati in 1567 as a monument to Cosimo I's defeat of Siena. Michelangelo is credited with the elegant design, based on an intriguing elliptical curve echoing those on the famous Medici tombs *(p103)*. The statues of the Four Seasons at each end were added in 1608 for Cosimo II's marriage to Maria of Austria. The bridge was restored after it was blown up by the Germans in 1944, and the statues were dredged up from the river bed.

Look west from here to the spectacular golden-yellow Palazzo Corsini (1648–56), with statues on the roof balustrade. It is one of the finest examples of Baroque architecture in Florence.

HIDDEN GEM
Museo Ferragamo

Fans of shoe designer Salvatore Ferragamo will adore this exquisite collection of his shoes, made for such stars as Marilyn Monroe and Sophia Loren. It's inside the Ferragamo store on Via de' Tornabuoni.

Via de' Tornabuoni

D7

This elegant street, running from Piazza degli Antinori to the Santa Trinita bridge, has been the city's most refined ever since the Renaissance, when leading families built their palazzi here. Nowadays this and several of the surrounding streets, especially Via della Vigna Nuova, are lined with high-fashion stores.

The Salvatore Ferragamo flagship store and museum occupies the imposing Palazzo Spini Feroni. The brand originated in Florence, as did Gucci, Roberto Cavalli, Enrico Coveri and Emilio Pucci, as well as the more recent Patrizia Pepe and Ermanno Scervino. Florence was the nation's fashion capital for centuries, long before Milan.

→ The Ponte Santa Trinita with its graceful curves, attributed to Michelangelo

Museo Marino Marini

D6 Piazza San Pancrazio 055 21 94 32 10am-5pm Mon, Wed-Sat Public hols museomarinomarini.it

The former church of San Pancrazio is now a museum devoted to the work of Italy's best-known abstract artist, Marino Marini (1901–80). Marini was born in Pistoia, where more of his work can be seen in the Palazzo del Comune and in the Centro Marino Marini *(p217)*. Marini studied art in Florence before moving on to teaching in Monza and in Milan. He sought to reinterpret Etruscan and medieval art forms and is noted for rugged and elemental bronzes, many on the theme of horse and rider.

↑ An abstract equestrian figure at the Museo Marino Marini

Palazzo Rucellai

D6 Via della Vigna Nuova 16

Built in 1446–51, this is one of the most ornate Renaissance palaces in the city. It was commissioned by Giovanni Rucellai, whose wealth derived from the family business, the import of a rare and costly red dye made from a lichen found only on Majorca. The dye was called *oricello*, from which the name Rucellai is derived.

The architect, Leon Battista Alberti, designed the palace almost as a textbook illustration of the major Classical orders. In ascending order of complexity, the pilaster strips on the ground floor are Doric, those above are Ionic and those on the top floor are Corinthian. Two symbols are carved into the entablature: the Rucellai's billowing sails of Fortune and the ring symbol of Lorenzo de'Medici – a reminder that Bernardo Rucellai formed an alliance with the Medici in the 1460s by marrying Lorenzo's sister, Lucrezia.

EAT & DRINK

Gilli

A historic café serving delicious cakes.

E6 Via Roma 1R caffegilli.com

Paszkowski

Opened in 1846, this charming café hosts daily concerts.

E6 Piazza della Repubblica 35R caffepaszkowski.it

Procacci

A deli-wine bar famed for its truffle specialities.

D6 Via de' Tornabuoni 64R procacci1885.it

I Fratellini

This tiny establishment is a classic stop for a quick glass or a panino.

F7 Via de' Cimatori 38R iduefratellini.it

A SHORT WALK
AROUND THE DUOMO

Distance 1 km (0.5 miles) **Nearest bus stop** Olio **Time** 15 minutes

Much of Florence was rebuilt during the Renaissance, but the eastern part of the city retains a distinctly medieval feel. A lot of what you can see on a stroll through the maze of tiny alleyways and hidden lanes would still be recognizable to Dante. His house, the Casa di Dante, still stands near the parish church where he first glimpsed his beloved, Beatrice Portinari. He would also recognize the Bargello and, of course, the Baptistry. One of the oldest streets is the Borgo degli Albizi. Now lined with Renaissance palaces, it follows the line of the ancient Roman road to Rome.

The dome, completed in 1436, was designed by Brunelleschi to dwarf even the great buildings of ancient Greece and Rome.

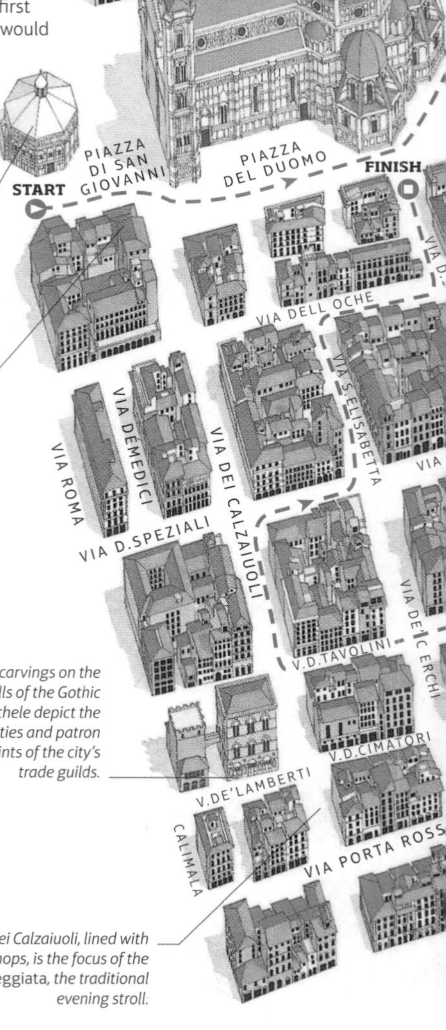

The vast Duomo holds up to 20,000 people. It is elegantly partnered by Giotto's Campanile and the Baptistry, with its decorative doors.

The Loggia del Bigallo was built in 1358. During the 15th century, abandoned children were kept here for three days. If their parents did not claim them, they were sent to foster homes.

The carvings on the walls of the Gothic Orsanmichele depict the activities and patron saints of the city's trade guilds.

Via dei Calzaiuoli, lined with smart shops, is the focus of the passeggiata, the traditional evening stroll.

↑ The elegant bell tower of the Badia Fiorentina

↑ Statues in the beautiful gallery of the Bargello

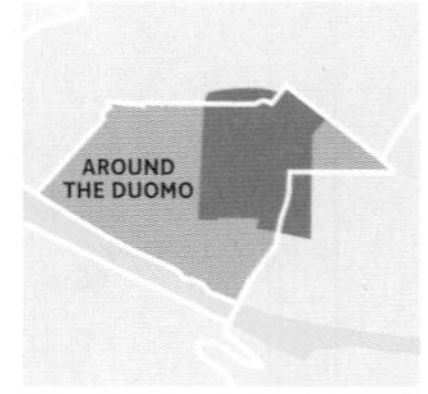

Locator Map

For more detail see p64

Did You Know?

Donatello designed one of the stained-glass windows in the cathedral dome.

The Museo dell'Opera del Duomo displays works that are related to the Duomo.

The Palazzo Nonfinito is now the anthropological museum.

Pegna, a mini-supermarket tucked away in the Via dello Studio, sells a range of gourmet treats, including chocolate, honey, wine, balsamic vinegar and olive oil.

Palazzo Salviati, now the head office of the Banca Toscana, has 14th-century frescoes in the main banking hall.

Santa Margherita de' Cerchi is where Dante married Gemma Donati in 1285.

The Bargello, the city's old prison, is home to a rich collection of applied arts and sculpture.

The Badia Fiorentina's bell regulated daily life in medieval Florence.

The Casa di Dante is a museum devoted to Dante's life and work.

VIA DELL'ORIUOLO
BORGO DEGLI ALBIZI
VIA DE' GIRALDI
VIA DEL PROCONSOLO
VIA DEL PRESTO
VIA DE PANDOLFINI
VIA DELL'ACQUA
ALIGHI ERI
VIA D. MAGAZZINI
VIA DELLA VIGNA VECCHIA
PIAZZA DI S. FIRENZE
VIA DELLA CONDOTTA
VIA DELL ANGUILLARA

0 metres 100
0 yards 100

N

The view from Piazzale Michelangelo at dusk

AROUND SANTA CROCE

In Roman times this area was home to an amphitheatre, the echoes of which can still be seen in the curved Via Torta and Piazza Peruzzi. Since the Middle Ages, however, the focal point of the neighbourhood has been Piazza Santa Croce, one of Florence's largest squares and the site of traditional events such as the Calcio Storico. The piazza is overlooked by the Gothic façade of the late 13th-century Santa Croce church, built with funds donated by the district's wealthy families. In medieval times tanners and wool dyers worked in this area using water from the Arno, and their trades are commemorated in road names such as Via delle Conce (tanneries) and Corso dei Tintori (dyers). Plans proposed in the 19th century to create an avenue linking Santa Croce to Piazza della Signoria were never carried out, but one successful project of that era was Piazzale Michelangelo, designed to add grandeur to the city when it was the national capital (1865–71). The area, along with the rest of the city, suffered from bomb damage during World War II, but out of the wreckage grew the Santa Croce leather school. Opened by the friars of Santa Croce and local leather artisans to teach war orphans a trade, it has helped to ensure the continuation of this important neighbourhood industry.

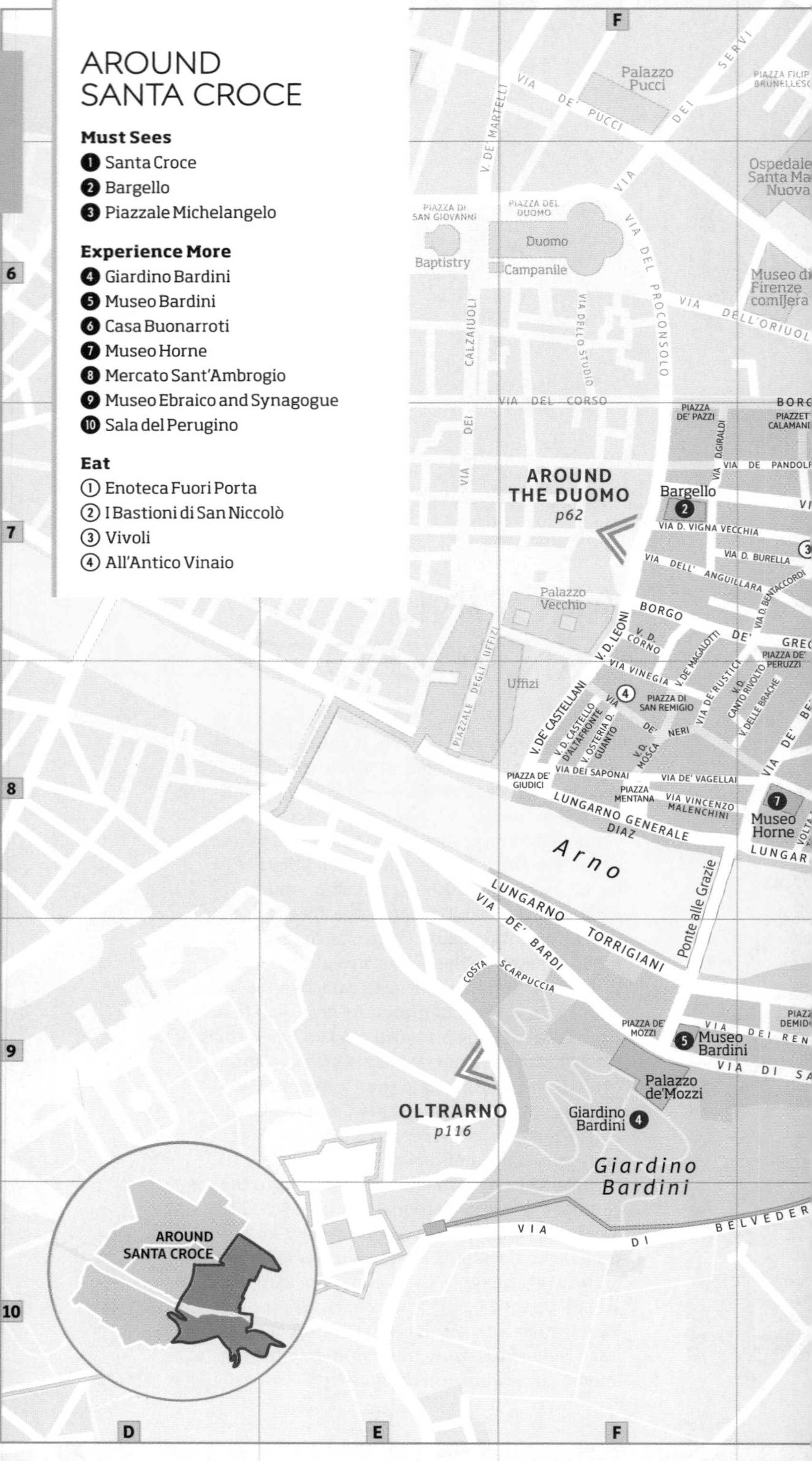

AROUND SANTA CROCE
Must Sees
1 Santa Croce
2 Bargello
3 Piazzale Michelangelo
Experience More
4 Giardino Bardini
5 Museo Bardini
6 Casa Buonarroti
7 Museo Horne
8 Mercato Sant'Ambrogio
9 Museo Ebraico and Synagogue
10 Sala del Perugino
Eat
① Enoteca Fuori Porta
② I Bastioni di San Niccolò
③ Vivoli
④ All'Antico Vinaio
F
Palazzo Pucci
Via de' Pucci
Via dei Servi
V. de' Martelli
Ospedale Santa Maria Nuova
Piazza di San Giovanni
Piazza del Duomo
Duomo
Baptistry
Campanile
Via del Proconsolo
Via dell'Oriuolo
Museo di Firenze com'era
Calzaiuoli
Via dello Studio
Via del Corso
Via dei
Piazza de' Pazzi
D.Giraldi
Via de Pandolfini
AROUND THE DUOMO
p62
Bargello
2
Via D. Vigna Vecchia
Via D. Burella
Via dell' Anguillara
V. D. Bentaccordi
Palazzo Vecchio
Borgo de' Greci
Piazza de' Peruzzi
V. D. Leoni
V. D. Corno
Via Vinegia
V. de' Magalotti
Via de' Rustici
Uffizi
Piazzale degli Uffizi
V. de' Castellani
Piazza di San Remigio
V. D. Canto Rivolto
V. delle Brache
Via de' Neri
V. D. Castello d'Altafronte
V. Osteria D. Guanto
V. D. Mosca
Piazza de' Giudici
Via dei Saponai
Via de' Vagellai
Piazza Mentana
Via Vincenzo Malenchini
7
Museo Horne
Lungarno Generale Diaz
Arno
Ponte alle Grazie
Lungarno Torrigiani
Via de' Bardi
Costa Scarpuccia
Piazza de' Mozzi
5
Museo Bardini
Via dei Renai
Via di San Niccolò
Palazzo de'Mozzi
OLTRARNO
p116
Giardino Bardini
4
Giardino Bardini
Via di Belvedere
AROUND SANTA CROCE
6
7
8
9
10
D
E
F

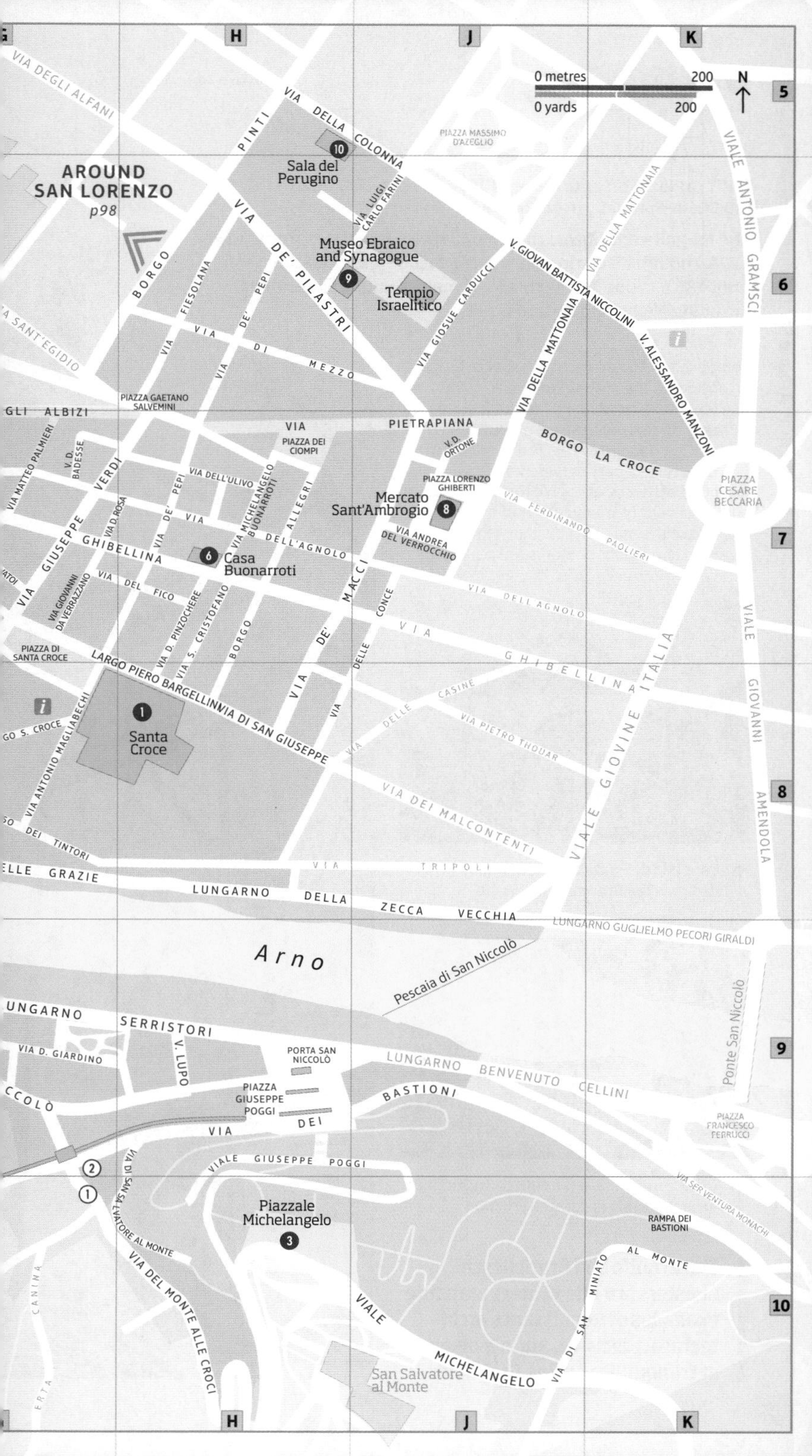
AROUND SAN LORENZO
p98
Sala del Perugino
Museo Ebraico and Synagogue
Tempio Israelitico
Mercato Sant'Ambrogio
Casa Buonarroti
Santa Croce
Piazzale Michelangelo
San Salvatore al Monte
Arno
Pescaia di San Niccolò
Ponte San Niccolò
0 metres 200
0 yards 200
N
VIA DEGLI ALFANI
VIA DELLA COLONNA
PINTI
BORGO
VIA DE' PILASTRI
VIA LUIGI CARLO FARINI
PIAZZA MASSIMO D'AZEGLIO
VIALE ANTONIO GRAMSCI
VIA DELLA MATTONAIA
V. GIOVAN BATTISTA NICCOLINI
V. ALESSANDRO MANZONI
VIA GIOSUE CARDUCCI
VIA FIESOLANA
VIA DE' PEPI
VIA DI MEZZO
VIA SANT'EGIDIO
PIAZZA GAETANO SALVEMINI
BORGO DEGLI ALBIZI
VIA PIETRAPIANA
PIAZZA DEI CIOMPI
V. D. ORTONE
BORGO LA CROCE
PIAZZA CESARE BECCARIA
VIA MATTEO PALMIERI
V. D. BADESSE
VIA VERDI
VIA DELL'ULIVO
VIA MICHELANGELO BUONARROTI
VIA ALLEGRI
PIAZZA LORENZO GHIBERTI
VIA FERDINANDO PAOLIERI
VIA GIUSEPPE VERDI
VIA D. ROSA
VIA GHIBELLINA
VIA DELL'AGNOLO
VIA ANDREA DEL VERROCCHIO
VIA DE' MACCI
VIA GIOVANNI DA VERRAZZANO
VIA DEL FICO
VIA D. PINZOCHERE
VIA S. CRISTOFANO
BORGO
VIA DELLE CONCE
VIALE GIOVANNI AMENDOLA
PIAZZA DI SANTA CROCE
LARGO PIERO BARGELLINI
VIA DI SAN GIUSEPPE
VIA DELLE CASINE
VIA PIETRO THOUAR
VIALE GIOVINE ITALIA
VIA ANTONIO MAGLIABECHI
BORGO S. CROCE
VIA DEI MALCONTENTI
DEI TINTORI
DELLE GRAZIE
VIA TRIPOLI
LUNGARNO DELLA ZECCA VECCHIA
LUNGARNO GUGLIELMO PECORI GIRALDI
LUNGARNO SERRISTORI
VIA D. GIARDINO
V. LUPO
PORTA SAN NICCOLÒ
PIAZZA GIUSEPPE POGGI
LUNGARNO BENVENUTO CELLINI
VIA DEI BASTIONI
PIAZZA FRANCESCO FERRUCCI
VIALE GIUSEPPE POGGI
VIA DI SAN SALVATORE AL MONTE
VIA DEL MONTE ALLE CROCI
VIA SER VENTURA MONACHI
RAMPA DEI BASTIONI
VIA DI SAN MINIATO AL MONTE
VIALE MICHELANGELO
COSTA SAN GIORGIO
ERTA CANINA

SANTA CROCE

H8 Piazza di Santa Croce 055 24 66 105 C, 14, 23
9:30am-5pm daily (from 2pm Sun); no visits during mass

The magnificent Gothic church of Santa Croce dates from 1294, though its distinctive marble façade was not added until 1863. Inside lie the tombs of many famous Florentines, including Michelangelo and Galileo.

Composed of 16 family chapels, Santa Croce is considered the largest Franciscan church in the world. Its spacious, airy interior is enhanced by the 14th-century frescoes of Giotto and his gifted pupil, Taddeo Gaddi. The Arnolfo and Brunelleschi Cloisters provide visitors with fine examples of Renaissance architectural precision, and a moment of tranquillity during their tour. The rest of the monastic buildings form a museum of religious painting and sculpture.

↑ Cappella de'Pazzi, a domed chapel designed by Brunelleschi in 1430

↑ Ornate interiors in the church, including an elaborately decorated crucifix

The Arnolfo and Brunelleschi Cloisters provide visitors with fine examples of Renaissance architectural precision, and a moment of tranquillity during their tour.

INSIDER TIP
Leather School

Tucked under a discreet archway inside the church's grounds is the Scuola del Cuoio, or leather school. Students travel from across the world to train in traditional methods at this family-run institution. Visitors can take in demonstrations or workshops, or simply buy the beautiful final products.

↑ The Neo-Gothic façade of the church, reclad in coloured marble in 1863

Notable Tombs

Leonardo Bruni

▲ A staunch republican, Leonardo Bruni became Chancellor of Florence first in 1410, and then again in 1427. Rossellino's effigy (1447) of the great humanist, depicted in serene old age, is a triumph of realistic portraiture.

Lorenzo Ghiberti

▶ Though Lorenzo Ghiberti (1378-1455) initially trained as a goldsmith, he instead found fame as a sculptor. He is best known as the creator of the magnificent doors of Florence's Baptistry *(p67)*, and is buried in Santa Croce along with his sons and assistants, Vittorio and Lorenzo.

Niccolò Machiavelli

Despite his religious scepticism, Machiavelli was buried here in 1527. The diplomat's monument, designed by Innocenzo Spinazzi, was finally erected more than 250 years after his death, in 1787.

Michelangelo

◀ Michelangelo never completed the *Pietà* he planned for his own tomb. The artist died in Rome, miles from his beloved Florence, but his body was brought back to Santa Croce as his chosen place of burial. His monument was designed in 1570 by Vasari. It is the first tomb visitors see upon entering the church, and the figures adorning it depict Painting, Architecture and Sculpture.

Galileo Galilei

▶ Condemned by the church in 1633 for his "heretic" beliefs, Galileo was denied a Christian burial until 1737, when a tomb designed by Giulio Foggini was erected.

2

BARGELLO

F7 Via del Proconsolo 4 055 238 86 06 (bookings: 055 294 883) 14, A 8:15am-4:20pm daily 1st, 3rd & 5th Mon & 2nd & 4th Sun of each month; 1 Jan, 1 May, 25 Dec

Located in the Palazzo del Bargello, an imposing, battlement-topped fortress, this museum has housed some of Italy's finest Renaissance sculptures since the mid-19th century.

Built in 1255 as the city's town hall, the Bargello is the oldest seat of government surviving in Florence. Its austere, sand-coloured walls surround a striking courtyard that is dotted with wide arches. In the 16th century, it was the residence of the chief of police and a prison, and executions were carried out here until 1786. After extensive renovation, it became one of Italy's first national museums in 1865. Today the Bargello houses a superb collection of Florentine Renaissance sculpture, with rooms dedicated to the work of Michelangelo, Donatello, Verrocchio, Giambologna and Cellini, as well as a collection of Mannerist bronzes and examples from the decorative arts.

BACCHUS STATUE

GALLERY GUIDE

To the right of the entrance hall, the Michelangelo Room is presided over by *Bacchus* (1497), commissioned when the artist was only 21. Other highlights by Michelangelo include his *David-Apollo* (c 1530), marble bust *Brutus* (c 1539) and the unfinished *Pitti Tondo* bas-relief (1505). The courtyard staircase leads up to the Upper Loggia, filled with statues of birds by Giambologna. To the right is the Donatello Room, which contains the panels for the Baptistry doors competition of 1401 and his famous statue of *David* (1450), the first nude by a western artist since Classical times. The Magdalen Chapel and Islamic Collection are also on the first floor. The Verrocchio Room, the Andrea and Giovanni della Robbia rooms, the Arms and Armour Collection and the Room of the Small Bronzes are on the second floor.

← An intricately painted plate, depicting two soldiers in combat

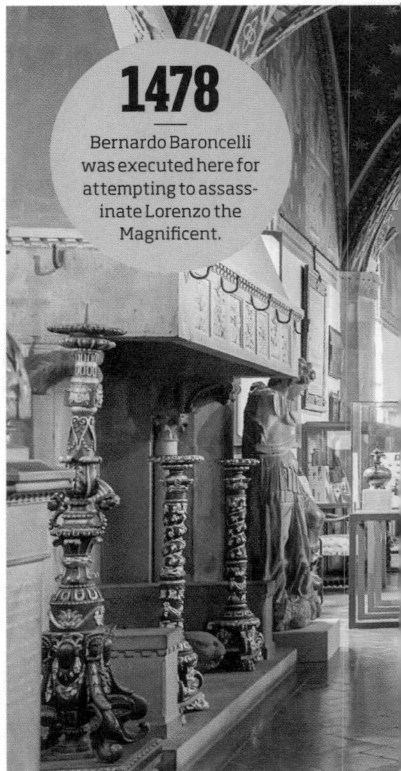

1 The daunting, heavily fortified exterior of the Bargello rises above the tightly packed streets of Florence.

2 Visitors can admire the impressive sculptures throughout the museum's many galleries.

3 A magnificent 16th-century sculpture by Bartolomeo Ammannati.

←

Exhibits in the museum, sitting beneath the Bargello's ornate 13th-century arches

3

PIAZZALE MICHELANGELO

H10

Of all the great Florentine viewpoints – such as the Duomo and Campanile – none offers such a magnificent panorama of the city's skyline as Piazzale Michelangelo.

Laid out in the 1860s by Giuseppe Poggi, and dotted with copies of Michelangelo's statues, this square's balconies attract many visitors and the inevitable massed ranks of souvenir sellers. The piazzale remains an evocative spot, however, especially when the sun sets over the Arno and distant Tuscan hills. In spring you can admire multi-coloured blooms at the iris garden in the square, and for more expansive views you can stroll even higher to the nearby San Miniato al Monte, a picturesque 11th-century church. There is a rose garden en route back towards downtown Florence, filled with 350 varieties and a series of sculptures.

Did You Know?

The creator of Pinocchio, Carlo Lorenzini, is buried in San Miniato's cemetery.

↑ Cityscape as seen from the Piazzale Michelangelo's renowned viewpoint

EAT

Enoteca Fuori Porta
Located on a steep street at the edge of the square, this local favourite combines traditional and contemporary flavours, and offers an excellent wine list.

G10 Via Monte alle Croci 10R
fuoriporta.it

I Bastioni di San Niccolò
A small restaurant with a lively atmosphere; head here for hearty Italian fare and truly exceptional pizzas.

G9 Via dei Bastioni 9R
055 247 67 60

1 The gorgeous interior of San Miniato al Monte is decorated with green and white marble.

2 This hillside building at the edge of the square was also designed by Poggi. Initially intended as a museum, it now houses a restaurant with a lush garden and spectacular views.

3 The church of San Miniato al Monte is part of an abbey that sits above the square.

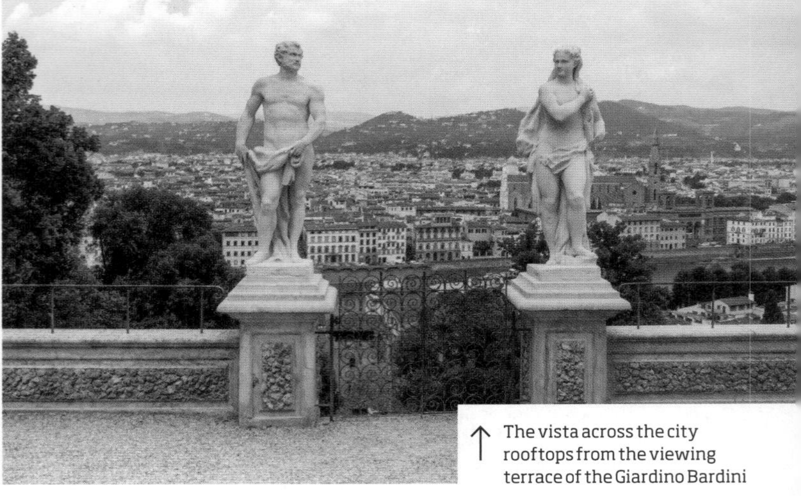

↑ The vista across the city rooftops from the viewing terrace of the Giardino Bardini

EXPERIENCE MORE

4 

Giardino Bardini

F9 Costa San Giorgio 2 Gardens: daily; villa: 10am-7pm Tue-Sun villabardini.it

There are magnificent views over Florence from this historic garden, which dates from medieval times and occupies a steep area of hillside near the Boboli Gardens. The garden has a lovely wisteria tunnel, an Italianate section with a formal staircase and panoramic terrace, an English landscape garden with a decorative Chinese area, and a collection of fruit trees. The adjacent Villa Bardini hosts exhibitions and a museum dedicated to the 20th-century artist Pietro Annigoni.

5 

Museo Bardini

F9 Via dei Renai 37 055 234 24 27 11am-5pm Fri-Mon 1 Jan, Easter Sun, 1 May, 15 Aug, 25 Dec

Stefano Bardini was a 19th-century antiquarian and avid collector of architectural materials. In 1883, he built this palazzo almost entirely from salvaged medieval and Renaissance masonry, including carved doorways, chimney pieces and staircases, and painted and coffered ceilings. The rooms are full of sculpture, paintings, armour, musical instruments, ceramics and antique furnishings.

6 

Casa Buonarroti

H7 Via Ghibellina 70 055 24 17 52 10am-4pm Wed-Mon 1 Jan, Easter Sun, 25 Apr, 1 May, 15 Aug, 25 Dec

Michelangelo (whose surname was Buonarroti) bought a group of three houses on this site as an investment in the early 16th century and spent a short time here. Subsequent generations of his family employed eminent artists to decorate rooms to celebrate the artist's life. The significant collection of his works includes two early reliefs, the *Madonna della Scala* and the *Battle of the Centaurs*.

CIBRÈO EATERIES

Opening his first restaurant in 1979, chef Fabio Picchi now has six very individual enterprises, clustered near the Mercato Sant'Ambrogio. The Florentine is passionate about his roots, even choosing the name Cibrèo to celebrate a local dish made with chicken livers. Cibrèo restaurant is the high-end showcase for his skills, but there is also a Cibrèo trattoria and a café; Ciblèo, serving Tuscan-Asian fusion; and the C.BIO store, which sells the group's own baked goods and has a fabulous deli counter. Picchi's wife Maria is behind the Teatro del Sale, an informal arts venue that welcomes new performers; it's possible to book a buffet dinner before shows.

Museo Horne

G8 Via de'Benci 6 055 24 46 61 10am-2pm Mon-Sat 1 Jan, Easter Sun & Mon, 25 Apr, 1 May, 15 Aug, 1 Nov, 25-26 Dec

This small collection of paintings, sculpture and decorative arts was left to the city by Herbert Percy Horne (1844–1916), the English art historian. It is housed in a splendid example of a Renaissance *palazzino* (small town house), built in 1489 for the Alberti family, who grew wealthy from the city's thriving cloth trade. Don't miss the kitchen, with Horne's superb collection of Renaissance pots, artisan tools and cooking utensils.

From the Horne Museum you can arrange a visit to the Casa Vasari, just around the corner. This is where Giorgio Vasari lived from 1557 until his death in 1574. The walls are decorated with rich frescoes painted by the artist himself.

Mercato Sant'Ambrogio

J7 Piazza Ghiberti 7am-2pm Mon-Sat mercatosantambrogio.it

Dating from 1873, this market is largely frequented by locals who come for the fresh fruit and vegetables, clothing and household goods on sale in the outside area as well as the speciality butchers and delis under cover. Prices are fair and there is an authentic feel to the place; and if all the tempting produce whets your appetite, there is the Trattoria da Rocco, which serves delicious and genuine Florentine specialities.

Did You Know?

Renaissance *palazzini* often had the kitchen on the top floor to avoid fumes rising through the house.

Museo Ebraico and Synagogue

H6 Via Farini 6 055 24 52 52 Oct-May: 10am-5:30pm, Sun-Thu, 10am-3pm Fri; Jun-Sep: 9:30am-6:30pm Sun-Thu, 9:30am-5pm Fri Jewish hols

The green copper-covered dome of Florence's main synagogue stands out on the horizon as you look down on the city from the surrounding hills. Housing a museum of ritual objects dating from the 17th century, the interior is truly stunning, decorated in a colourful Moorish style, with sumptuous frescoes and mosaics, inlaid marble floors and stained-glass windows.

Sala del Perugino

H5 Via della Colonna 9 055 288 88 03 2:30-5:30pm Tue & Thu School holidays

An entrance through the Liceo Michelangelo school leads to the vaulted chapterhouse of the former Santa Maria Maddalena dei Pazzi convent, inside which is the magnificent, large-scale *Crucifixion and Saints* fresco painted by Perugino (1493-6). The beautifully preserved fresco is in three sections, following the arches of the room, unified by the lovely background, a detailed and serene landscape of wooded hills and winding streams.

↓ *Three Saints* by Pietro Lorenzetti, in the Museo Horne

EAT

Vivoli

The city's oldest gelateria, dating from 1930. It is still run by the Vivoli family.

G7 Via dell'Isola degli Stinchi 7R vivoli.it

All'Antico Vinaio

Expect quality local produce at several locations on one street.

F8 Via de' Neri allanticovinaio.com.

Diners at the historic Mercato Centrale

AROUND SAN LORENZO

The Renaissance character of this area is the legacy of the Medici dynasty. Cosimo Il Vecchio commissioned the great artists and sculptors of the time to create numerous monuments, including the family's first residence, the Palazzo Medici Riccardi, and the churches of San Marco and San Lorenzo. Santa Maria Novella was also decorated with important artworks during the Renaissance, while the piazza on which the church sits was the location of the annual Palio dei Cocchi chariot race established at this time. In 1563 Europe's first art school was founded at the Accademia by Vasari (under Medici patronage); its Galleria was added in 1784 to inspire the students.

Following the relocation of the Medicis to Oltrarno in the 16th century, San Lorenzo became more working class. The Santa Maria Novella railway station was inaugurated in 1848 and in 1874 the Mercato Centrale was built to rehouse market stalls banished from the redesigned Piazza Repubblica. In the 20th century the area's status as the city's main transport hub was cemented with the construction of the new Santa Maria Novella train station (1935). Commissioned by the Fascist government to replace the 19th-century building, the plain, blocky structure embodies the functionalist architecture of the time.

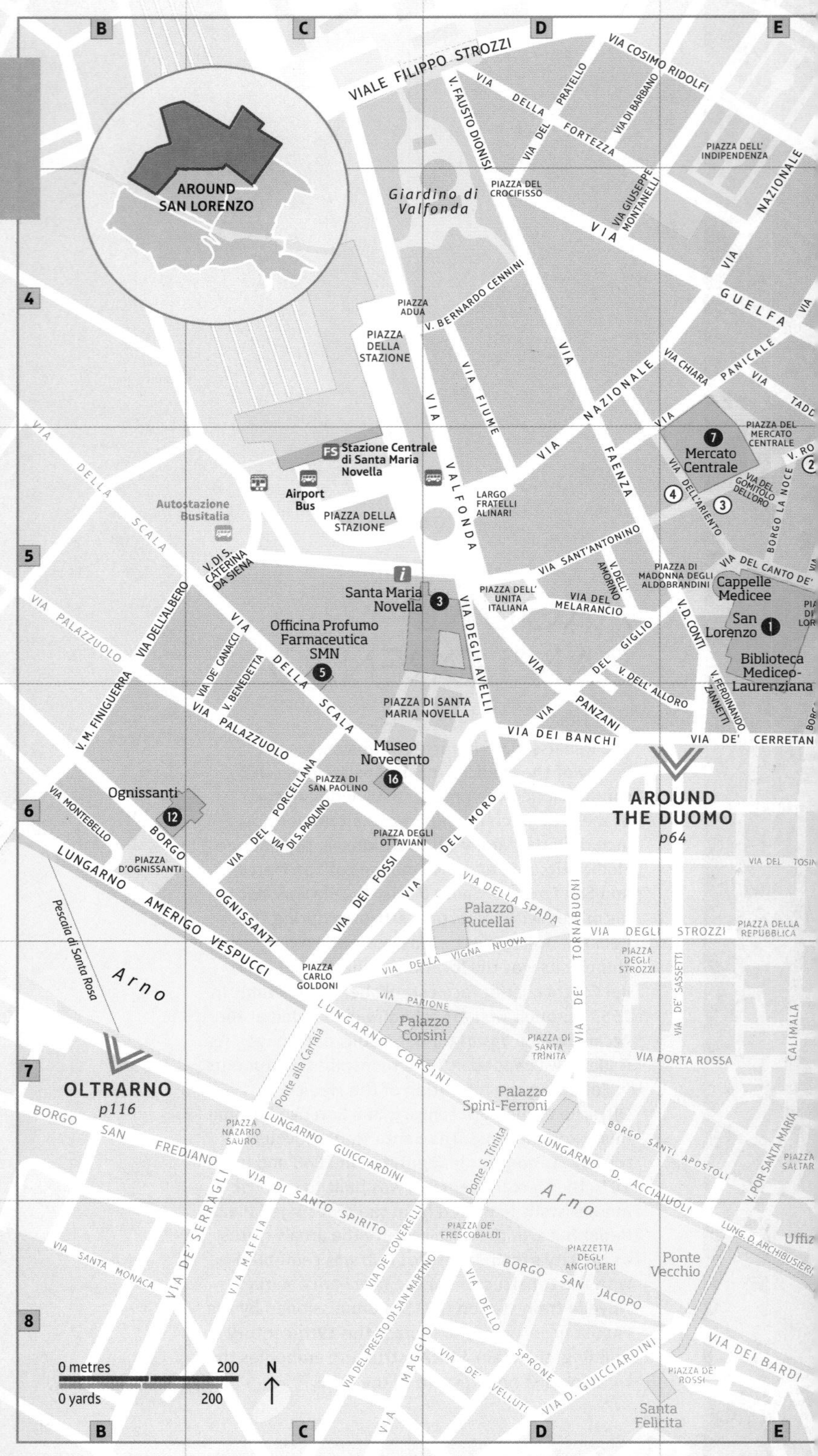

AROUND SAN LORENZO
Giardino di Valfonda
Stazione Centrale di Santa Maria Novella
Airport Bus
Autostazione Busitalia
Santa Maria Novella
Officina Profumo Farmaceutica SMN
Museo Novecento
Ognissanti
Mercato Centrale
Cappelle Medicee
San Lorenzo
Biblioteca Mediceo-Laurenziana
Palazzo Rucellai
Palazzo Corsini
Palazzo Spini-Ferroni
Ponte Vecchio
Santa Felicita
AROUND THE DUOMO
p64
OLTRARNO
p116
Arno
0 metres 200
0 yards 200
N

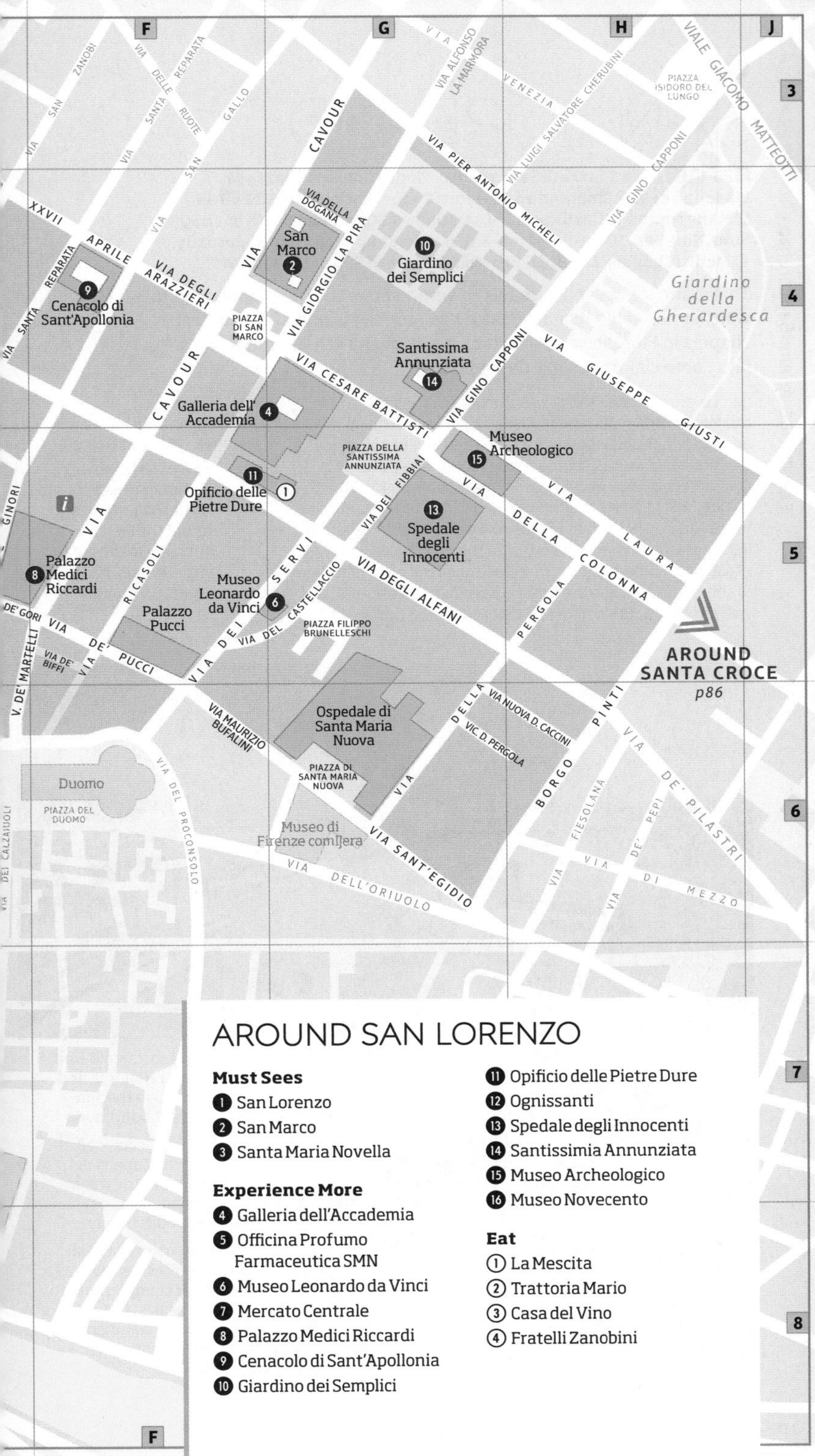

AROUND SAN LORENZO
Must Sees
1 San Lorenzo
2 San Marco
3 Santa Maria Novella
Experience More
4 Galleria dell'Accademia
5 Officina Profumo Farmaceutica SMN
6 Museo Leonardo da Vinci
7 Mercato Centrale
8 Palazzo Medici Riccardi
9 Cenacolo di Sant'Apollonia
10 Giardino dei Semplici
11 Opificio delle Pietre Dure
12 Ognissanti
13 Spedale degli Innocenti
14 Santissimia Annunziata
15 Museo Archeologico
16 Museo Novecento
Eat
① La Mescita
② Trattoria Mario
③ Casa del Vino
④ Fratelli Zanobini
AROUND SANTA CROCE p86
San Marco
Giardino dei Semplici
Cenacolo di Sant'Apollonia
Giardino della Gherardesca
Santissima Annunziata
Galleria dell' Accademia
Museo Archeologico
Opificio delle Pietre Dure
Spedale degli Innocenti
Palazzo Medici Riccardi
Museo Leonardo da Vinci
Palazzo Pucci
Ospedale di Santa Maria Nuova
Duomo
Piazza del Duomo
Museo di Firenze com'era
Piazza di San Marco
Piazza della Santissima Annunziata
Piazza Filippo Brunelleschi
Piazza di Santa Maria Nuova
Piazza Isidoro del Lungo
Via Cavour
Via XXVII Aprile
Via degli Arazzieri
Via della Dogana
Via Giorgio La Pira
Via Cesare Battisti
Via Gino Capponi
Via Giuseppe Giusti
Via della Colonna
Via Laura
Via dei Servi
Via dei Fibbiai
Via degli Alfani
Via del Castellaccio
Via Ricasoli
Via de' Pucci
Via de' Gori
Via de' Biffi
V. de' Martelli
Via Maurizio Bufalini
Via della Pergola
Via Nuova d. Caccini
Vic. d. Pergola
Borgo Pinti
Via Sant'Egidio
Via dell'Oriuolo
Via del Proconsolo
Via de' Pilastri
Via di Mezzo
Via Fiesolana
Via de' Pepi
Via Pier Antonio Micheli
Via Alfonso La Marmora
Via Venezia
Via Luigi Salvatore Cherubini
Viale Giacomo Matteotti
Via San Gallo
Via San Zanobi
Via Santa Reparata
Via delle Ruote
Via dei Calzaiuoli
F
G
H
J
3
4
5
6
7
8

SAN LORENZO

E5 Basilica: Piazza di San Lorenzo; Medici Chapels: Piazza di Madonna degli Aldobrandini Medici Chapels tickets: 055 29 48 83 Many routes Basilica: Mar-Oct: 10am-5:30pm Mon-Sat (from 1:30 Sun), Nov-Feb: 10am-5pm Mon-Sat; Medici Chapels: 8:15am-5pm daily Medici Chapels: 1st, 3rd & 5th Mon, 2nd & 4th Sun of the month

This rustic-looking basilica has towered above the neighbourhood to which it has given its name since the 1400s. It is one of the largest chapels in Florence and – built as it was over a 4th-century church – lays some claim to being the oldest.

San Lorenzo as seen today was the parish church of the Medici family, and they lavished their wealth on its adornment. Brunelleschi rebuilt the church in Renaissance Classical style in 1419, although the façade was never completed. In 1520 Michelangelo began work on the Medici tombs, before designing the Biblioteca Mediceo-Laurenziana in 1524 to house the family's collection of manuscripts; the library's.Mannerist staircase is one of the artist's most innovative designs The church is the burial place of all principal members of the Medici family, from Cosimo il Vecchio to Cosimo III, as well as other notable figures such as the artist Donatello.

INSIDER TIP
Market Price

The San Lorenzo outdoor market sprawls through the streets around the Mercato Centrale. Head here for leather goods, and be prepared to haggle.

1 The terracotta-coloured rooftops of the church and dome rise above the San Lorenzo neighbourhood.

2 The highly decorated interior of the Capella dei Principi houses the tombs of 49 members of the dynastic Medici family.

3 The square behind San Lorenzo is presided over by a monument commissioned by Cosimo I,the first Grand Duke of Tuscany, to commemorate his father, Giovanni delle Bande Nere.

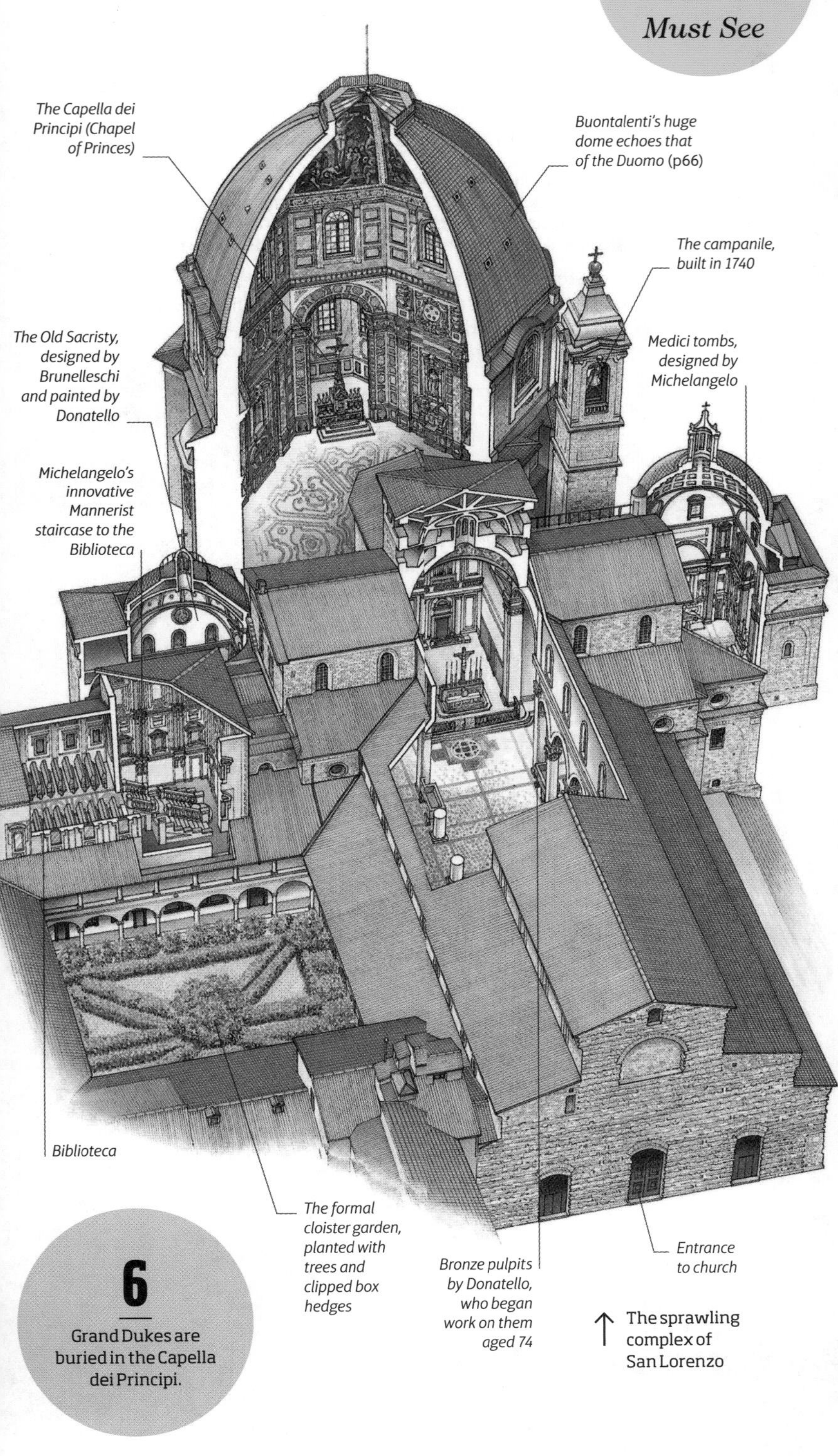

↑ The sprawling complex of San Lorenzo

6

Grand Dukes are buried in the Capella dei Principi.

2

SAN MARCO

G4 Piazza di San Marco Church: 055 28 76 28; museum: 055 238 86 08 (reservations: 055 29 48 83) Many routes Church: 7am-noon, 4-8pm daily; museum: 8:15am-1:50pm Mon-Fri, 8:15am-4:50pm Sat & Sun Museum: 2nd & 4th Mon & 1st, 3rd & 5th Sun of month; 1 Jan, 1 May, 25 Dec

Still in use as a church today, this perfectly preserved Dominican monastery also houses the Museo di San Marco, which is home to the world's largest collection of works by Fra Angelico (1395–1455).

The convent of San Marco was founded in the 13th century and enlarged in 1437, when Dominican monks from nearby Fiesole moved here at the invitation of Cosimo il Vecchio. He paid a considerable sum to have the convent rebuilt by his favourite architect, Michelozzo, whose simple cloisters and cells are the setting for a remarkable series of devotional frescoes (c 1438–45) by Fra Angelico. Two cells were reserved for Cosimo il Vecchio, so that he could retreat to the convent to meditate and pray. Today the monastery also serves as a museum, where Fra Angelico's most important paintings can be admired.

Did You Know?

San Marco is home to Europe's first public library, which opened in 1441 and contained 400 books.

THE "MAD MONK"

Girolamo Savonarola (1452-98), prior of San Marco, became popular for his calls for Christian renewal. When France threatened invasion in 1494, Florence expelled the ruling Medici family and installed a republic with the friar at the helm. Savonarola led campaigns against the excesses of the Renaissance, but enraged Pope Alexander VI with his radicalism, and he was executed in 1498. At San Marco you can see several relics of the "Mad Monk", including his cloak and part of the beam he was hanged from.

↑ The broad façade of San Marco church

→ *The Annunciation* (c 1440) by Fra Angelico, which demonstrates the artist's mastery of perspective

The richly decorated interior of San Marco

SANTA MARIA NOVELLA

D5 Piazza di Santa Maria Novella A, 6, 11, 36, 37 Check website for details 8 & 25 Dec chiesasantamarianovella.it

Part monastery and part museum, this basilica is fronted by a spectacular green-and-white marble façade. The interior is no less striking, with works by artists including Masaccio, Giotto and Ghirlandaio on display.

Built by the Dominicans from 1279 to 1357, the Gothic church of Santa Maria Novella houses some of the most important works of art in Florence. Beside the church is a cemetery walled in with *avelli* (grave niches), which continue along the façade and the wall beyond. The cloisters form a museum, within which the frescoes in the Spanish Chapel show the Dominicans as whippets – *domini canes*, or hounds of God – rounding up the "stray sheep".

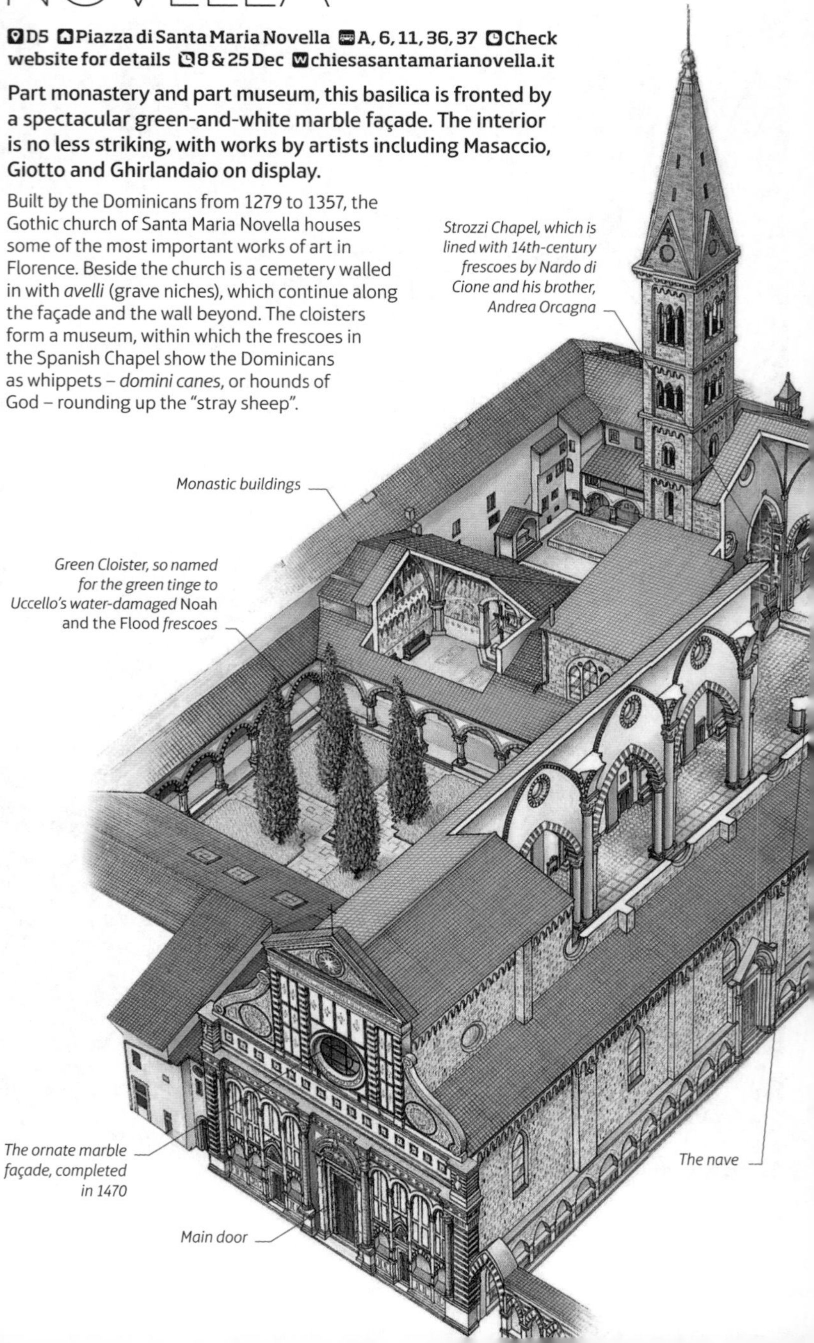

Strozzi Chapel, which is lined with 14th-century frescoes by Nardo di Cione and his brother, Andrea Orcagna

Monastic buildings

Green Cloister, so named for the green tinge to Uccello's water-damaged Noah and the Flood *frescoes*

The ornate marble façade, completed in 1470

Main door

The nave

1 The striking marble façade of Santa Maria Novella is bathed in golden Italian sunlight.

2 The interior of the church complex is patterned with magnificent ancient frescoes.

3 *The Presentation of the Virgin at the Temple* is part of Ghirlandaio's famous fresco series that adorns the walls of the Tornabuoni Chapel (named for the family who commissioned the paintings).

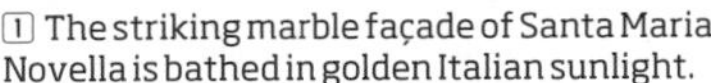

The walls of the old cemetery, which are decorated with the emblems and badges of wealthy Florentines

↑ The beautiful monastical complex of Santa Maria Novella

HOLY TRINITY (C 1427)

Masaccio pioneered perspective in painting, using architectural illusion to create a three-dimensional effect. In this fresco, his most famous work, the figures form a triangle, symbolizing the Holy Trinity. The viewer's eye is drawn upwards to the figures of Christ and God the Father at the apex. The Virgin and St John are depicted as real people, rather than idealized figures. Lorenzo Lenzi, Masaccio's patron, kneels opposite his wife.

EXPERIENCE MORE

Galleria dell'Accademia

G4 Via Ricasoli 60 Information: 055 238 86 09; booking: 055 29 48 83 8:15am-6:50pm Tue-Sun 1 Jan, 1 May, 25 Dec

The Academy of Fine Arts in Florence was founded in 1563 and was the first school in Europe set up to teach drawing, painting and sculpture. The art collection displayed in the gallery was formed in 1784 with the aim of providing students with material to study and copy.

Since 1873, many of Michelangelo's most iconic works have been in the Accademia, most famously *David* (1504). This colossal Classical statue, 5.2 m (17 ft) tall, depicts the biblical hero who killed the giant Goliath. It was commissioned by the city of Florence and positioned in front of the Palazzo Vecchio. This established Michelangelo, then aged 29, as the foremost sculptor of his time. In 1873, it was moved to the Accademia, to protect it from the weather and pollution. A copy now stands in the original position in Piazza della Signoria *(p68)*; a second can be seen in the Piazzale Michelangelo *(p94)*.

Michelangelo's other masterpieces here include a statue of St Matthew, finished in 1508, and the *Quattro Prigionieri* (the four prisoners), which were sculpted between 1521 and 1523 and intended to ornament the tomb of Pope Julius II. The muscular figures struggling to free themselves from the stone are among the most dramatic of his works. The statues were moved to the Grotta Grande in the Boboli Gardens in 1585, where casts of the originals can now be seen.

Also here are important paintings by 15th- and 16th-century contemporaries of Michelangelo such as Fra Bartolomeo, Filippino Lippi, Bronzino and Ridolfo del Ghirlandaio. They include the *Madonna del Mare* (Madonna of the Sea), attributed to Botticelli (1445–1510), and *Venus and Cupid* by Jacopo Pontormo (1494–1556), based on a preparatory drawing by Michelangelo. Also on display is an elaborately painted wooden chest, the *Cassone Adimari*. Dating from around 1440, it originally held a bride's trousseau, and is covered with details of Florentine daily life, clothing and architecture. The bridal party is pictured standing in front of the Baptistry.

Pacino di Bonaguida's *Tree of Life* (1310) is a prominent painting among the Byzantine and late 13th- and 14th-century religious art, much of which is stylized and heavily embossed with gold.

The Salone della Toscana (Tuscany Room) is full of 19th-century sculpture and paintings by members of the Accademia, and a series of original plaster models by the sculptor Lorenzo Bartolini, a professor at the Accademia

Did You Know?

A replica *David* made for London's V&A Museum came with a detachable fig leaf for modesty.

→ Michelangelo's *David*, effortlessly dominating the Accademia gallery

Tuscan produce at its finest on display at the Mercato Centrale ↑

from 1839 until his death in 1850. His work includes busts of the poet Lord Byron and the composer Franz Liszt.

5 

Officina Profumo Farmaceutica SMN

C5 Via della Scala 16 9am-8pm daily smnovella.it

First opened in 1612 by Dominican friars at Santa Maria Novella, this unique perfumery has sold popular remedies and perfumes for over 400 years. The history of its aromatic waters can be traced all the way back to the 14th century, when they were used as a disinfectant during plague outbreaks. The frescoed premises, which include a museum and a tearoom, conjure up a real atmosphere of times gone by, and the ornate shop sells perfumes, cosmetic creams and natural remedies still made to the recipes used by the friars.

FINE FRAGRANCE

Florence's master perfumers have been among the world's best for centuries. In addition to the historic Officina Profumo Farmaceutica di Santa Maria Novella, Dr Vranjes *(Via della Spada 9R)* has become a well-known name for luxury fragrances for the home and person, while Lorenzo Villoresi works on a smaller scale at his distinctive San Niccolò boutique-atelier.

6 

Museo Leonardo da Vinci

G5 Via dei Servi 66R 10am-7pm daily (to 6pm Nov-Mar) mostredi leonardo.com

This small museum contains more than 40 life-size models created from da Vinci's original plans – an awe-inspiring collection of inventions that show just how far ahead of his time the genius was. There are flying machines, contraptions destined for military use and examples of civil engineering, and visitors are free to turn handles, move levers and generally interact with the various items. Another room is dedicated to some of his greatest works of art, while a third has a display of video mapping on the human body to show how anatomical studies were fundamental to developments in the world of art and sculpture. The museum shop has excellent model kits of da Vinci's inventions as well as books and souvenirs.

7 Mercato Centrale

E5 Via dell'Ariento 10-14 Ground-floor food market: 7am-2pm Mon-Sat; first floor: 10am-midnight daily mercatocentrale.it

At the heart of the San Lorenzo street market is the bustling Mercato Centrale, Florence's busiest food market. It is housed in a vast two-storey building of cast-iron and glass, built in 1874 by Giuseppe Mengoni. The ground-floor stalls sell meat, poultry, fish, hams, oils and cheeses. There are also Tuscan takeaway foods such as *porchetta* (roast suckling pig), *lampredotto* (pig's intestines) and *trippa* (tripe). The first floor functions as a large bar/ restaurant, and also has a bank, a bookshop and a cooking school. On the mezzanine you will find a pizzeria and a restaurant.

↑ A nobleman from the fresco of *The Procession of the Magi (inset)* in Palazzo Medici Riccardi

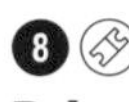

Palazzo Medici Riccardi

F5 Via Cavour 1 055 276 03 40 8:30am-7pm Thu-Tue (last adm 5pm) 1 May, 25 Dec

Home of the Medici for 100 years from 1444, the palazzo was later acquired by the Riccardi family and now houses government offices. It was built to an austere design by Michelozzo for Cosimo il Vecchio, who rejected Brunelleschi's original plans as too flamboyant – Cosimo did not want to flaunt his wealth.

Through the main door, the courtyard walls are covered in ancient Roman masonry fragments. Donatello's statue *David* (now in the Bargello) used to be here, but today the place of honour is given to Bandinelli's marble *Orpheus*.

Only a few rooms inside are open to the public. In the Cappella dei Magi is a colourful fresco of *The Procession of the Magi* painted in 1459–60 by Benozzo Gozzoli. It depicts several members of the Medici dynasty *(p54)*. The Sala di Luca Giordano is named after the Neapolitan artist who painted its walls with *The Apotheosis of the Medici* in High Baroque style in 1683.

Pre-booking is advisable in the busy season.

Cenacolo di Sant'Apollonia

F4 Via XXVII Aprile 1 055 238 86 07 8:15am-1:50pm daily 1st, 3rd & 5th Sun, 2nd & 4th Mon of the month

The cloister and refectory of what was originally a convent for Camaldolite nuns are now used by the students of Florence University. On the main wall of the refectory is a fresco of *The Last Supper*, painted in 1445–50, one of the few surviving works by Andrea del Castagno. He was a pupil of Masaccio and among the first Renaissance artists to experiment with perspective. Judas sits isolated in the foreground of the picture, disrupting its balance and breaking up the long white strip of tablecloth. He has the face of a satyr: a mythological creature, half-man, half-goat, often used in Renaissance paintings to represent evil.

> **Donatello's statue *David* (now in the Bargello) used to be here, but today the place of honour is given to Bandinelli's marble *Orpheus*.**

10

Giardino dei Semplici

G4 Via Micheli 3 055 275 74 02 Apr-Sep: 10am-7pm Thu-Tue; Oct-Mar: 10am-4pm Sat & Sun 1 Jan, 6 Jan, 25 Apr, Easter Sun & Mon, 1 May, 13-17 Aug, 1 Nov, 24-26 Dec, 31 Dec

The word "Semplici" refers to the medicinal plants, or "simples", grown and used by medieval apothecaries. This historic herb garden was set up in 1545 by Niccolò Tribolo for Cosimo I and retains its original layout, but the plant collection today includes tropical specimens as well as flora native to Tuscany.

Also of interest are the large 19th-century glasshouses and an impressive selection of monumental trees. Up to 30 m (100 ft) tall, they include a yew tree planted from seed in 1720 and a cork oak planted in 1805; the trunk of which has a circumference of over 4 m (13 ft).

11 

Opificio delle Pietre Dure

G5 Via degli Alfani 78 055 265 11 8:15am-2pm Mon-Sat Public hols

Situated in the former monastery of San Niccolò, the *opificio* (factory) was founded in the 16th century through the patronage of the Medici dukes and dedicated to the Florentine craft of producing inlaid pictures using marble and semiprecious stones. The tradition has flourished over the centuries and the *opificio* now runs a national institute teaching the craft. There is a small museum displaying 19th-century workbenches, tools, vases and portraits showing *pietre dure* work, as well as exquisite marbles and semiprecious stones dating to Medici times. Several *pietre dure* table tops are on display. Since 1975, the institution has incorporated the Florentine centre for art restoration, which uses highly advanced techniques.

EAT & DRINK

La Mescita

A traditional hostelry with a handful of tables, serving panini and hearty dishes.

G5 Via degli Alfani 70R
338 992 2640

Trattoria Mario

This historic eatery offers a lunch menu of typical local dishes.

E5 Via Rosina 2R
trattoria-mario.com

Casa del Vino

This place is ideal for a glass of Chianti and a snack.

E5 Via dell' Ariento 16R Sun
casadelvino.it

Fratelli Zanobini

An atmospheric wine-bar; expect standing room only.

E5 Via Sant'Antonino 47R
055 239 68 50 Sun

←

Part of the herb gardens growing "simples" at the Giardino dei Semplici

↑ The façade of the Ognissanti, an example of Baroque architecture

12 Ognissanti

B6 Borgo Ognissanti 42 055 239 87 00 7:45am-noon, 4:45-6:30pm Mon-Sat; refectory: 9am-1pm Mon & Sat Fri morning, first and last Mon of month

All Saints was the church of the Vespucci, one of whose members, the 15th-century navigator Amerigo, gave his name to the Americas. He is depicted in a Ghirlandaio fresco in the second chapel on the right. The major artwork here, however, is Giotto's *Crucifix*, painted on wood; newly restored, its brilliant colours are breathtaking.

Ognissanti is also the burial place of Sandro Botticelli. His fresco of *St Augustine* (1480) is on the south wall. Alongside the church is a cloister and a refectory in which Ghirlandaio's fresco *The Last Supper* (1480), with its background of birds and trees, can be seen.

13 Spedale degli Innocenti

G5 Piazza della Santissima Annunziata 12 055 203 73 08 10am-7pm daily 1 Jan, Easter, 25 Dec

Built in the early 15th century as an orphanage, the most beautiful feature of the Hospital of the Innocents is its elegant colonnades by Brunelleschi, a masterpiece of early Renaissance architecture. The rounded arches are interspersed with sky-blue terracotta roundels with images of babies added by Andrea della Robbia at a later date. Look out for the *rota*, a rotating stone to the left of the portico where unwanted children could be left anonymously to the care of the orphanage.

The institute continues to work for children's rights to this day. It also has a museum with around 80 paintings including works by Botticelli and Ghirlandaio, as well as a display on the history of the organization. There are views across the rooftops of Florence and the Duomo from the top-floor terrace café.

14 Santissima Annunziata

G4 Piazza della Santissima Annunziata 055 26 61 81 7:30am-12:30pm, 4-6:30pm daily (also 8:45-9:45pm Sun)

The Church of the Holy Annunciation was founded by the Servite order in 1250 and rebuilt by Michelozzo between 1444 and 1481. There is a series of early 16th-century frescoes in the atrium by Mannerist artists Rosso Fiorentino, Andrea del Sarto and Jacopo Pontormo, but many have suffered from damp and are fading. The most celebrated are *The Journey of the Magi* (1511) and *The Birth of the Virgin* (1514), by del Sarto.

The church contains one of the most revered shrines in Florence, a painting of the Virgin Mary begun in 1252 by a monk. Devout Florentines believe it was finished by an angel. Nine chapels radiate from the sanctuary. The central one contains the tomb of Giambologna, with bronze reliefs and a crucifix he sculpted for his own resting place.

Through the door in the north transept of the church is the Chiostro dei Morti (Cloister of the Dead), originally used as a burial ground and packed with memorial stones. The fresco above the entrance porch is by Andrea del Sarto. Painted in 1525, it shows the Holy Family resting on their

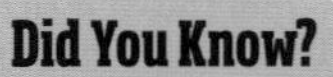

Did You Know?

Many newly-weds visit Santissima Annunziata to present a bouquet of flowers to the Virgin.

Sepulchral and richly decorated, the interior of Santissima Annunziata

↑ The ancient Etruscan François Vase in the Museo Archeologico

flight to Egypt and is usually known as *La Madonna del Sacco*, since Joseph is depicted leaning on a sack.

15 

Museo Archeologico

G5 Via della Colonna 36 055 235 75 8:30am–7pm Tue–Fri, 8:30am–2pm Sat–Mon 2nd, 4th and 5th Sun of the month, 1 Jan, 1 May, 25 Dec

The Archaeological Museum is in a palazzo built by Giulio Parigi for the Princess Maria Maddalena de'Medici in 1620. It now exhibits outstanding collections of Etruscan, Greek, Roman and ancient Egyptian artifacts, the latter including a complete chariot of bone and wood found near Thebes that dates from the 15th century BC.

A section on the second floor is dedicated to Greek vases, with a room given over to the François Vase, found in an Etruscan tomb at Fonte Rotella near Chiusi *(p188)*. Painted and signed in 570 BC, it is decorated with six rows of black and red figures depicting scenes from Greek mythology. The Etruscan collection was very badly damaged by the 1966 floods in Florence *(p55)*, so since then restoration work has been carried out on the pieces.

On the first floor there are two famous bronzes. The *Chimera (p178)*, sculpted in the 4th century BC, is a mythical lion with a goat's head and a serpent for a tail, shown here cowering in terror. It was ploughed up in a field near Arezzo in 1553 and presented to Cosimo I de'Medici by Giorgio Vasari. The *Arringatore* (Orator) was found c 1566 near Lake Trasimeno in central Italy and is inscribed with the name of an Etruscan aristocrat, Aulus Metullus. The sculpture dates from the 1st century BC, and the figure, splendidly dressed in a Roman toga, appears to be addressing his audience.

IT'S AMERICA, NOT COLUMBIA

Masters of perspective, Florentine artists made excellent navigators and mapmakers. When Columbus returned from his historic transatlantic voyage, King Ferdinand of Spain hired Amerigo Vespucci, from the Florentine merchant family, to verify this new route to the Indies. On his voyage Vespucci soon realized that Columbus had instead discovered a new continent, describing his findings in letters home to Florence. His colleagues quickly drew up the new landmass and named it America, in tribute to Vespucci.

16 

Museo Novecento

C6 Piazza Santa Maria Novella 10 Apr–Sep: 11am–2pm Thu, 11am–11pm Fri, 11am–8pm Sat–Wed; Oct–Mar: 11am–2pm Thu, 11am–7pm Fri–Wed museonovecento.it

Housed in a lovely former convent opposite the church of Santa Maria Novella *(p106)*, this fine museum was inaugurated in 2014. Displaying around 400 works in chronological order, it offers visitors a comprehensive picture of Italian art from the early 20th century to the present day. Temporary exhibitions focusing on individual artists or themes are held regularly while the rich permanent collections include works by Giorgio Morandi, Giorgio de Chirico, Filippo de Pisis, Mario Sironi and Renato Guttuso as well as a series of portraits by local artist Otone Rosai. Arts and crafts workshops for children can be booked.

A SHORT WALK AROUND SAN LORENZO

Distance 1 km (0.5 miles) **Nearest bus stop** Santa Maria Maggiore **Time** 15 minutes

This area has the mark of Cosimo il Vecchio, founder of the Medici dynasty, who commissioned San Lorenzo and the Palazzo Medici Riccardi. In much of the area, and especially around the Mercato Centrale, a huge general market fills the streets, its colourful awnings almost obscuring the various monuments. The market is a reminder that Florence has always been a city of merchants. Many of the products on sale – leather goods and silk, wool and cashmere garments – are great value, especially if, like the Florentines, you are prepared to bargain.

Built in 1874, the Mercato Centrale is packed with fish, meat and cheese stalls downstairs, while a dining hall is located upstairs.

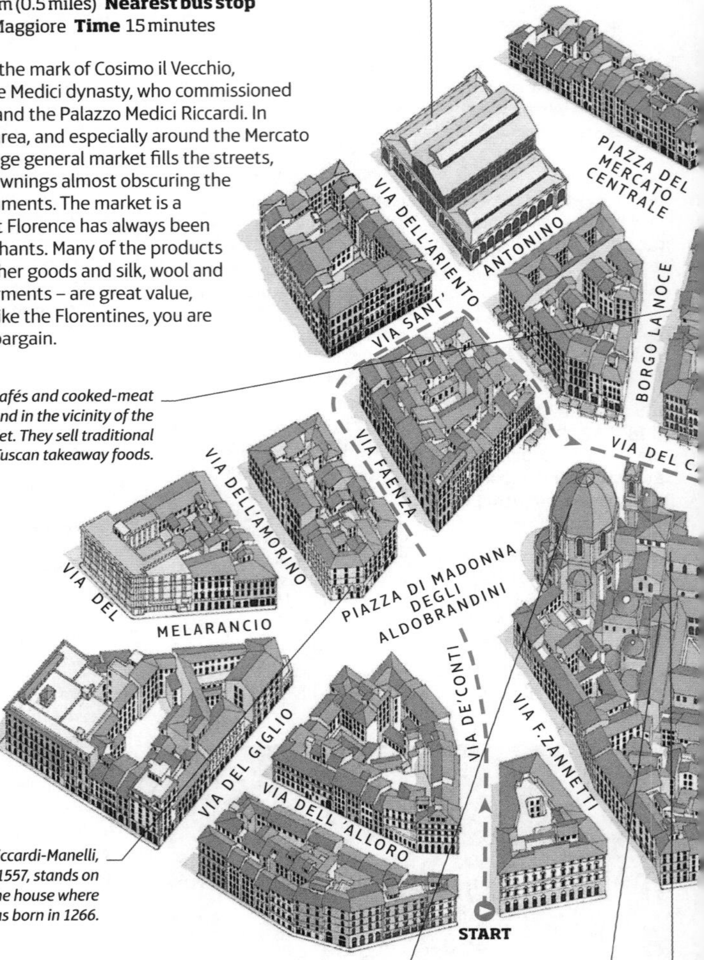

Cheap cafés and cooked-meat stalls abound in the vicinity of the market. They sell traditional Tuscan takeaway foods.

Palazzo Riccardi-Manelli, begun in 1557, stands on the site of the house where Giotto was born in 1266.

The Cappelle Medicee are situated in San Lorenzo. Michelangelo designed the New Sacristy and two Medici tombs, and some of his pencil sketches survive on the walls inside.

Biblioteca Mediceo-Laurenziana

The unfinished façade of San Lorenzo belies the noble interior, which was designed for the Medici by Brunelleschi in 1425–46.

Did You Know?

The Biblioteca Riccardiana holds a 14th-century manuscript of Dante's *Divine Comedy*.

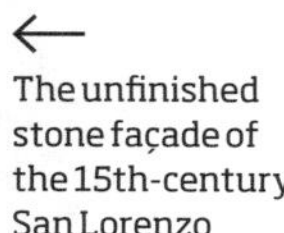

The unfinished stone façade of the 15th-century San Lorenzo

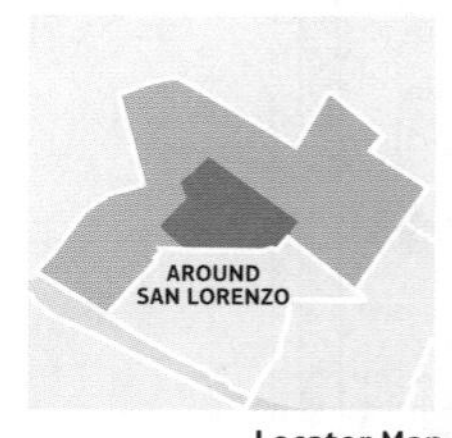

Locator Map

For more detail see p100

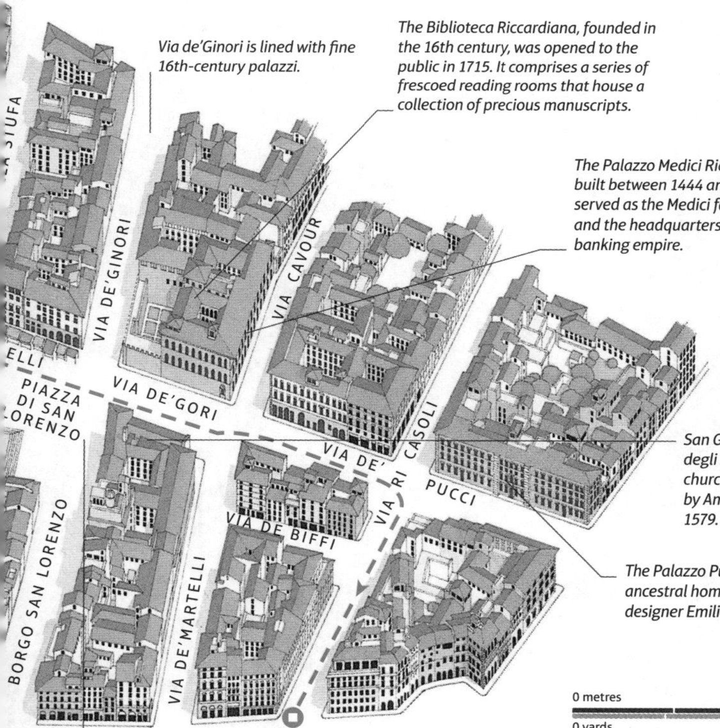

Via de'Ginori is lined with fine 16th-century palazzi.

The Biblioteca Riccardiana, founded in the 16th century, was opened to the public in 1715. It comprises a series of frescoed reading rooms that house a collection of precious manuscripts.

The Palazzo Medici Riccardi, built between 1444 and 1464, served as the Medici family home and the headquarters of their banking empire.

San Giovannino degli Scolopi church was begun by Ammannati in 1579.

The Palazzo Pucci is the ancestral home of the late designer Emilio Pucci.

VIA DE'GINORI

VIA CAVOUR

VIA DE'GORI

PIAZZA DI SAN LORENZO

VIA DE' PUCCI

VIA RI CASOLI

VIA DE BIFFI

VIA DE'MARTELLI

BORGO SAN LORENZO

FINISH

0 metres 100

0 yards 100

N

Giovanni delle Bande Nere, Grand Duke Cosimo I's father, is depicted in battle dress in a statue by Baccio Bandinelli (1540).

→

The beautifully decorated interior of San Lorenzo

Alfresco dining in Oltrarno

OLTRARNO

Literally "across the Arno", the Oltrarno was not incorporated into the city until the final set of defensive walls was built in 1333. Initially the poorest area of town, separated from the grander centre by the river, things changed when the Medici household moved to the Palazzo Pitti in the mid-16th century. Built a century earlier by Luca Pitti with the aim of outdoing the splendour of the rival Medici and Strozzi palazzi, it was bought by Eleonora di Toledo, wife of Cosimo I, who believed that the relatively rural setting would be beneficial to her poor health. The Medicis expanded the palazzo still further and although their presence drew other aristocrats to this part of town, the area retained its original character, particularly around Santo Spirito and Borgo San Frediano. Here, in the many artisan workshops and trattorias serving genuine home cooking, is where the authentic side of Florence is most evident. In recent years it has become the city's trendiest neighbourhood, thanks to its bohemian atmosphere and its shielded location away from the main tourist sights. The proliferation of independent boutiques and buzzing bars and eateries has only added to its appeal.

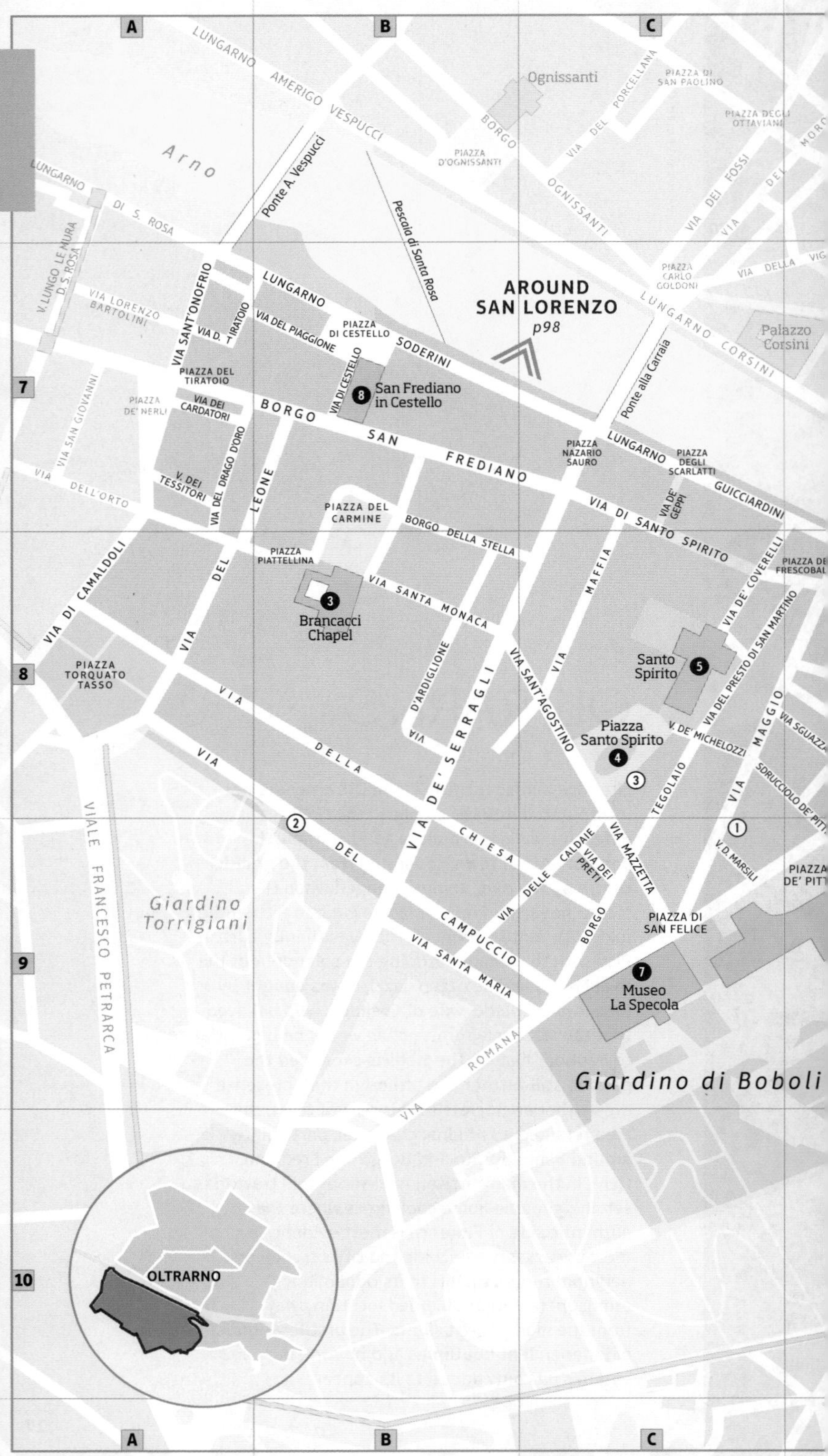

AROUND SAN LORENZO
p98
Arno
Giardino Torrigiani
Giardino di Boboli
OLTRARNO
San Frediano in Cestello
Brancacci Chapel
Santo Spirito
Piazza Santo Spirito
Museo La Specola
Ognissanti
Palazzo Corsini
Ponte A. Vespucci
Pescaia di Santa Rosa
Ponte alla Carraia
LUNGARNO AMERIGO VESPUCCI
LUNGARNO DI S. ROSA
LUNGARNO SODERINI
LUNGARNO CORSINI
LUNGARNO GUICCIARDINI
BORGO SAN FREDIANO
VIA DI SANTO SPIRITO
VIA DE' SERRAGLI
VIA SANT'AGOSTINO
VIA MAGGIO
VIA DELLA CHIESA
VIA DEL CAMPUCCIO
VIA ROMANA
VIALE FRANCESCO PETRARCA
PIAZZA DEL CARMINE
PIAZZA TORQUATO TASSO
PIAZZA DI SAN FELICE
PIAZZA NAZARIO SAURO
PIAZZA DI CESTELLO
PIAZZA D'OGNISSANTI
PIAZZA CARLO GOLDONI

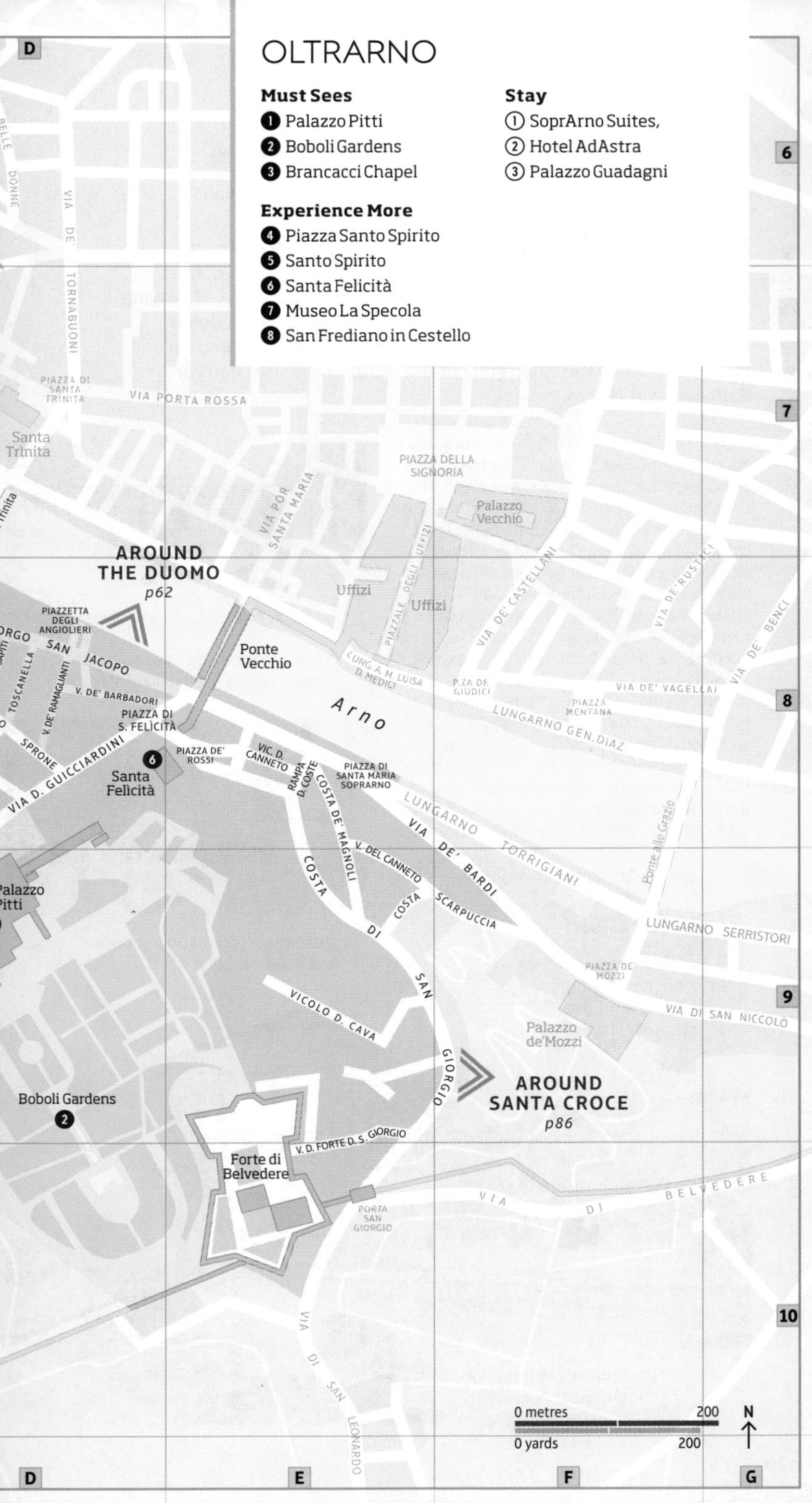

OLTRARNO
Must Sees
1 Palazzo Pitti
2 Boboli Gardens
3 Brancacci Chapel
Experience More
4 Piazza Santo Spirito
5 Santo Spirito
6 Santa Felicità
7 Museo La Specola
8 San Frediano in Cestello
Stay
① SoprArno Suites,
② Hotel AdAstra
③ Palazzo Guadagni
AROUND THE DUOMO
p62
AROUND SANTA CROCE
p86
Ponte Vecchio
Arno
Santa Trinita
Palazzo Vecchio
Uffizi
Santa Felicità
Palazzo Pitti
Boboli Gardens
Forte di Belvedere
Palazzo de'Mozzi
PIAZZA DELLA SIGNORIA
PIAZZA DI SANTA TRINITA
VIA PORTA ROSSA
VIA POR SANTA MARIA
VIA DE' TORNABUONI
PIAZZALE DEGLI UFFIZI
VIA DE' CASTELLANI
VIA DE' RUSTICI
VIA DE' BENCI
VIA DE' VAGELLAI
PIAZZETTA DEGLI ANGIOLIERI
BORGO SAN JACOPO
V. DE' BARBADORI
PIAZZA DI S. FELICITÀ
VIA D. GUICCIARDINI
PIAZZA DE' ROSSI
VIC. D. CANNETO
PIAZZA DI SANTA MARIA SOPRARNO
LUNGARNO TORRIGIANI
VIA DE' BARDI
COSTA DE' MAGNOLI
V. DEL CANNETO
COSTA SCARPUCCIA
COSTA DI SAN GIORGIO
VICOLO D. CAVA
LUNGARNO GEN. DIAZ
PIAZZA MENTANA
P.ZA DE GIUDICI
LUNG. A. M. LUISA D. MEDICI
LUNGARNO SERRISTORI
PIAZZA DE' MOZZI
VIA DI SAN NICCOLÒ
Ponte alle Grazie
V. D. FORTE D. S. GIORGIO
PORTA SAN GIORGIO
VIA DI BELVEDERE
VIA DI SAN LEONARDO
0 metres 200
0 yards 200
N
D E F G
6 7 8 9 10

1

PALAZZO PITTI

D9 Piazza de' Pitti D, 11, 36, 37 8:15am-6:50pm Tue-Sun 1 Jan, 1 May, 25 Dec uffizi.it/palazzo-pitti

Although the palace still bears the name of its original owner, it is best known as a residence of the Medici family. Today four separate museums are housed across this sprawling Renaissance site, displaying a wealth of artistic and decorative treasures. The star collection is that of the Palatine Gallery: frescoed by Pietro da Cortona and second only to the Uffizi, it contains one of the world's best selections of Raphaels and Titians.

The Palazzo Pitti, begun in 1457, was originally built for the banker Luca Pitti. The Medici are responsible for its huge scale, however, after they bought the palazzo a century later when building costs bankrupted Pitti's heirs. The family enlarged the palace and developed it into its current shape. It became the dynasty's main residence and subsequently all Florentine rulers lived here. Today, the richly decorated rooms exhibit treasures from the Medici collection *(p122)* and the Habsburg-Lorraine court.

The Palatine Gallery is home to a vast art collection amassed by the Medici family and the Habsburg-Lorraine duchies in the 1600s and 1700s, and it opened to the public in 1833. Other attractions include the royal apartments, the Medici collection of jewellery and treasures, the gallery of modern art, and an exhibition of 18th-, 19th- and 20th-century Italian clothing.

↑ Visitors gathering in the cobbled street outside the Palazzo Pitti

↑ Priceless artworks on display in the Palatine Gallery

Did You Know?

Napoleon used the palace as his Florentine residence during his reign over Italy.

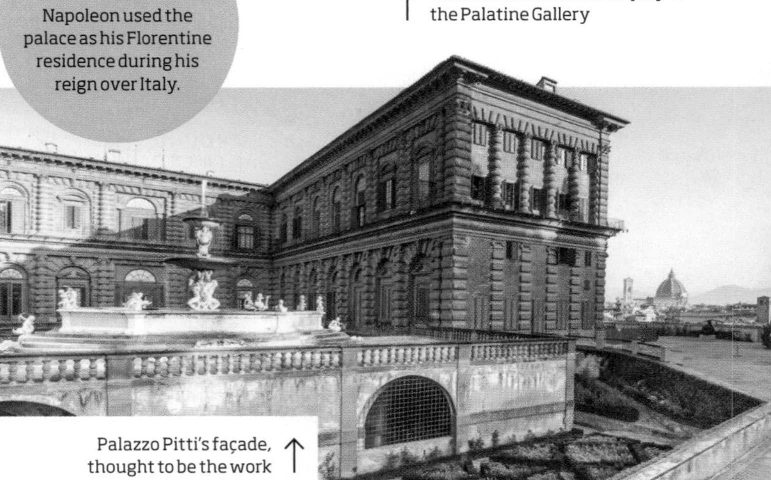

Palazzo Pitti's façade, thought to be the work of Brunelleschi ↑

INSIDER TIP
Arty Audio

Artworks in the Palatine Gallery are hung as they would have been while the Medici family lived here. The sheer size of the collection can be overwhelming, so we recommend picking up an audio guide.

A spectacularly gilded and frescoed ceiling within the Palazzo Pitti ↑

The glass chandeliers of Palazzo Pitti's Sala Bianca ("White Room"), dangling above its exhibits

The Palatine Gallery

The gallery contains a superb collection of works dating from the Renaissance and Baroque. They are hung as the 17th- and 18th-century Grand Dukes wished, placed purely for their effect, regardless of subject or chronology. Rooms 4 to 8 are painted with Baroque ceiling frescoes begun by Pietro da Cortona and finished by his pupil Ciro Ferri, which allegorize the education of a prince by the gods. The other rooms in the gallery were private apartments and their decor ranges from the opulent to the severe.

Although some of the Medici collection has been transferred to the Uffizi over the years, the Palatine Gallery is still packed with masterpieces by artists such as Botticelli, Perugino, Titian, Andrea del Sarto, Pontormo, Tintoretto, Veronese, Caravaggio, Rubens and Van Dyck, among others. There are approximately 1,000 paintings here, providing a vast survey of 16th- and 17th-century European painting.

Impressive artworks can be found in every corner of the Palatine Gallery

Royal Apartments

▶ The Royal Apartments on the first floor of the south wing of the palazzo were built in the 17th century. They are decorated with frescoes by various Florentine artists and a series of portraits of the Medici by the Flemish painter Justus Sustermans, who worked at the court between 1619 and 1681. In the late 18th and early 19th centuries, the apartments were completely revamped in Neo-Classical style by the Dukes of Lorraine when they succeeded the Medici dynasty as the rulers of Florence *(p54)*.

The apartments are lavishly appointed with ornate gold and white stuccowork ceilings and rich decoration. Their varied ownership is revealed in the inconsistent design, which embraces three distinct artistic periods.

Tesoro dei Granduchi

This museum is on the ground and mezzanine floors - below the Palatine Gallery - in the rooms used by the Medici as their summer apartments. It displays the massive private wealth of the Medici dynasty: the collection encompasses rare and beautiful examples of ancient Roman glassware, ivory, carpets, crystal and amber, and fine works by Florentine and German goldsmiths. The pride of the collection are 16 *pietre dure* vases, displayed in the Sala Buia. These belonged to Lorenzo the Magnificent and are from the ancient Roman and Byzantine periods.

The family's lavish tastes are reflected in the museum's polished ebony furniture inlaid with semiprecious marbles and stones. Portraits of the Medici hang throughout the rooms, including a series of the Grand Duchesses, and Cosimo I and his family carved in an onyx cameo.

LA VELATA

Raphael did many portraits, usually of Madonnas, and several of his best are in these collections. *La Velata* (1516) is his masterpiece of portraiture, displaying his mastery of colour, light and form. The sitter is most likely La Fornarina, his Roman girlfriend. Other works by Raphael in the Palatine include *Portrait of a Woman* and *Madonna of the Chair*.

Galleria d'Arte Moderna

Here, the paintings span the period from 1784 to 1924; many of them were amassed by the Dukes of Lorraine. The present museum has combined this collection with pictures donated by the state and various private collectors. The museum contains Neo-Classical, Romantic and religious works, but probably the most important collection is of the group of late 19th-century artists known as the Macchiaioli (spot-makers), similar to French Impressionists. This collection was given to the city of Florence in 1897 by the art critic Diego Martelli, and includes paintings by Giovanni Fattori and Giovanni Boldini. Two works by Camille Pissarro hang in the same room.

Museo della Moda e del Costume

◀ Opened in 1983, this gallery is on the ground floor of the Palazzo Meridiana. It was designed in 1776 by Gaspare Maria Paoletti and is home to more than 6,000 pieces. The exhibits reflect the changing tastes in the courtly fashion of the late 18th century up to the 1920s. Some items of 20th-century haute couture are also on display, from big-hitting designers such as Valentino, Armani, Versace and Saint Laurent.

2

BOBOLI GARDENS

D9 Piazza de' Pitti D, 11, 36, 37 8:15am–4:30pm daily (later closing during summer, check website for full details) 1st & last Mon of month; 1 Jan & 25 Dec uffizi.it/giardino-boboli

Unfurling down the hill behind the Palazzo Pitti are the Boboli Gardens, captivating any visitor with their lush greenery. Spend a couple of hours exploring the elegant lawns, dramatic amphitheatre and hidden grottoes of these manicured 16th-century gardens.

The Boboli Gardens were laid out for the Medici in 1550, one year after they bought the Palazzo Pitti. A perfect example of stylized Renaissance gardening, they were opened to the public in 1766. The more formal parts of the gardens, nearest the palazzo, consist of box hedges clipped into symmetrical geometric patterns. These lead to wild groves of ilex and cypress trees, planted to create a contrast between artifice and nature; both gardens are dotted with statues of varying styles and periods. There are splendid views, too, over the city. In 2017, fashion house Gucci pledged €2 million to restore the gardens to their former glory.

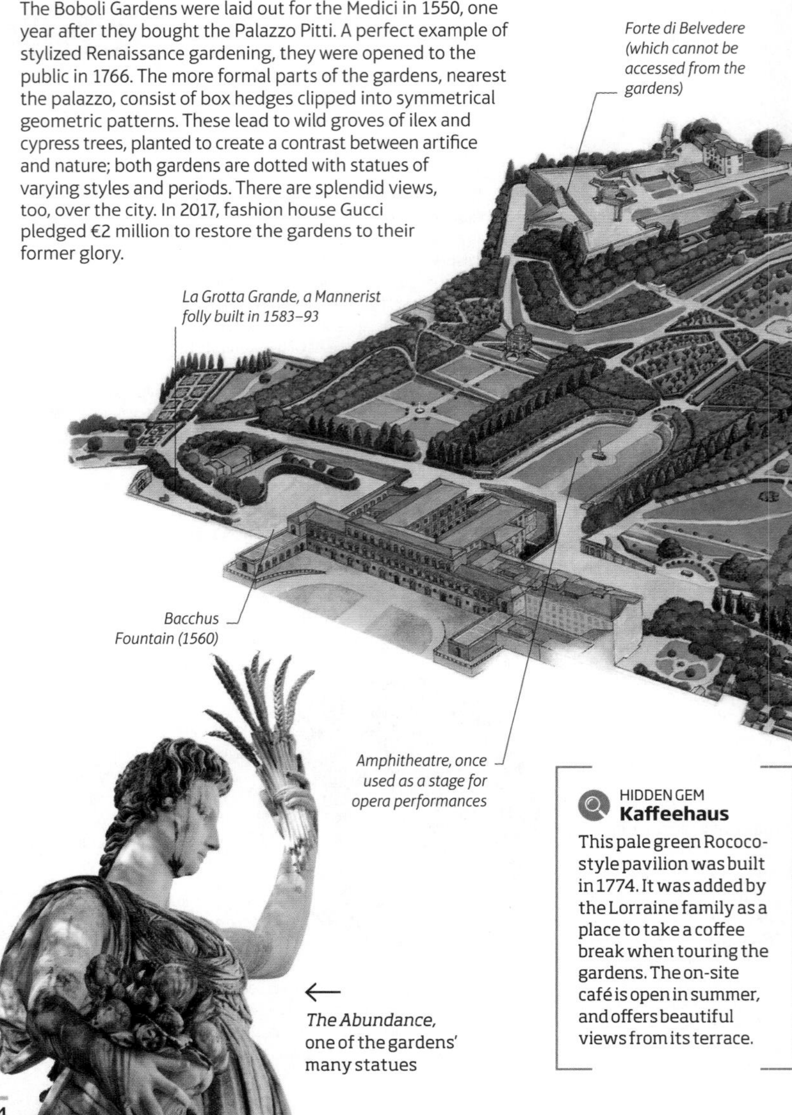

← *The Abundance*, one of the gardens' many statues

HIDDEN GEM
Kaffeehaus

This pale green Rococo-style pavilion was built in 1774. It was added by the Lorraine family as a place to take a coffee break when touring the gardens. The on-site café is open in summer, and offers beautiful views from its terrace.

1 La Grotta Grande is one of the most spectacular sites in the gardens. Its walls are decorated with mother-of-pearl, shells and dramatic artificial stalactites.

2 Classical sculptures are dotted throughout the Boboli Gardens.

3 *Tindaro Screpolato* (1998), by Polish artist Igor Mitoraj, is a vast bronze statue that contrasts with the older works on display.

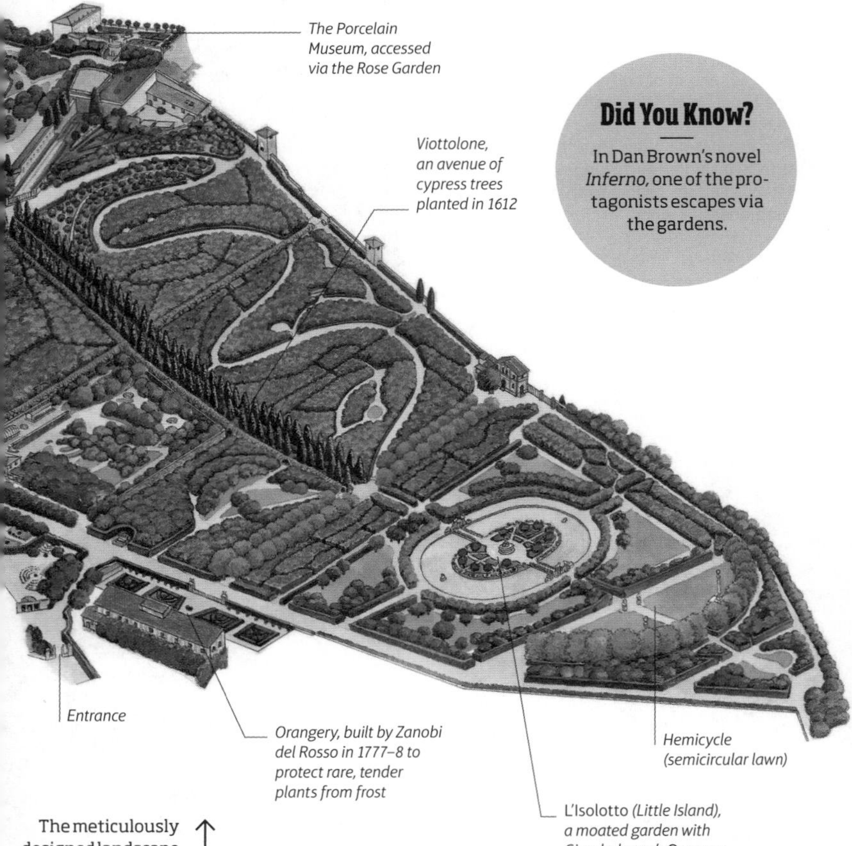

The Porcelain Museum, accessed via the Rose Garden

Viottolone, an avenue of cypress trees planted in 1612

Did You Know?

In Dan Brown's novel *Inferno*, one of the protagonists escapes via the gardens.

Entrance

Orangery, built by Zanobi del Rosso in 1777–8 to protect rare, tender plants from frost

Hemicycle (semicircular lawn)

L'Isolotto *(Little Island), a moated garden with Giambologna's* Oceanus Fountain *(1576) in the centre*

The meticulously designed landscape of the gardens ↑

3

BRANCACCI CHAPEL

B8 Piazza del Carmine 055 276 82 24, (reservations: 055 276 85 58) D 9:30am-1pm, 2-5pm Mon-Sat, 9:30am-12:30pm Sun Tue, public hols

The church of Santa Maria del Carmine was built in the 15th century, but nearly destroyed by a fire in 1771. The chapel's magnificent frescoes were fortunately spared and remain the site's main draw today.

The most famous of the church's frescoes is *The Life of St Peter* series in the Brancacci Chapel, commissioned by the Florentine merchant Felice Brancacci in around 1424. Masolino began the work in 1425, but many of the scenes are by his pupil, Masaccio, who died before completing the cycle. Filippino Lippi finished the work 50 years later, in 1480. Masaccio's use of perspective in *The Tribute Money* and the realism of his figures in *The Expulsion of Adam and Eve* placed him in the vanguard of Renaissance painting. Many great artists, including Michelangelo, later visited the chapel to study his pioneering work.

→ Exterior of Santa Maria del Carmine, within which stands the renowned chapel

1 The figures in *The Temptation of Adam and Eve* are shown as two realistically rendered naked youths.

2 This portion of *The Raising of the Son of Theophilus and Saint Peter Enthroned* shows the aftermath of a resurrection.

3 This detail from *Saint Peter Healing the Sick with His Shadow* depicts invalids being cured as Peter passes.

INSIDER TIP
Zoom In

Art fans may find it worthwhile to invest in a pair of binoculars before visiting the chapel. Some of the frescoes are fairly far off the ground, but you'll want to take in all the finer details.

↑ The magnificent Renaissance interior of the Brancacci Chapel

EXPERIENCE MORE

Piazza Santo Spirito

C8

This part of Florence is best appreciated by wandering around the square and its market, looking at the many furniture restorers' workshops and medieval palazzi and taking a break in one of the attractive bars and cafés. The biggest house here is the Palazzo Guadagni (1505), on the corner with Via Mazzetta. The top floor, now a hotel, has a wide, open loggia with a fantastic view of the neighbourhood. The first of its kind to be built in the city, the loggia was soon copied by other 16th-century Florentine aristocrats in their own palazzi.

Santo Spirito

C8 Piazza Santo Spirito 055 21 00 30 9:30am-12:30pm, 4-5:30pm Thu-Sat & Mon-Tue, 11:30am-12:30pm, 4-5:30pm Sun Wed

The Augustinian foundation of this church dates from 1250. The present building has an unfinished 18th-century façade, which dominates the northern end of Piazza Santo Spirito. Brunelleschi designed the church in 1435, but it was not completed until the late 1400s, well after his death.

Inside, the harmony of the proportions has been somewhat spoiled by the elaborate Baroque baldacchino and the High Altar. There are 38 side altars, decorated with 15th- and 16th-century Renaissance paintings and sculpture, among them works by Cosimo Rosselli, Domenico Ghirlandaio and Filippino Lippi.

In the north aisle, a door beneath the organ leads to a vestibule with an ornate coffered ceiling. It was designed by Simone del Pollaiuolo, more commonly known as Cronaca, in 1491.

All that survives of the monastery that stood next to Santo Spirito is the refectory, the **Cenacolo di Santo Spirito**, now a small museum. Inside is a fresco, *The Crucifixion* (1360–65), attributed to the followers of Andrea Orcagna and his brother Nardo di Cione. In a city that has a wealth of Renaissance art, this is a rare and beautiful example of High Gothic religious work.

FIESOLE

Just 7 km (4 miles) from Florence, the attractive town of Fiesole makes an easy day trip. The ancient Etruscan settlement is a popular retreat from the city thanks to its hilltop position, which attracts cool breezes and offers a panoramic view over Florence in the valley below. Bus 7 leaves from Piazza San Marco three times an hour for Fiesole, taking around 20 minutes.

Cenacolo di Santo Spirito
055 28 70 43
10am-5pm Sat & Mon, 1-5pm Sun 1 Jan, Easter Sun, 1 May, 15 Aug, 25 Dec

Santa Felicità

E8 Piazza di Santa Felicità 055 21 30 18 9am-noon, 3:30-6:30pm Mon-Sat

A church has stood on this site since the 4th century, but the current building dates from the 11th century. It was extensively remodelled by Ferdinando Ruggieri in 1736–9, but some original Gothic features and the porch added by Vasari in 1564 were retained.

The Capponi family chapel to the right of the entrance houses two works by Mannerist artist Jacopo da Pontormo: a panel depicting *The Deposition* and an *Annunciation* fresco. Painted

Brunelleschi's vaulted arcades with side altars, Santo Spirito

↑ The church of San Frediano, blending in with the low roofline

in 1525–8, they make use of vivid colours, such as salmon pink, light green, apricot and gold. The roundels at the base of the ceiling vault depict the *Four Evangelists*, also painted by Pontormo, with help from his pupil Agnolo Bronzino.

Museo La Specola

C9 Via Romana 17 9:30am-4:30pm Tue-Sun Mon, public hols msn. unifi.it

This unusual museum is in the Palazzo Rottigiani, built in 1775 and now used by the natural science faculty of Florence University. The name "La Specola" refers to the observatory built on the roof of the building by Grand Duke Pietro Leopoldo in the late 18th century. It now contains the museum, which has a zoological section exhibiting vast numbers of preserved animals, insects and fish, and an anatomical section with some very realistic 18th-century wax models showing grotesque aspects of human physiology and disease. Not for the faint-hearted!

Did You Know?

The English poets Elizabeth and Robert Browning lived in Oltrarno after eloping in 1847.

San Frediano in Cestello

B7 Piazza di Cestello 055 21 58 16 10-11:30am, 4:30-6pm Mon-Sat; 5-6:30pm Sun

The San Frediano area, with its small, low houses, has long been associated with the wool and leather industries. The parish church of San Frediano in Cestello stands beside the Arno, looking across the river. It has a bare-stone exterior with a large dome that is a local landmark. It was built in 1680–89 by Antonio Maria Ferri: inside, the fresco and stuccowork are typical of the late 17th/early 18th centuries.

STAY

SoprArno Suites

Vintage furnishings, original frescoes and wooden floors characterize this stylish yet friendly small hotel.

C8 Via Maggio 35 soprarnosuites.com

Hotel AdAstra

Quiet but characterful, with a wide terrace overlooking gardens. Each of the 14 rooms has very individual, often quirky, decor.

B9 Via del Campuccio 53 adastraflorence.com

Palazzo Guadagni

In prime position at the heart of the Oltrarno neighbourhood, this 16th-century palazzo offers 15 comfortable rooms. The top-floor loggia is ideal for relaxing with a drink.

C8 Piazza Santo Spirito 9 palazzoguadagni.com

A SHORT WALK

OLTRARNO

Distance 1.2 km (0.75 miles) **Nearest bus stop** Frescobaldi **Time** 20 minutes

For the most part, the Oltrarno is a homely area of small houses, quiet squares and shops selling antiques, bric-a-brac and foodstuffs. The Via Maggio, a busy thoroughfare, breaks this pattern, but step into the side streets and you can escape the bustle. The restaurants serve authentic, reasonably priced food, and the area is full of studios and workshops restoring antique furniture. Among the things to see are Santo Spirito Church and Palazzo Pitti, one of the city's largest palaces, which contains an art collection second only to that of the Uffizi.

The 16th-century fountain and gargoyle in Piazza de' Frescobaldi were designed by Buontalenti, as was the façade (1593–4) of the nearby church of Santa Trinita.

Ponte Santa Trinita

START

Simplicity is the keynote of Santo Spirito, Brunelleschi's last church. It was completed after his death in 1446.

The Cenacolo di Santo Spirito was the refectory of a monastery that once stood here. It contains a dramatic fresco attributed to Orcagna (c 1360).

The Palazzo di Bianca Cappello (1579) is covered in ornate sgraffito.

Between 1846 and 1861, Casa Guidi was the home of the poets Robert Browning and Elizabeth Barrett Browning.

Traditional inlaid mosaics can be purchased at this shop, Pitti Mosaici.

Locator Map
For more detail see p118

Elaborate fountain on the corner of Piazza de'Frescobaldi

Palazzo Guicciardini was the birthplace of historian Francesco Guicciardini, a friend and contemporary of Niccolò Machiavelli.

Four museums are contained within the Palazzo Pitti (p120), *including one with an outstanding collection of paintings.*

Did You Know?

The nearby San Niccolò district is home to lots of great-value bars and restaurants.

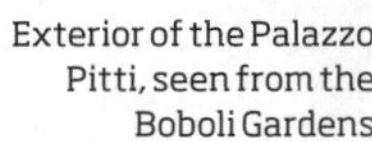

Exterior of the Palazzo Pitti, seen from the Boboli Gardens

EXPERIENCE TUSCANY

The rooftops of Siena

GETTING TO KNOW TUSCANY

Rolling hills and charming villages, delicious food and fine wine, cities of art and colourful traditions, plus a varied coastline with a sprinkling of islands – Tuscany really does have it all. Beyond the famous destinations such as Pisa and Siena, there are plenty of fascinating quiet corners to be explored.

PAGE 138

NORTHEAST TUSCANY

Inspirational and spiritual, this corner of the region combines the timeless landscapes of steep wooded hillsides, chosen by religious orders for their most remote communities, with the agricultural plains. Affluent and industrious towns such as Prato and Pistoia house unexpected artistic treasures, while the wide expanses of farmland are punctuated by the occasional, perfectly proportioned, Renaissance villa – a legacy of the Medici family, who originated here. Lying comparatively off the beaten track, this area offers a peaceful respite from the tourist hotspots elsewhere.

Best for
Hill walking, chestnuts and discovering lesser-known towns and villages

Home to
Mugello

Experience
A horse trek in hilly Mugello

PAGE 152

CENTRAL TUSCANY

A far cry from frenetic Florence nearby, the gentle hills of the Chianti region have an appealingly slow pace of life. Locals greet each other by name and take the time to chat; their understandable pride in living in this delightful area is apparent in the well-kept villages with their traditional shops and eateries. San Gimignano, famous for its wine and one of Tuscany's most attractive historic centres, is a magnet for artists from all over the world. They come to draw and paint, often opening studios and taking root in this welcoming part of the region.

Best for
Wine-tasting and traditional eateries

Home to
Chianti, Volterra, San Gimignano

Experience
Cycling through vineyards

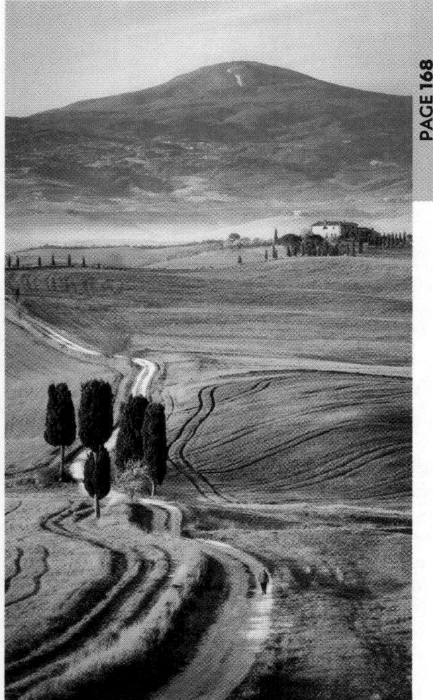

PAGE 168

SOUTHEAST TUSCANY

Nature and architecture intermingle in this part of Tuscany, particularly in Siena. The atmosphere in the city at Palio time is intense, noisy and colourful, and anyone from the vicinity will be asked their *contrada* (district) before their name. Throughout the area, the genuine, open and rather earthy local character is expressed by a vibe that is both energetic and relaxed – as epitomized by the flavours of the world-class local wines, Brunello di Montalcino and Vino Nobile di Montepulciano.

Best for
Timeless landscapes

Home to
Siena, Arezzo, Cortona

Experience
Hunting for truffles near Siena

→

PAGE 192

NORTHWEST TUSCANY

A land of many talents, northwest Tuscany is home to a famous local rivalry between Pisa and Livorno, which is no less strongly felt today than it was during Medici rule. Nonetheless, the area is the most pioneering, forward thinking corner of Tuscany. The busy working port town of Livorno has always been an open-minded melange of cultures, while Pisa is home to one of the country's most populous universities, with a variegated and lively nightlife. Further north, the marble favoured by Michelangelo and other sculptors is a constant presence, important for both the economy and culture.

Best for
Opera and sculpture

Home to
Pisa, Lucca

Experience
A tour of a marble quarry

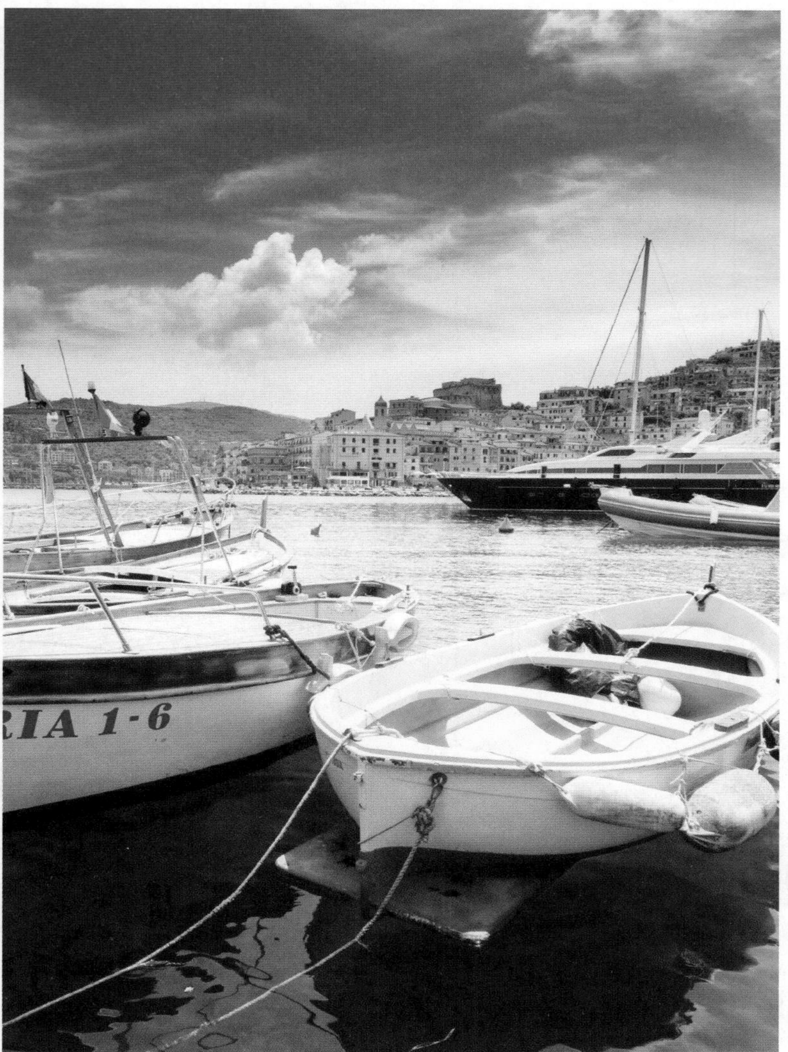

PAGE 220

SOUTHWEST TUSCANY

This part of the region is a curious combination of prestigious and elemental. It is home to some of Italy's most exclusive resorts, including Monte Argentario, where yacht owners frequent the classy boutiques and restaurants of Porto Ercole and Porto Santo Stefano. Just a few kilometres away, however, are the wild expanses of the Maremma and evocative natural areas such as the Orbetello nature reserve, a favourite among birdwatchers. Popular with divers, Elba and the other islands of the Tuscan Archipelago have a strongly independent character that makes them highly alluring.

Best for

Natural wonders and ancient Etruscan remains

Home to

The Tuscan Archipelago

Experience

Views of the spectacular coastline aboard a boat tour

Mountain-bike riders head towards Mount Calvana

NORTHEAST TUSCANY

It's little wonder that this beautiful area, characterized by the forests and mountains of the Mugello and Casentino, has produced many of history's most inspired artists – from Giotto and Fra Angelico (both from Vicchio) to Piero della Francesca (San Sepolcro) and Michelangelo (Caprese Michelangelo). In medieval times the region attracted religious hermits seeking isolation, and several impressive monasteries and convents were built; the mountain-top sanctuary of La Verna is reputed to be the place where St Francis received the stigmata.

The Medici family were already important landowners in Mugello by the late Middle Ages, long before they founded the Grand Duchy of Tuscany, and they constructed a legacy of elegant villas across the countryside. They also founded the towns of Firenzuola (1332) and Scarperia (1306), the latter of which became – and still is – a major knife-making centre. The textiles industry in Prato also began in medieval times, and the city remains a world leader in the field to this day.

NORTHEAST TUSCANY

Must See

1 Mugello

Experience More

2 Borgo San Lorenzo
3 Vicchio
4 Scarperia
5 Palazzuolo sul Senio
6 Marradi
7 Parco di Pratolino
8 Prato
9 The Casentino
10 Camaldoli Monastery
11 La Verna Monastery
12 Vallombrosa Abbey
13 Poppi
14 Caprese Michelangelo
15 Sansepolcro
16 Anghiari

NORTHEAST
TUSCANY
Faenza
Forlì
Cesenatico
La Strada
Modigliana
Dovadola
Predappio
Medola
Tredozio
Borello
Galeata
San Benedetto
in Alpe
Premilcuore
EMILIA-ROMAGNA
Mercato
Saraceno
Santa Sofia
Spinello
Pennabilli
Campigna
San Piero in Bagno
Ca Renicci
Sant'Agata
Feltria
Badia Tedalda
10
CAMALDOLI
MONESTERY
Stia
Verghereto
Badia
Prataglia
Balze
Marecchia
POPPI
13
LA VERNA
MONASTERY
11
Sestino
Montalone
Bibbiena
Chiusi della Verna
Arno
Badia
Tedalda
THE CASENTINO
Pieve Santo
Stefano
Viamaggio
Borgo Pace
9
Chitignano
Poggio
Masserecci
1548m
Rassina
14
CAPRESE
MICHELANGELO
Alpe di
Catenaia
Lago di
Montedoglio
Talla
Val Tiberina
SANSEPOLCRO
15
Subbiano
ANGHIARI
16
San Giustino
CENTRAL
TUSCANY
p152
SOUTHEAST
TUSCANY
p168
Arezzo
Monterchi
Città di Castello
Val di Chiana
Palazzo del
Pero
Monte Favalto
1082m
Rigutino
Morra
Trestina
Castiglion Fiorentino
Cortona
0 kilometres 10
0 miles 10
N

Silver fog rolling through the hills of the Mugello valley ↑

❶

MUGELLO

S2 Via Palmiro Togliatti 45 & Borgo San Lorenzo; www.mugellotoscana.it

The unspoiled, wooded slopes of Mugello form a natural gateway from Florence and Tuscany through the Apennines to northern Italy.

Mugello has attracted travellers since Etruscan times, thanks to its location on the Via degli Dei – an ancient route from Florence that passes through the mountains and across the border to Emilia Romagna. Although the path is still popular with walkers and cyclists, the area has remained largely untouched by mass tourism, and rural traditions continue to flourish. Farming has always been fundamental to the economy here, and Mugello's specialities are famously flavoursome.

Mugello's distinctive grey stone, Pietra Serena, has been popular with architects and sculptors since the Renaissance. The area's villages are all built from it, as are the pavements of Florence. Steve Jobs was so impressed by the latter that he chose Pietra Serena for flooring at Apple stores worldwide.

THE MEDICIS AND MUGELLO

The Medici family originated in Mugello and owned numerous properties there, inspiring other influential Florentine families to follow suit. Trebbio and Cafaggiolo castles were designed by Michelozzo for Cosimo il Vecchio, while the 16th-century Fortezza San Martino was built for Cosimo I.

Did You Know?

Every year thousands of fans descend on Mugello to watch the Italian MotoGP, held here since 1994.

EAT

People often come off the motorway for Mugello's famed food. Here are a few favourite pit stops.

Badia di Moscheta
Via di Moscheta 898, Firenzuola Mon & Tue
badiadimoscheta.it

€€€

La Selva di Frena
Via Frena 1422, Firenzuola Mon & Tue
laselvadifrena.com

€€€

Il Paiolo
Via Cornocchio 1F, Barberino di Mugello
Tue ilpaiolo.eu

€€€

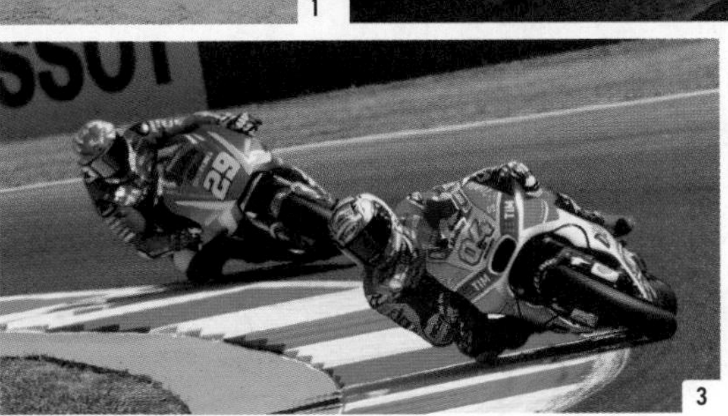

1 Cafaggiolo Castle was designed for Cosimo il Vecchio and was a favourite haunt of Lorenzo the Magnificent.

2 The village of Dicomano lies at the bottom of one of Mugello's gentle slopes.

3 Motorbike races are held at the popular Mugello Circuit near Borgo San Lorenzo.

EXPERIENCE MORE

Borgo San Lorenzo

S3 FS 🚌 i Largo La Vacchini; 055 845 62 30

Substantially rebuilt after an earthquake in 1919, this is the largest town of the Mugello. The parish church, the **Pieve di San Lorenzo**, has an odd Romanesque campanile, circular in its lower stages and hexagonal above. In the apse, the wall paintings (1906) are by the Art Nouveau artist Galileo Chini.

The interior of the **Villa Pecori Giraldi** incorporates splendid Art Nouveau features by the Chini family dating from the mid-19th century onwards. The building hosts the Museo Chini – a collection of vases, plates and other decorative items made by the family's firm of artistic manufacturers. Also in the villa is an interactive museum for children, with rooms dedicated to music, science, art and exploration. To the west of Borgo San Lorenzo is the Castello del Trebbio, with beautiful gardens.

Pieve di San Lorenzo
Via Cocchi 4
Mon-Sat, Sun pm

Villa Pecori Giraldi
Piazzale Lavacchini 1
Museo Chini: Apr-Oct: 9am-1pm & 3-7pm Thu-Sun; Nov-Mar: 10am-1pm & 3-7pm Sat-Sun; Piccolo Museo dei Bambini: 10am-12:30pm & 3-6:30pm Sat-Sun all year
museochini.it

Vicchio

S3 FS i Corso del Popolo 53; 055 8448355

The peaceful town of Vicchio is where Giotto, who pioneered the break from stylized Byzantine art towards a naturalistic style, was born in 1267. His birthplace, the **Casa di Giotto**, is an idyllic spot just outside the town. It has displays about the artist and exhibitions of local art. Close to the house is the attractive 13th-century church of San Martino and the Sentiero dei Pittori footpath that links to the centre as well as to the bridge where, according to Vasari, the artist Cimabue came across the young Giotto intent on drawing a sheep; he became mentor to the shepherd boy. Beato (Fra) Angelico was also born in Vicchio and the town's museum, the **Museo di Arte Sacra Beato Angelico**, houses religious art brought here from rural churches in the area to protect it. There are combined entry tickets for the Giotto house and the Fra Angelico museum.

INSIDER TIP
Barberino Outlet

With 120 shops, including some top labels and brands, this retail park is a popular day trip for shoppers. There's a handy shuttle bus service from Florence with a journey time of just 30 minutes.

Casa di Giotto
Località Vespignano
3:30-7:30pm Thu-Fri, 10am-1pm & 3:30-7:30pm Sat-Sun

Museo di Arte Sacra Beato Angelico
Piazza Don Milani
3:30-7:30pm Thu-Fri, 10am-1pm & 3:30-7:30pm Sat-Sun

↓ Castello del Trebbio, a Medici villa built for Cosimo il Vecchio

←

The Palazzo dei Capitani (Palace of the Captains) in Palazzuolo sul Senio

The Senio river runs through this pretty and peaceful village characterized by grey stone houses and surrounded by wooded hillsides.

Scarperia

S2 · Piazza dei Vicari 1 · prolocoscarperia.it

The town of Scarperia has been an important centre for blade-making since the 16th century and several artisans (such as Giglio at Via delle Oche 48) still practise the craft, making beautiful knives of all kinds, cutlery and other related items. The **Museo dei Ferri Taglienti** is a modern, interactive museum dedicated to the art of knife-making that can be found within the Palazzo dei Vicari on the central piazza. This statuesque 14th-century building has a striking façade studded with the heraldic shields of past governors (including terracottas by the Della Robbia school); a frescoed interior, and a bell tower clock by Brunelleschi.

Museo dei Ferri Taglienti

Piazza dei Vicari · Wed-Sun · museoferritaglienti scarperia.it

Palazzuolo sul Senio

S2 · Piazza Ettore Alpi 1; 055 8046125

The Senio river runs through this pretty and peaceful village characterized by grey stone houses and surrounded by wooded hillsides with plenty of opportunities for walking and mountain biking. In the village, the late 14th-century **Palazzo dei Capitani** hosts the Museo delle Genti di Montagna, dedicated to local mountain life, and the Museo Archeologico Alto Mugello, with local archaeological finds.

The church of Santo Stefano has decorations by the Chini school and there is an admirable *Via Crucis* by Tito Chini in Santi Antonio da Padova e Carlo Borromeo church.

Palazzo dei Capitani

Piazza Alpi 4 · Jul-Aug: 10am-12pm & 4-7pm (closed Mon); May-Oct: 10am-12pm & 3-6pm Fri-Sun (closed Fri May & Oct); Nov-Apr: 3-6pm Sat-Sun

→

Entering the Palazzo dei Vicari in Scarperia, with its Renaissance frescoes

6 Marradi

S2 FS Via Castelnaudary 5 pro-marradi.it

The attractive town of Marradi stands on the Lamone river. It has a rather more elegant character than most other towns and villages of the Apennines, thanks to the noble families who built grand palazzi such as the 16th-century Palazzo Torriani (now a hotel), which includes Art Nouveau decorations by Galileo Chini.

Surrounded by woodland, Marradi is particularly famous for its exceptional chestnuts, celebrated at an annual festival held in October, and for its good food in traditional trattorias. It's also a great base for walkers, with footpaths that include a relatively unchallenging route that leads from the centre to the ruins of the 6th-century hilltop castle, Rocca di Castiglionchio, with great views.

INSIDER TIP
Lago di Bilancino

A ten-minute drive from Parco di Pratolino, this lake is an idyllic place to cool off in summer. Its nature reserve has birdwatching trails while the Bahia Café and pizzeria has loungers, perfect for watching the sunset.

7 Parco di Pratolino

S3 Via Fiorentina 276, Vaglia Apr-Oct: 10am-8pm Fri-Sun (to 6pm Oct)

In the early 19th century the Grand Duke of Tuscany Ferdinand III demolished the original villa here, built for Francesco I de' Medici in 1568, due to its poor state of repair. However, he also transformed the vast estate into a beautiful landscaped garden, with a good network of footpaths meandering past fountains, artificial caves and areas of woodland. The hexagonal chapel by Bernardo Buontalenti and the towering statue by Giambologna of a giant, representing the Apennines, are among the remaining 16th-century features while the former stables now host an exhibition of Medici theatre equipment.

STAY

Locanda Senio

Comfortable country-chic style, with a traditional restaurant, a small wellness suite and an open-air pool.

Via Borgo dell'Ore 1, Palazzuolo sul Senio locandasenio.com

Castello di Nipozzano

Four exclusive guest rooms are attached to the 11th-century Nipozzano castle and wine estate.

Via di Nipozzano, Pelago nipozzano.com

UNA Poggio dei Medici

The 70 rooms of this comfortable hotel have balconies or private gardens. There's an 18-hole golf course, open-air pool and small gym.

Via San Gavino 27, Scarperia golf poggiodeimedici.com

The Lamone river, flowing past the town of Marradi, famed for its chestnuts

Prato

R3 Piazza della Carceri 15; 0574 241 12

Prato has been one of Italy's most important textile-manufacturing cities since the 13th century. It also attracts pilgrims from all over Italy, who come to see the Virgin's Girdle, a prized relic kept in the **Duomo** on the main square. The Pulpit of the Holy Girdle is to the right of the church's façade, its frieze of dancing cherubs by Donatello (1438). Inside, the first chapel on the left holds the Virgin's Girdle, which is displayed from the pulpit on religious holidays. Frescoes by Agnolo Gaddi (1392–5) relate how the girdle reached Prato. In 1141, a local merchant married a woman from Palestine who had inherited it from the Apostle Thomas. The Virgin herself had let the girdle, a length of knotted cord, fall from the sky into Thomas's hands at the time of the Assumption.

Donatello's original panels for the Pulpit of the Holy Girdle are on display in the Museo dell'Opera del Duomo. The museum also houses the reliquary (1446) made for the Girdle by Maso di Bartolomeo, and *St Lucy* by Filippino Lippi.

Just off the central Piazza del Comune, the **Museo Civico** houses the altar painting *The Story of the Holy Girdle*, by Bernardo Daddi (1312–48), and Filippo Lippi's *Madonna del Ceppo* (c 1452–3).

Prato's second important church, **Santa Maria delle Carceri**, stands on the site of a prison *(carceri)* on whose wall an image of the Virgin miraculously appeared in 1484. With its harmoniously proportioned interior, the domed church (1485–1506) is a fine work by Renaissance architect Giuliano da Sangallo. Andrea della Robbia created the blue-and-white glazed terracotta roundels of the *Evangelists* (1490). To the right of the church is the imposing Castello dell'Imperatore (1237), built by the German Holy Roman Emperor Frederick II during his campaign to conquer Italy.

The history of Prato's textile industry, the basis of its wealth, is charted in the **Museo del Tessuto**. Located on the city's southern outskirts, it houses historic looms and examples of lush Renaissance velvets, embroidery, lace and damask.

Near the Prato Est Autostrada exit, in an interesting modern building, the **Centro per l'Arte Contemporanea Luigi Pecci** is used for changing displays of contemporary art, concerts and films.

Duomo
Piazza del Duomo 0574 26 23 Duomo: daily; Museo dell'Opera del Duomo: Mon, Wed-Sun & hols

Did You Know?

Prato is the birthplace of *cantucci*, the almond biscuits Tuscans love to dip into sweet Vin Santo wine.

Museo Civico
Palazzo Pretorio, Piazza del Comune 19
0574 183 6302 Mon, Wed-Sun

Santa Maria delle Carceri
Piazza delle Carceri
7am-noon, 4-7pm daily

Museo del Tessuto
Via Puccetti 3 Tue-Sun
museodeltessuto.it

Centro per l'Arte Contemporanea Luigi Pecci
Viale della Repubblica 277 Tue-Sun
centropecci.it

Prato's Duomo, the Cattedrale di Santo Stefano

9

The Casentino

S3 FS

The vast Casentino region, an area of tiny villages among hills covered with ancient woodland, lies to the north of Arezzo. The River Arno rises here, on the slopes of Monte Falterona. Countless streams run down the valleys to join it, creating stunning waterfalls.

Another attraction of the area is its selection of historic working monasteries, such as Camaldoli and La Verna, where the various orders continue to offer hospitality to travellers and make and sell produce. The ecclesiastical buildings make a good focal point for woodland walks, especially in autumn: the area is renowned for its abundant mushroom crops.

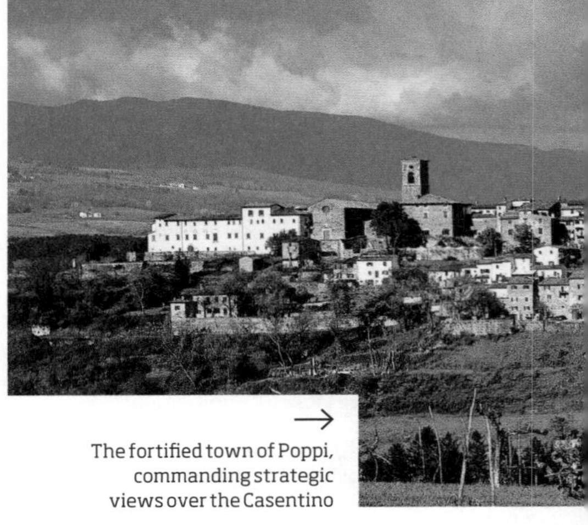

→ The fortified town of Poppi, commanding strategic views over the Casentino

Camaldoli Monastery

S3 9am-1pm, 2:30-7:30pm daily (to 7pm winter) camaldoli.it

This Casentino monastery was founded in 1046 and today houses 40 Carthusian monks.

The original *eremo* (hermitage) lies 2.5 km (1.5 miles) up a narrow, winding road from the monastic complex through dense ancient forest; some of the most ecologically rich in Europe, it has been a National Park since 1991. The monks still tend this magnificent beech and chestnut woodland, as their predecessors have done for nearly 1,000 years.

The hermitage dates back to 1012 when San Romualdo (St Rumbold) came here with a small group of followers to cut themselves off completely from the outside world. The monks lead a more gregarious life now, running a small café in the monastery below and making soaps, toiletries and liqueurs that they sell in their pharmacy.

↓ The tranquil Camaldoli Monastery, which lies deep in ancient woods

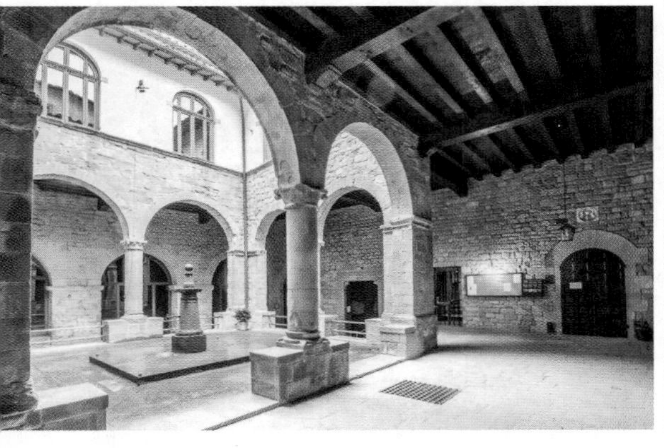

Did You Know?

The poet William Wordsworth and writer Mary Shelley both visited Vallombrosa.

11 

La Verna Monastery

T3 0575 53 41 6:30am-10pm daily (to 7:30pm winter)

The rocky outcrop on which La Verna monastery stands, surrounded by woodland, was split, according to legend, by an earthquake when Christ died on the Cross. The site was given to St Francis in 1213 by Count Orlando Cattani, and it was here, in 1224, that the saint was miraculously marked with the stigmata – the wounds of Christ.

Today the monastery complex, with its churches, chapels and museum, is both a popular tourist destination and a charismatic religious centre. There is accommodation for both travellers and pilgrims, the refectory serves meals all year round, and the monks make and sell cosmetics, natural remedies and liqueurs.

Vallombrosa Abbey

S3 monaci.org

Although a short way outside the Casentino, Vallombrosa shares the characteristics of its woodland monasteries, and walks to and around the abbey are very scenic, with plenty of picnic spots. The Vallombrosan order was founded by St Giovanni Gualberto Visdomini in 1038. He aimed to persuade like-minded aristocrats to join him in relinquishing their wealth and adopting a life of great austerity. Contrary to these worthy ideals, the order grew wealthy and powerful during the 16th and 17th centuries. It was then that this fortress-like abbey was built.

Today's monks have a more modest and tranquil lifestyle, tending to the arboretum and herb gardens and producing liqueurs, jam, honey, cosmetics and even gin, on sale at the Antica Farmacia. This and the general areas of the abbey, including the frescoed church and a museum, are open daily. Visits to the monastic quarters and the magnificent library can be arranged through tour companies or by appointment.

FOOTPATHS AND MOUNTAIN BIKE ROUTES

Both the Mugello and Casentino areas offer a wealth of tracks and trails of all kinds, including ancient cobbled roads through woodland. Although both areas have plenty of steep mountain slopes, there is also a good choice of paths for an easy stroll. It's excellent mountain biking territory too *(see www.mugelloinbike.it)*.

Poppi

S3 Via Cesare Battisti 23; 0575 52 96 82

The older part of Poppi is located high above the town's bus and train termini. Its splendid castle, the imposing **Castello di Poppi**, can be seen from up to 5 km (3 miles) away. Just south of the town is the **Zoo Fauna Europa**, which specializes in the conservation of endangered European species such as the Apennine wolf and the lynx.

Visible from Poppi, a short drive to the northwest up the Arno valley, is the 11th-century Castello di Romena, where Dante stayed as a guest of the local rulers in the early 14th century. Romena's *pieve*, dating to 1152, is a typical example of a Romanesque village church.

Castello di Poppi
0575 52 99 64 Apr-Oct: daily; Nov-Mar: Thu-Sun

Zoo Fauna Europa
Via del Parco Zoo 16
9am-sunset daily
parcozoopoppi.it

STAY

Il Borro

Il Borro offers country-chic accommodation in charming stone houses around a stunning medieval village, plus self-catering villas elsewhere on the estate. Non-residents are welcome to shop at the craft workshops or join a wine-tasting tour. There's a choice of dining, a spa, two pools, horse riding and golf.

Località Borro 1, San Giustino Valdarno
ilborro.it

↑ Piero della Francesca's masterly *Resurrection*, in Sansepolcro's Museo Civico

14

Caprese Michelangelo

 T4 🚌 ℹ Via Capoluogo 1; 0575 79 37 76

Michelangelo Buonarroti was born in Caprese on 6 March 1475, while his father served as the town's *podestà* – a combination of magistrate, mayor and chief of police. His birthplace is now a museum, the **Comune Casa Natale Michelangelo**, housing photos and copies of the artist's work. The town walls feature modern sculptures and have fine views over the alpine landscape. Michelangelo attributed his keen mind to the mountain air he breathed here as a child.

INSIDER TIP
Palio della Balestra

Held in Sansepolcro, this festival, which dates from the time of the Renaissance, involves a colourful costumed crossbow tournament between Sansepolcro locals and rivals from the Umbrian town of Gubbio. It takes place in the Piazza Torre di Berta on the second Sunday of September.

Comune Casa Natale Michelangelo

 Casa del Podestà, Via Capoluogo 1 0575 79 37 76 Jun-Sep: daily (call ahead for times); Oct-May: Wed-Mon

15

Sansepolcro

T4 🚌 ℹ Via Matteotti 8; 0575 74 05 36

Sansepolcro is a busy industrial town, famous as the birthplace of the artist Piero della Francesca (1410–92). The building in which he was born, on Via Aggiunti, houses a small foundation dedicated to his work, but sadly not the life-size fresco *Hercules* he painted on the first floor; this was taken down and transported to a museum in Boston, USA in the early 20th century. However, the **Museo Civico**, housed in the 14th-century Palazzo Comunale, contains a fine collection of his work. The most famous is the fresco *The Resurrection* (1463), in which a curiously impassive Christ strides out of his tomb. The sleeping soldiers at his feet, in their Renaissance armour, seem trapped in time, while the son of God takes possession of a primitive, eternal landscape. The soldier in brown, second from the left, is thought to be a self-portait of the artist. Other works by Piero are displayed in the same room, notably the *Madonna della Misericordia* (1462).

Sansepolcro is home to a number of other major works. Don't miss Luca Signorelli's 15th-century *Crucifixion* (also in the Museo Civico) and

Did You Know?

Despite it involving thousands of troops, only one person was killed in the Battle of Anghiari.

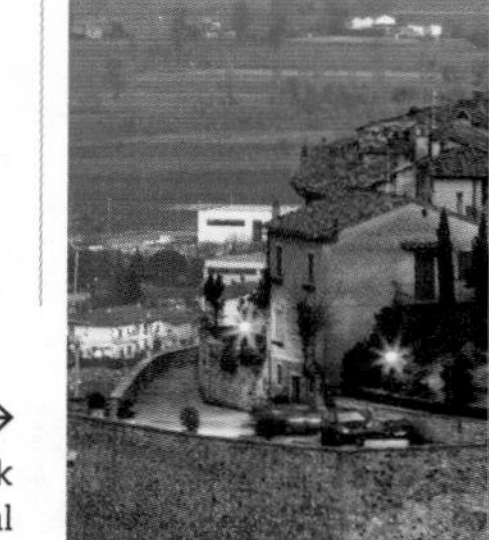

→ Lights appearing at dusk to illuminate the medieval town of Anghiari

Rosso Fiorentino's Mannerist *Deposition*, in San Lorenzo church on Via Santa Croce.

Museo Civico

Via Aggiunti 65 0575 73 22 18 Mid-Jun-mid-Sep: 10am-1:30pm, 2:30-7pm daily; mid-Sep-mid-Jun: 10am-1pm, 2:30-6pm daily 1 Jan, 25 Dec

Anghiari

T4 Via Matteotti 103; 0575 74 92 79

Surrounded by sturdy stone walls, the medieval town of Anghiari makes a striking sight and the pretty centre with its artisan workshops is a pleasure to explore. Anghiari came under Florentine rule in 1440 after a famous battle against the Milanese, the subject of a lost fresco Leonardo da Vinci was commissioned to paint in Florence's Palazzo Vecchio.

Several major works, including Jacopo della Quercia's fine wooden *Madonna* (1420), can be seen at the **Museo Statale di Palazzo Taglieschi**. There are also displays of locally made furniture and toys.

Santa Maria delle Grazie is the town's main church. Dating to the 18th century, it contains a High Altar and tabernacle from the della Robbia workshops and a 15th-century *Madonna and Child* painted by Matteo di Giovanni.

The Misericordia, a charitable organization, was founded in the 13th century to look after ailing pilgrims on their way to Rome. Today, it operates Tuscany's ambulance service. A small museum here, the **Museo della Misericordia**, records their work.

Museo Statale di Palazzo Taglieschi

Piazza Mameli 16 0575 78 80 01 Tue-Sun 1 Jan, 1 May, 25 Dec

Santa Maria delle Grazie

Via Propositura Daily

Museo della Misericordia

Via Francesco Nenci 13 0575 78 95 77 By appointment

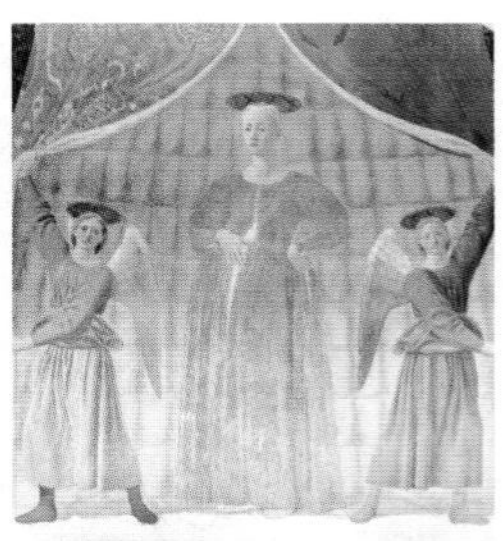

MONTERCHI

A ten-minute drive southeast of Anghiari, the village of Monterchi contains a cemetery chapel chosen in 1460 by Piero della Francesca for his *Madonna del Parto* (Pregnant Madonna), possibly because his mother may be buried here. The restored fresco, with its haunting portayal of a weary, pensive Virgin, is now in the Museo Madonna del Parto on Via della Reglia. There is no entry charge for pregnant visitors.

Sunrise in San Gimignano

CENTRAL TUSCANY

Stretching between Florence and Siena, much of central Tuscany is taken up by the vine-clad hills and olive groves of the Chianti Classico area. Wine production began here in the ancient Etruscan era, at which time the local tradition of alabaster work was also established in Volterra. It was during the medieval period that wine-making became firmly established as a major trade – some of the wineries founded at this time, including Ricasoli and Antinori, are still in operation. Prosperity also came to the walled towns of San Gimignano and Monteriggioni thanks to their position on the Via Francigena, a pilgrimage route from Canterbury to Rome that passed through the western part of the region. Central Tuscany's position between Florence and Siena meant that it was caught in the middle of centuries of feuding between the two cities, and the hills are dotted with numerous castles and villas that grew out of the conflict. In recent years, many of these have been converted into wineries or prestigious holiday accommodation.

CENTRAL TUSCANY

Must Sees

1. Chianti
2. Volterra
3. San Gimignano

Experience More

4. San Giovanni Valdarno
5. Colle di Val d'Elsa
6. Monteriggioni
7. Empoli
8. Vinci

San Piero a Sieve
Borgo San Lorenzo
San Godenzo
Mugello
Vicchio
Vaglia
Dicomano
Prato
Bivigliano
Monte Falterona
1654m
Londa
Pratolino
NORTHEAST
TUSCANY
p138
Campi
Bisenzio
Poggio A Caiano
Fiesole
Rufina
Stia
Signa
Florence
Consuma
FLORENCE
p56
Pontassieve
Pelago
Pratovecchio
Lastra
a Signa
Bagno
A Ripoli
Arno
Rignano
sull'Arno
Casentino
Vallombrosa
Poppi
Pesa
Cerbaia
Impruneta
Reggello
Greve
San Casciano
in Val di Pesa
Incisa in Val d'Arno
Poggio Masserecci
1548m
Figline
Valdarno
CHIANTI
SAN GIOVANNI
VALDARNO
Tavernelle
Val di Pesa
Terranuova
Bracciolini
Certaldo
San
Donato
Montevarchi
Barberino
Val d Elsa
Chianti
Levane
SAN
GIMIGNANO
Radda
in Chianti
Poggibonsi
Castellina
in Chianti
Gaiole in Chianti
COLLE DI
VAL D'ELSA
Capannole
Brolio
MONTERIGGIONI
Elsa
Arbia
Casole d'Elsa
Castelmauro
Siena
SOUTHEAST
TUSCANY
p168
Rapolano Terme
Lucignano
Rosia
Monteroni
d'Arbia
Asciano
Sinalunga
Merse
Ombrone
Monte Oliveto
Maggiore
Torrita
di Siena
San
Galgano
San Lorenzo
a Merse
San Giovanni
d'Asso
Monticiano
Buonconvento
Bagni di Petriolo
Montalcino
Roccatederighi
Roccastrada
0 kilometres
10
0 miles
10
N

1

CHIANTI

S4 chianti.com

Chianti is one of Tuscany's best-known and most beautiful wine regions. The Medici Grand Duke Cosimo III first officially defined this vineyard-dotted stretch of countryside between Florence and Siena for Chianti wine production in 1716.

The gentle slopes and wide-open panoramas just south of Florence lead to more hilly terrain as you journey through Chianti towards Siena, with a proliferation of winding roads and quaint villages built in the typical honey-coloured stone. There are numerous historic abbeys and hilltop castles, many of which now house wineries and frequently offer tours, tastings and accommodation. Wine has been fundamental to the Chianti area for centuries, and the excellent Casa del Chianti Classico visitor centre in Radda is the perfect place to find out more.

CHIANTI WINE GUIDE

Regular Chianti is made in much of Tuscany - such as in Pisa, Arezzo or Pistoia - but in 1932 the term "Classico" was added for wines made exclusively within the defined Chianti area. These prestigious wines must be made with at least 80 per cent Sangiovese grapes. A Chianti Classico Riserva is one of these wines, aged for 24 months, while a Gran Selezione is made from grapes grown on the same estate and is aged for 30 months.

Sunrise over the rolling hills of Chianti, which are dotted with historic buildings *(inset)* ↑

Did You Know?

On average, around 38 million bottles of Chianti Classico are produced each year.

1 The cellars of Chianti are packed with huge barrels that store the region's eponymous wine.

2 L'Eroica is a vintage cycling event that winds through Chianti.

3 The neatly ordered rows of a vineyard in Panzano are bathed in Tuscan sunshine.

①   

Greve in Chianti

Piazza Matteotti 10; 0558 54 52 71

Although larger than the other Chianti communities, Greve, which is named after the pretty river passing through the centre, is no less appealing. The town is focused around an unusual triangular piazza, lined with porticoes housing characterful eateries, shops and bars. A panoramic road leads up to the delightful walled hilltop village of Montefioralle nearby.

② 

Panzano in Chianti

W panzano.com

This quiet hill village features wide views across the Chianti countryside. A footpath leads to the San Pietro alle Stinche church, hidden among the trees, which was once part of a medieval castle. Dario Cecchini's butcher's shop on Via XX Luglio is also well worth a visit.

EAT

Here are three of Chianti's best butcher-eateries.

Antica Macelleria Cecchini

Via XX Luglio 11, Panzano in Chianti
9am-4pm daily
dariocecchini.com

Macelleria Falorni

Piazza G Matteotti 66, Greve in Chianti
9am-7pm Mon-Sat; 10am-7pm Sun
falorni.it

Stiaccini

Via Ferrucio 33, Castellina in Chianti
9am-2:30pm & 4:45-7:30pm Mon-Sat
macelleria stiaccini.com

3 

Castellina in Chianti

Castellina in Chianti is reached via scenic roads that meander through the rolling Tuscan hills. Upon arrival, the attractive town centre is built around a 15th-century castle with an unusual tower that can be seen from miles around. The hilltop town, one of the largest in Chianti, can trace its origins back to Etruscan times, and there are still a handful of accessible ancient remains that visitors can explore. There is also a wide selection of places to drink, shop and eat, some of which can be found in the atmospheric underground walkway – Via della Volte – that winds beneath the walls of the town.

4 

Radda in Chianti

Piazza Castello 6; 10am-1pm & 3-7pm daily

Located at the heart of the Chianti region, hilltop Radda offers striking panoramas from its narrow side-streets, which host an assortment of traditional restaurants and bars. These include Casa Porciatti, a good butcher-eatery run by the Prociatti family. Radda became the centre of power in the Chianti region in 1384 and the Palazzo della Podestà, built in the 15th century and studded with coats of arms of past mayors, still houses the local authorities.

GALLO NERO

Chianti Classico's black cockerel symbol originates from a 13th-century attempt to fix the boundary between Florence and Siena at the place where a horseman from each of the cities met, having left at cockcrow. Florence's black cockerel woke early, having been starved for days beforehand. This gave the Florentine a headstart and he covered more ground, so the two met just south of Castellina.

↑ The Badia a Passignano, an 11th-century abbey complex in Chianti

Did You Know?

Records show that Chianti has exported wine to England since the 1600s.

⑤ Gaiole in Chianti

Via Ricasoli 3; 0577 744711

This pretty village has a stream running around its centre. The numerous castles near Gaiole include Brolio, the largest winery in the Chianti Classico area, which was built in 1041 but owes its current Neo-Gothic style to 19th-century intervention by the influential Ricasoli wine-making family. Also within easy reach is the attractive 13th-century Meleto – with tours available through its frescoed rooms and wine cellar – and the Badia a Coltibuono estate, which comprises some 800 hectares filled with vines, olive trees and good woodland walks.

⑥ Badia a Passignano Abbey

Badia a Passignano

The impressive structure of this isolated 11th-century abbey complex incorporates additions from successive centuries, including a 15th-century cloister and towers. It was founded on a stretch of road between Greve in Chianti and Sambuca, another tiny town in the region. The interior features some admirable frescoes, including the *Last Supper* by the Ghirlandaio brothers in the refectory.

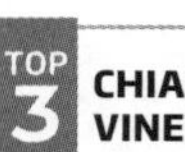

CHIANTI VINEYARDS

Badia a Coltibuono
Gaiole in Chianti
An organic winery in an 11th century abbey.

Antinori
San Casciano Val di Pesa
One of Tuscany's leading winemakers.

Castello di Volpaia
Radda in Chianti
Wine has been made here since 1172.

⑦ Sant'Andrea in Percussina

Lying not far from the medieval hill town of San Casciano Val di Pesa, this hamlet is where the exiled Niccolò Machiavelli wrote his famous political treatise, *The Prince* (1513). The wine estate owned by Machiavelli and his family, the 500-year-old Villa Machiavelli, continues to produce Chianti Classico, and his house and garden are open for tours.

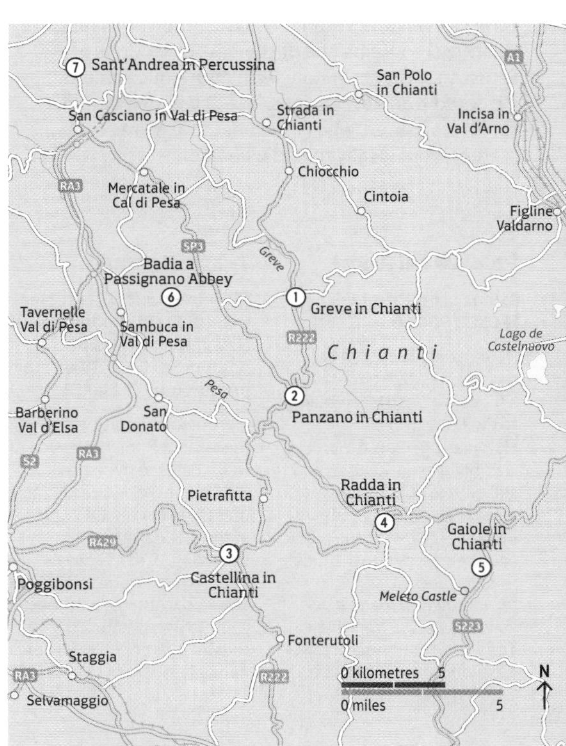

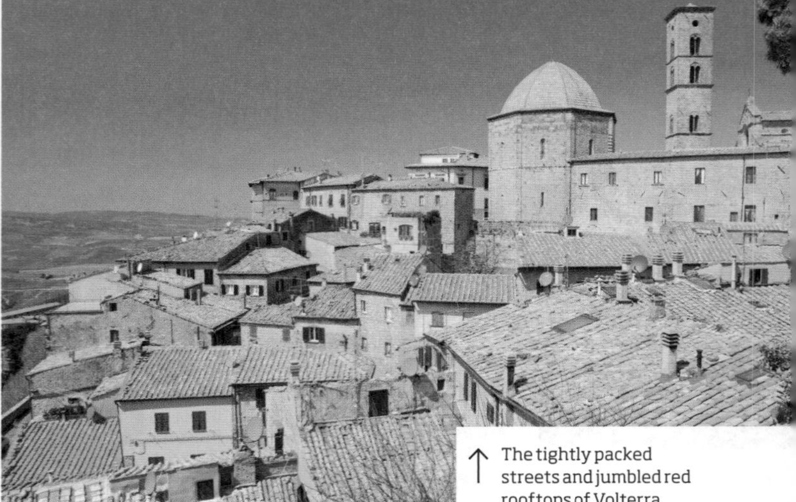

The tightly packed streets and jumbled red rooftops of Volterra

2

VOLTERRA

R4 Via G Turazza 2; www.volterratur.it

Situated, like many Etruscan cities, on a high plateau, Volterra offers uninterrupted views over the surrounding hills. In many places the ancient Etruscan walls still stand, and the renowned Museo Guarnacci contains one of the best collections of Etruscan artifacts in Italy, with numerous exhibits gathered from local tombs. The city is also famed for its craftsmen, who carve beautiful white statues from locally mined alabaster.

Palazzo dei Priori

Piazza dei Priori 1 0588 860 50

Dominating Piazza dei Priori, this fine palazzo (built 1208–57) bears a close resemblance to the Palazzo Vecchio in Florence *(p68)*. It is the oldest civic building in Tuscany, and still houses Volterra's local authorities. Parts of the interior are open to the public and the frescoes on the first floor include the splendid *Annunciation in the Sala del Consiglio*, dating from 1383. The views from the bell tower are particularly impressive.

Teatro Romano

Viale Ferruci Mid-Mar-Oct: 10:30am-5:30pm daily; Nov-mid-Mar: 10am-4:30pm Sat & Sun (weather permitting) 1 Jan, 25 Dec

Just outside the city walls, the ancient Roman theatre – which dates to the 1st century BC – is one of the best-preserved in Italy. Enough of the original structure (including 19 rows of seats, built on a natural slope) has survived to enable an almost complete reconstruction. The theatre is not open to visitors during heavy rain.

Pinacoteca e Museo Civico

Via dei Sarti 1 0588 875 80 Mid-Mar-Oct: 9am-7pm daily; Nov-mid-Mar: 10am-4:30pm daily 1 Jan, 25 Dec

Volterra's excellent art gallery is situated in the 15th-century Palazzo Minucci-Solaini. There is a significant emphasis on Florentine artists, who are responsible for many of the

The Deposition (1521) by Rosso Fiorientino, in the Pinacoteca e Museo Civico

gallery's best works. In Ghirlandaio's *Christ in Majesty* (1492), Christ hovers above an idealized Tuscan landscape. It was meant for the San Giusto monastery, which was abandoned after a landslip like the one shown in the middle distance of the work and beyond. Luca Signorelli's *Madonna and Child with Saints* (1491) shows his debt to Roman art through the reliefs on the base of the Virgin's throne, while his delicate *Annunciation* (1491) is another beautiful composition.

The museum's main exhibit is Rosso Fiorentino's Mannerist work *The Deposition* (1521). Attention is focused on the grief-stricken figures in the foreground and the pallid, empty shell of Christ's body, its dead weight symbolizing that his spirit is elsewhere.

Tickets for the Pinacoteca e Museo Civico also allow entry into the Ecomuseo dell' Alabastro *(p163)*.

Did You Know?

The alabaster festival is held near the feast day for St Luke, patron saint of artisanal workers.

④ 

Museo d'Arte Sacra

Chiesa di Sant'Agostino 0588 877 33 11am-6pm Tue-Sun 1 Jan, 1 May, 25 Dec

This museum, which relocated to the imposing church of Sant'Agostino in 2017, contains sculpture and architectural fragments from the Duomo *(p162)*, which is also known for its art, and a number of other local churches.

The main exhibit is a 15th-century della Robbia terracotta of St Linus, Volterra's patron saint. The collection also has a range of church bells from the 11th to the 15th centuries, some church silver and several intricate illuminated manuscripts.

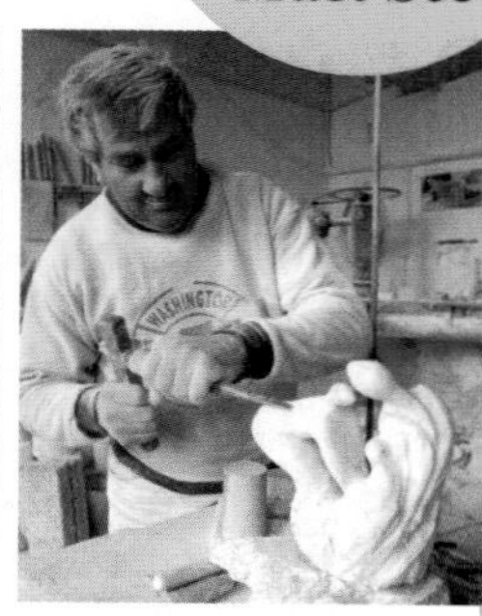

VOLTERRA'S ALABASTER

The locally quarried alabaster, prized for its smooth translucency, was once known as the "stone of the gods" and has been worked in Volterra since Etruscan times. A number of crafts studios in the city still make and sell items in alabaster, including Alab'Arte *(Via Don Minzoni 18)*. Volterra even hosts a three-day alabaster festival each October, which features everything from exhibitions to music.

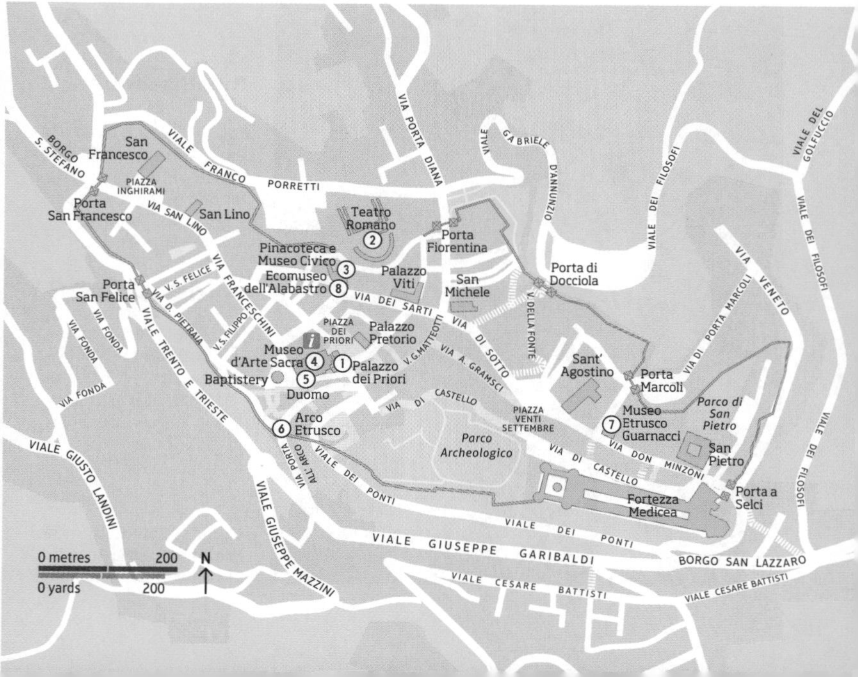

San Francesco
Borgo S. Stefano
Porta San Francesco
Piazza Inghirami
Viale Franco Porretti
Via San Lino
San Lino
Teatro Romano ②
Via Porta Diana
Viale Gabriele D'Annunzio
Porta Fiorentina
Pinacoteca e Museo Civico ③
Ecomuseo dell'Alabastro ⑧
Palazzo Viti
San Michele
Porta di Docciola
Viale dei Filosofi
Viale del Golfuccio
Via Veneto
Porta San Felice
V. S. Felice
Via Franceschini
Via dei Sarti
Via di Sotto
V. della Fonte
Via di Porta Marcoli
Via Fonda
Via D. Pietraia
Viale Trento e Trieste
V. S. Filippo
Piazza dei Priori
Palazzo Pretorio
V. G. Matteotti
Via A. Gramsci
Museo d'Arte Sacra ④
① Palazzo dei Priori
Baptistery
⑤ Duomo
Sant'Agostino
Porta Marcoli
Parco di San Pietro
Via di Castello
Piazza Venti Settembre
⑦ Museo Etrusco Guarnacci
⑥ Arco Etrusco
Parco Archeologico
Via Don Minzoni
San Pietro
Viale Giusto Landini
Via Porta all'Arco
Viale dei Ponti
Porta a Selci
Fortezza Medicea
Viale Giuseppe Mazzini
Viale Giuseppe Garibaldi
Borgo San Lazzaro
Viale Cesare Battisti
0 metres 200
0 yards 200
N

Duomo

Piazza San Giovanni
Daily

Work on Volterra's cathedral began in 1120, on the site of a pre-existing church, and continued intermittently over the next two centuries.

Inside the cathedral, a Romanesque wood-carving of *The Deposition* (1228) stands to the right of the High Altar. The altar itself is flanked by graceful marble angels carved by Mino da Fiesole in 1471; they face an elegant tabernacle, by the same artist, which is adorned with the figures of Faith, Hope and Charity.

The nave, remodelled in 1581, has an unusual coffered ceiling with stucco figures of bishops and saints painted in rich blue and gold. The pulpit, in the middle of the nave, dates from 1584, but was created using sculptural reliefs from the late 12th and early 13th centuries. The *Last Supper* panel, facing into the nave and thought to be the work of the Pisan artist Guglielmo Pisano, has a number of humorous details, including a monster snapping at the heels of Judas. Nearby, in the north aisle, Fra Bartolomeo's *The Annunciation* (1497) hangs above an altar in one of the side chapels.

More sculptures are housed in the oratory off the north aisle, near the main entrance. The best is a tableau of the Epiphany, preserved behind glass. The remarkably humane painted terracotta figures of the Virgin and Child in the foreground are believed to be by Zaccaria da Volterra (1473–1544), a local sculptor.

GREAT VIEW
Roman Remains

The best viewing point to see the remains of Volterra's Roman baths, which date from the 4th century, and theatre is off Via Guarnacci. This ancient site was covered up during the Middle Ages and excavations only began in the 1950s.

Arco Etrusco

Follow Via Porta all'Arco from the centre of Volterra to find the Arco Etrusco, which once formed part of the city's

Did You Know?

The language of the Etruscans has not yet been fully deciphered, so some artifacts remain unread.

Visitors gathering outside the Romanesque façade of Volterra's Duomo

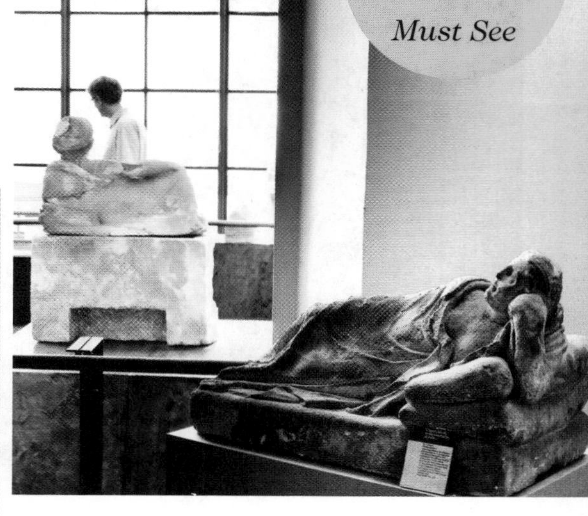

→ Exhibits on display at the Museo Etrusco Guarnacci

ancient walls. One of Volterra's more unusual sights, the Etruscan arch is in fact part Roman.

Only the columns and the severely weathered basalt heads, representing Etruscan gods, date to the 6th-century BC original. The features of each head are now barely visible, and though many legends surround them, no one can say for certain what they were intended to represent.

Museo Etrusco Guarnacci

Via Don Minzoni 15 0588 863 47 9am-7pm daily (Nov-mid-Mar: 10am-4:30pm) 1 Jan, 25 Dec

The pride of the Guarnacci Museum is its collection of 600 Etruscan funerary urns. Intricately carved, they offer a unique insight into Etruscan customs and beliefs.

The museum's two main exhibits are on the first floor. Room 20 contains the terracotta "Married Couple" urn, on which the elderly couple atop the lid are portrayed realistically, with careworn faces. Room 22 contains the elongated bronze known as *Ombra della Sera* (Shadow of the Evening), a name given by the poet Gabriele d'Annunzio, who said that the bronze reminded him of the shadow thrown by a human figure in the dying light of the evening sun. It probably dates from the 3rd century BC, but it is difficult to confirm this as the figure was cast with no clothes or jewellery to indicate rank, status or date. Indeed, it is only by chance that it survived. Ploughed up by a farmer in 1879, it was used as a fire poker until someone recognized it as a masterpiece of Etruscan art.

Ecomuseo dell'Alabastro

Via dei Sarti

Housed in the 13th-century Torre Minucci, adjacent to Palazzo Minucci Solaini and the Pinacoteca *(p160)*, this museum recounts the history of alabaster in the Volterra area from Etruscan times to the present day, covering techniques and materials, styles, and the social and economic conditions of alabaster workers. The most noteworthy exhibit is an ancient Etruscan funerary urn in alabaster.

THE ETRUSCANS

Tuscany is named after the Etruscans, who settled central Italy around the 8th century BC, from northern Lazio to the Umbrian Apennines. Little is known about them beyond scant Roman records and a handful of surviving (mostly funerary) artifacts *(right)*. According to myth, they came from Asia Minor (along with Tuscany's familiar cypress tree), enjoyed an advanced culture, with relative equality between the sexes, and excelled at engineering - they taught the Romans the art of draining land for farming. Many aspects of Roman religion can be attributed to the Etruscans, including animal sacrifice and divination. After a fierce war with Rome, the Etruscans came under Roman rule, signalling their end as a distinct civilization.

San Gimignano's skyline, bristling with medieval towers ↑

3

SAN GIMIGNANO

R4 Porta San Giovanni Piazza del Duomo 1; www.sangimignano.com

The "city of beautiful towers" – which were built in the 13th century both as a display of wealth and to serve as private fortresses – is one of the best-preserved medieval towns in Tuscany. Its main square is ringed by a jumble of unspoiled 13th- and 14th-century palazzi, while the two major streets, Via San Matteo and Via San Giovanni, still retain their medieval feel.

1

Duomo

Piazza del Duomo
Hours vary, check website
duomo sangimignano.it

The plain façade of this 12th-century Romanesque church belies its interior – it is one of the most frescoed churches in Italy. Further art from the Duomo is found in the Museo d'Arte Sacra, accessed via the Piazza Pecori.

2

Rocca di Montestaffoli

Piazza Propositura
Daily

The 14th-century Rocca, or fortress, now has only one surviving tower, following its dismantling by Cosimo I de' Medici in the 16th century. It encloses a public garden filled with fig and olive trees.

3

Museo Civico

Palazzo del Popolo
0577 28 63 00 Apr-Sep: 10am-7:30pm daily; Oct-Mar: 11am-5:30pm daily 31 Jan

This museum is housed in the Palazzo del Popolo (town hall). Its tower, finished in 1311, is the tallest in the town, at 54 m (175 ft); it is open to the public and offers stunning views. In the first public room, the Sala di Dante, an inscription records the poet's plea to the city council in 1300 to support the Florence-led Guelph (pro-Pope) alliance. The floor above has a small art collection, with works by Pinturicchio and Memmo di Filippucci.

4

Sant'Agostino

Piazza Sant'Agostino
0577 90 70 12 7am-noon, 3-7pm Tue-Sun (from 10am Dec-Mar)

Consecrated in 1298, this church's simple façade contrasts sharply with the heavily decorated Rococo interior (c 1740). Of note in the Cappella di San Bartolo is an elaborate marble altar, completed by Benedetto da Maiano in 1495.

DRINK

Vernaccia di San Gimignano Wine Museum

Try San Gimignano's famed white wine (and lesser-known reds, rosé and Vin Santo) at this regional wine museum. A fascinating multimedia experience also recounts the history and culture surrounding the wines.

Via della Rocca 1
sangimignanomuseo vernaccia.com

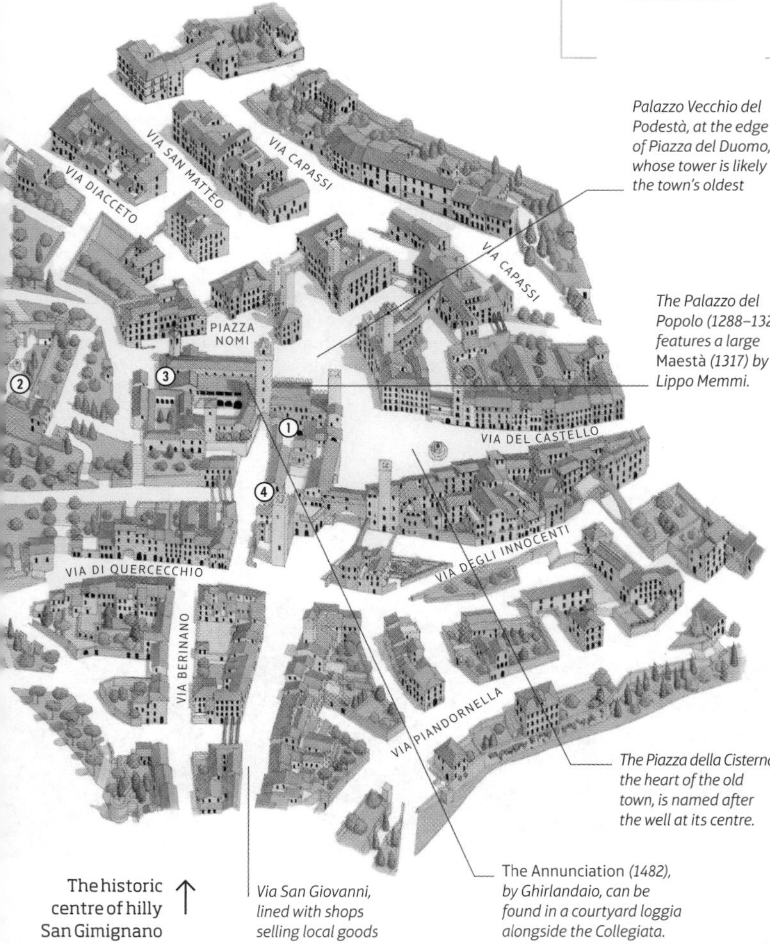

VIA SAN MATTEO
VIA CAPASSI
VIA DIACCETO

Palazzo Vecchio del Podestà, at the edge of Piazza del Duomo, whose tower is likely the town's oldest

VIA CAPASSI
PIAZZA NOMI

The Palazzo del Popolo (1288–1323) features a large Maestà *(1317) by Lippo Memmi.*

VIA DEL CASTELLO
VIA DI QUERCECCHIO
VIA DEGLI INNOCENTI
VIA BERINANO
VIA PIANDORNELLA

The Piazza della Cisterna, the heart of the old town, is named after the well at its centre.

The historic centre of hilly San Gimignano

Via San Giovanni, lined with shops selling local goods

The Annunciation *(1482), by Ghirlandaio, can be found in a courtyard loggia alongside the Collegiata.*

EXPERIENCE MORE

San Giovanni Valdarno

S4 FS Piazza Cavour 3

Tuscany's most important river, the Arno, gives its name to the Valdarno area and San Giovanni is the most important of the new towns built by the Florentines in the late 13th century. The striking Palazzo d'Arnolfo, which dates from the town's founding, houses the Museo delle Terre Nuove, dedicated to the phenomenon of new towns in medieval Europe. Della Robbia terracottas are among those decorating the palazzo to recall successive rulers.

Renaissance pioneer Masaccio was born here in 1401 and his birthplace, the Casa Masaccio, is now a centre for contemporary arts. The 15th-century Basilica di Santa Maria delle Grazie contains some impressive contemporary paintings, including an *Annunciation* by Fra Angelico; look out, in the atrium, for another Della Robbia terracotta.

5

Colle di Val d'Elsa

R4 FS Via Campana 43; 0577 92 27 91

Colle di Val d'Elsa has a lower and an upper town. The Mannerist Palazzo Campana, built on an aqueduct in 1539, forms a gateway to Colle Alta, the upper town, which is of great medieval architectural interest. In the modern lower town, shops sell locally made crystal glass. This has been a major glass-making centre since the 14th century and 98 per cent of Italy's crystal glass (and 14 per cent of the world's) is made here. While the glass museum in the lower town is undergoing works, most of its collection is on display in the ancient Palazzo dei Priori in the upper town. On the same street, Via del Castello, the Romanesque church of Santa Maria has a simple bell tower and a stone façade inlaid with brickwork. A tabernacle by Pier Francesco Fiorentino shows scenes from the lives of the Madonna and Child. Nearby in a pretty piazza is the Duomo, another simple yet dignified building.

Via Gracco del Secco is dominated at its eastern end by the Porta Nova. This large Renaissance fortress, with its two heavily fortified towers, was built in the 15th century to guard against attack from the Volterra road. Here, also, is the monumental San Pietro complex of former monastic buildings; inside, the Museo San Pietro has Siena school paintings and some fine Etruscan pottery. There are also some 14th-century hunting scenes by Bartolo di Fredi, and an early wooden crucifix by Marco Romano.

INSIDER TIP
Living History

Travel back in time at the Archeodromo Poggibonsi, a re-created 9th-century village that comes to life every Sunday afternoon with costumed "villagers" re-enacting ancient pastimes *(www.archeodromopoggibonsi.it)*.

↑ The lovely upper town of Colle di Val d'Elsa, with the Santa Maria bell tower

↑ Dining al fresco in the tranquil main square of Monteriggioni

Monteriggioni

R4 Piazza Roma 23; 0577 30 48 10

Monteriggioni is a gem of a medieval hilltop town. It was a garrison town, encircled by high walls with 14 heavily fortified towers, built to guard the northern borders of Siena's territory against invasion by Florentine armies.

The walls, still perfectly preserved, are best viewed from the Colle di Val d'Elsa road. Within, the sleepy village has a large piazza, a pretty Romanesque church, crafts shops, restaurants and shops selling the excellent local Castello di Monteriggioni wines.

Empoli

R3 Via Giuseppe del Papa 98; 0571 76 115

An industrial town, Empoli is worth visiting for the excellent **Museo della Collegiata**, with its collection of Renaissance paintings and sculpture. Of particular interest are Masolino's *Pietà* fresco (1425) and a marble font by Rossellino, dating from 1447.

Empoli's arcaded main square, Piazza Farinata degli Uberti, is surrounded by 12th-century buildings, notably the church of Sant'Andrea, with its black-and-white marble façade. The large fountain (1827), with water nymphs and lions, is by Luigi Pampaloni.

In the Magazzino del Sale, a 14th-century salt warehouse on Via Ridolfi, the Museo del Vetro recounts the history of local glass-making, including displays of glass objects, particularly in the Empoli speciality green glass.

Museo della Collegiata
Piazza della Propositura 3 0571 762 84 Tue–Sun Pub & relig hols

Vinci

R3 toscananel cuore.it

This hilltop town was the birthplace of Leonardo da Vinci (1452–1519). To celebrate his extraordinary genius, the 13th-century castle in the centre of the town is now the **Museo Leonardiano**. Among the displays are wooden models of Leonardo's machines and inventions, based on the drawings from his notebooks, copies of which are shown alongside. These range from his conception of a car, to an armoured tank and even a machine-gun. A pair of skis, designed for walking on water, show that he could occasionally miss the mark.

In nearby Santo Stefano church is the font in which Leonardo was baptized. His actual birthplace, the **Casa di Leonardo**, is 2 km (1 mile) from the town centre. There is not much to see at this simple farmhouse, but it's a lovely walk through poppy fields.

Museo Leonardiano
Castello dei Conti Guidi 0571 560 55 Daily

Casa di Leonardo
Anchiano 0571 560 55 Daily

RENAISSANCE VILLAS

Built in 1480 for Lorenzo de' Medici, the Villa Medicea di Poggio a Caiano was Italy's first Renaissance-style villa. Today it hosts the Museo della Natura Morta still-life museum.

The nearby Villa di Artimino, designed by Buontalenti in 1594, is known as the "Villa of a Hundred Chimneys" because of the ornate chimney pots crowding the roof. Now a hotel, it offers wine tastings.

↓ Wooden model made from the so-called "bicycle sketch" by Leonardo da Vinci

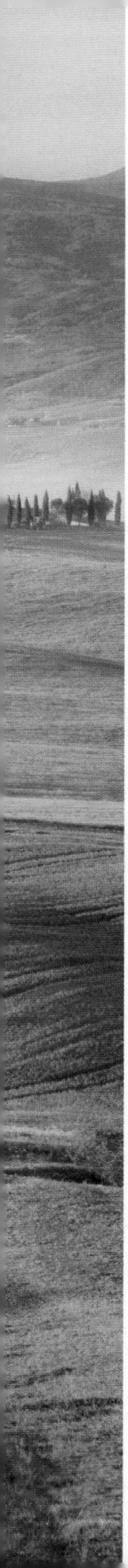

Cypress trees along a winding road near Pienza

SOUTHEAST TUSCANY

Legends say that the spectacular city of Siena was founded by the son of Remus (founder, with brother Romulus, of Rome). In reality, the hilly site was first settled by the Etruscans – along with Arezzo, Cortona and Chiusi, one of the most powerful centres of ancient Etruria – before becoming a military colony in Roman times. Siena grew in importance during the Middle Ages, thanks both to its location on the Via Francigena, an ancient pilgrimage route to Rome, and to its astute money-lending enterprises; Monte dei Paschi di Siena, founded in 1472, is the world's oldest operating bank. A thriving republic for four centuries, Siena was conquered in 1555 by long-term rival Florence, following a vicious siege.

Medici leader Lorenzo the Magnificent was a particular fan of this part of Tuscany, appreciating the tasty pecorino sheep's cheese from Pienza and enjoying the Val d'Orcia spa waters. Having remained largely rural with a low-profile wine-making industry, the region first released its prime product, Brunello di Montalcino, in 1865. Nowadays it is one of Italy's most prestigious wines.

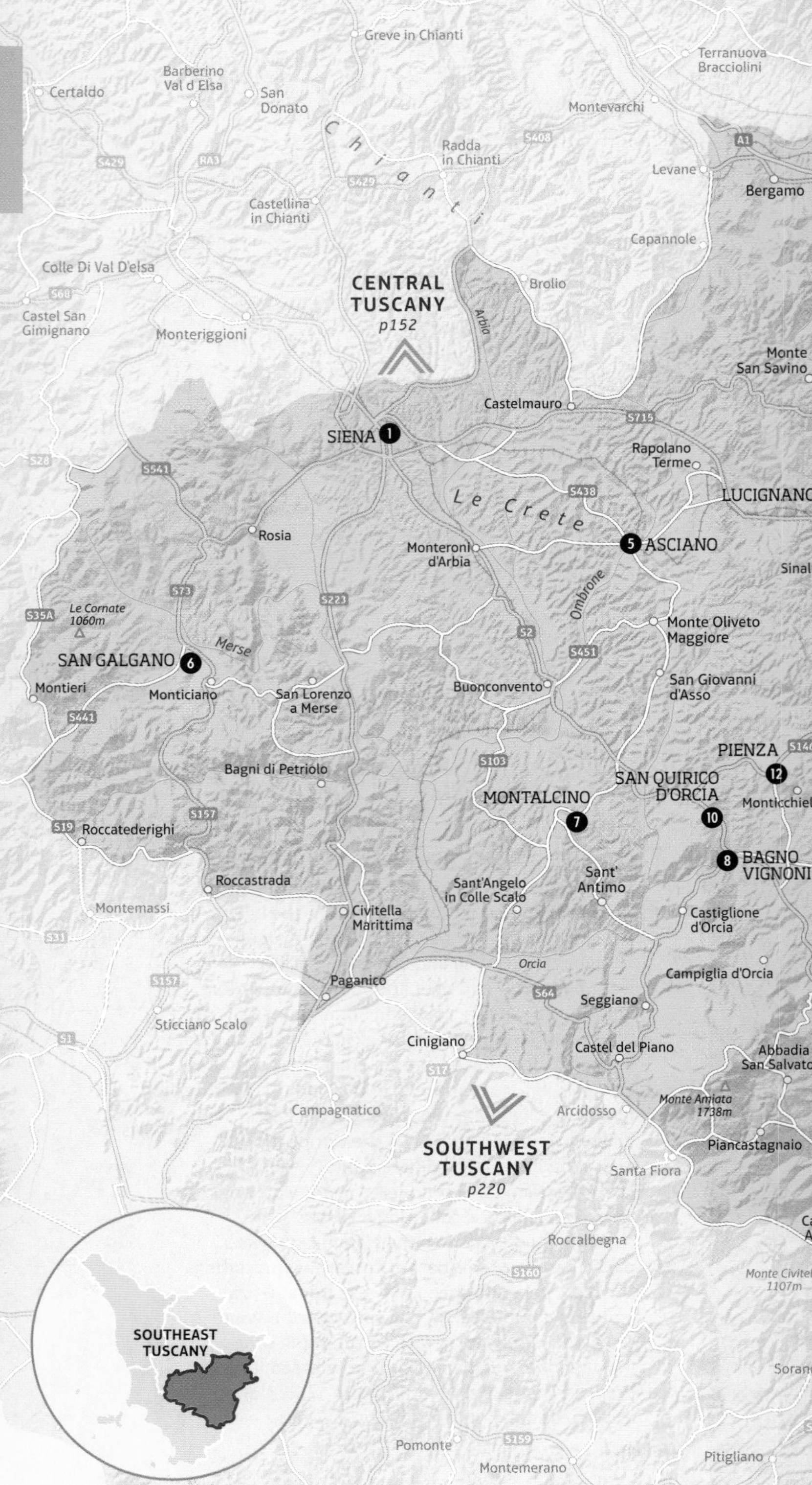

Greve in Chianti
Terranuova Bracciolini
Certaldo
Barberino Val d Elsa
San Donato
Montevarchi
Chianti
Radda in Chianti
Levane
Bergamo
Castellina in Chianti
Capannole
Colle Di Val D'elsa
Brolio
Castel San Gimignano
Monteriggioni
CENTRAL TUSCANY
p152
Arbia
Monte San Savino
Castelmauro
SIENA 1
Rapolano Terme
Le Crete
LUCIGNANO
Rosia
Monteroni d'Arbia
5 ASCIANO
Ombrone
Le Cornate 1060m
Monte Oliveto Maggiore
Merse
SAN GALGANO 6
Montieri
Monticiano
San Lorenzo a Merse
Buonconvento
San Giovanni d'Asso
PIENZA
SAN QUIRICO D'ORCIA
12
Bagni di Petriolo
MONTALCINO
Monticchiello
7
10
Roccatederighi
8 BAGNO VIGNONI
Roccastrada
Sant'Angelo in Colle Scalo
Sant' Antimo
Montemassi
Civitella Marittima
Castiglione d'Orcia
Orcia
Campiglia d'Orcia
Paganico
Seggiano
Stricciano Scalo
Cinigiano
Castel del Piano
Abbadia San Salvatore
Campagnatico
Arcidosso
Monte Amiata 1738m
SOUTHWEST TUSCANY
p220
Piancastagnaio
Santa Fiora
Roccalbegna
Monte Civitella 1107m
SOUTHEAST TUSCANY
Sorano
Pomonte
Montemerano
Pitigliano

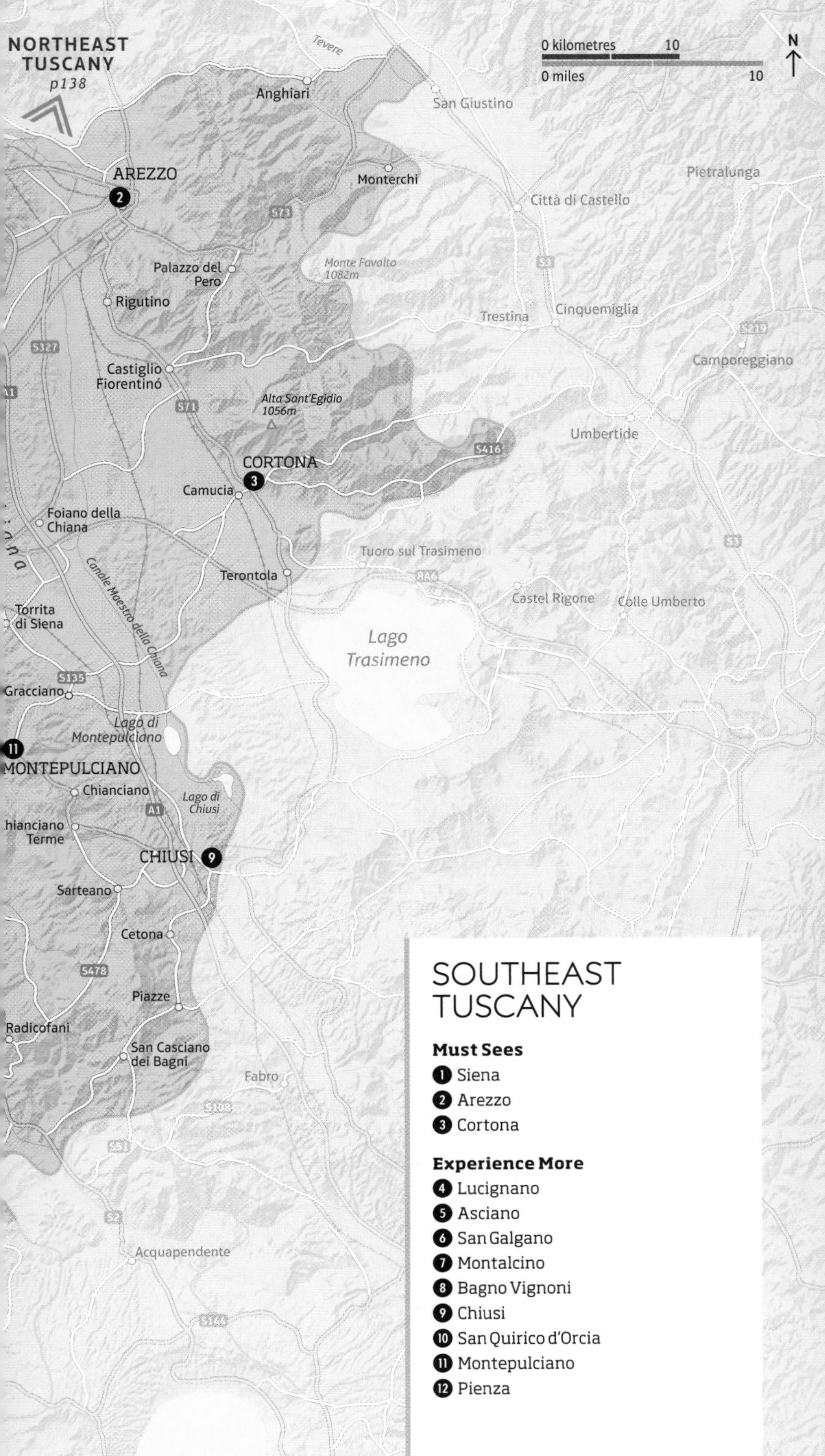

SOUTHEAST TUSCANY

Must Sees

1. Siena
2. Arezzo
3. Cortona

Experience More

4. Lucignano
5. Asciano
6. San Galgano
7. Montalcino
8. Bagno Vignoni
9. Chiusi
10. San Quirico d'Orcia
11. Montepulciano
12. Pienza

1 SIENA

R4 Piazza Stazione Piazza San Domenico
Piazza del Campo 56; 9am-7pm daily; 0577 28 05 51
terresiena.it

Siena is a city of steep medieval alleys surrounding the Piazza del Campo. The buildings around the square symbolize the golden age of the city, between 1260 and 1348, when wealthy citizens contributed to a major programme of civic building. Siena's decline began in 1348 when the Black Death arrived, killing a third of the population; 200 years later, many more died when the Florentines sieged and eventually won the city. The victors repressed all further development in Siena, and the city largely remains frozen in time, crammed with renovated medieval buildings.

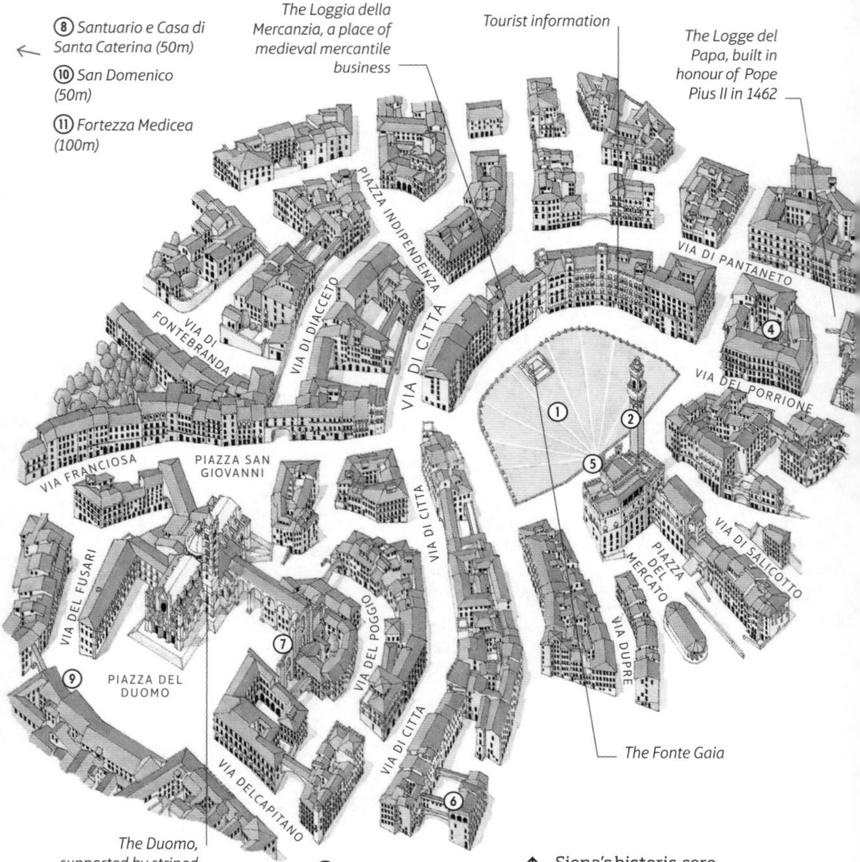

⑧ Santuario e Casa di Santa Caterina (50m)

⑩ San Domenico (50m)

⑪ Fortezza Medicea (100m)

The Loggia della Mercanzia, a place of medieval mercantile business

Tourist information

The Logge del Papa, built in honour of Pope Pius II in 1462

PIAZZA INDIPENDENZA
VIA DI PANTANETO
VIA DI FONTEBRANDA
VIA DI DIACCETO
VIA DI CITTA
VIA DEL PORRIONE
VIA FRANCIOSA
PIAZZA SAN GIOVANNI
VIA DI SALICOTTO
PIAZZA DEL MERCATO
VIA DEL FUSARI
VIA DEL POGGIO
VIA DUPRE
PIAZZA DEL DUOMO
VIA DELCAPITANO

The Fonte Gaia

The Duomo, supported by striped black-and-white marble pillars

③ Pinacoteca Nazionale (500m)

↑ Siena's historic core, centred around Piazza del Campo

↑ Siena's medieval townhouses, built up the city's gentle slopes

Piazza del Campo

The shell-shaped, 12th-century Piazza del Campo is bordered by elegant palazzi. Its focal point is an elaborate fountain: the Fonte Gaia, a rectangular marble basin decorated by statues. The fountain that can be seen today is a 19th-century copy of the original, which was carved by Jacopo della Quercia in 1409–19. This was removed to preserve it from the ravages of the weather. The reliefs on the fountain depict Adam and Eve, the Madonna and Child, and the Virtues. Water is fed into it by a 25-km- (15-mile-) long aqueduct, which has brought fresh water into the city from the hills since the 14th century.

Torre del Mangia

Piazza del Campo 0577 292 615 10am-7pm (mid-Oct-Feb: to 4pm)

The bell tower to the left of the Palazzo Pubblico is the second-highest in Italy, at 102 m (330 ft). Built by the brothers Muccio and Francesco di Rinaldo between 1338 and 1348, it is named after the first bell-ringer, who was nicknamed *Mangiaguadagni* (literally "eat the profits") because of his great idleness. (Since it was the bell-ringer's responsibility to warn the citizens of impending danger, this was worrisome.) There are 505 steps to the top of the tower, but climbers are rewarded with wonderful views across southeast Tuscany.

Pinacoteca Nazionale

Via San Pietro 29 0577 28 11 61 8:15am-7:15pm Tue-Sat, 9am-1pm Sun & Mon 1 Jan, 1 May, 25 Dec

Housed in the 14th-century Palazzo Buonsignori, this gallery contains important works by the Siena school. Lorenzetti's *Two Views*, produced in the 14th century, are early examples of landscape painting, and Pietro da Domenico's *Adoration of the Shepherds* (1510) shows how the art of the Siena school remained stylized long after Renaissance naturalism had influenced the rest of Europe. There is also a striking *Deposition* (1502) by Sodoma.

STAY

Palazzo Borghesi
Fresco-lined rooms in a 15th-century palace.

Via San Pietro 3 palazzoborghese siena.it

La Villa di STR
Refined, airy rooms in a delightful villa.

Viale Vittorio Veneto 11 lavilladistr.it

Hotel Santa Caterina
Comfortable hotel with a panoramic garden.

Via Piccolomini 7 0577 221105

Frances' Lodge
Lovely farmhouse with great views of Siena.

Strada di Valdipugna 2 franceslodge.eu

Palazzo Piccolomini

Via Banchi di Sotto 52 0577 247 145 Admission at 9:30am, 10:30am & 11:30am Mon-Sat, by appt only 1st two weeks in Aug & public hols

This imposing palazzo was built in the 1460s by Rossellino for the wealthy Piccolomini family. It houses the state archives, including the Tavolette di Biccherna – 13th-century municipal ledgers, with covers by Sano di Pietro, Ambrogio Lorenzetti, Domenico Beccafumi and others.

Palazzo Pubblico

Piazza del Campo 1 0577 292 226

The Palazzo Pubblico serves as the town hall, but the state rooms, which contain historic frescoes and works of art, are open to the public as part of the Museo Civico. The main council chamber is called the Sala del Mappamondo, after a map of the world painted by Ambrogio Lorenzetti in the early 1300s. One wall is covered by Simone Martini's *Maestà* (Virgin in Majesty; 1315). Opposite is Martini's fresco of the mercenary Guidoriccio da Fogliano (1330). The walls of the adjacent chapel are covered with frescoes by Taddeo di Bartolo, and the choir stalls (1428) feature wooden panels inlaid with biblical scenes.

The Sala della Pace contains the famous *Allegory of Good and Bad Government*, a pair of 1338 frescoes by Ambrogio Lorenzetti. The Sala del Risorgimento is covered with late 19th-century frescoes illustrating events leading up to the unification of Italy.

Accademia Musicale Chigiana

Palazzo Chigi Saracini, Via di Città 89 For concerts and exhibitions, check website for details chigiana.it

Founded by Count Guido Chigi Saracini in 1932, the Accademia holds masterclasses for the principal musical instruments. Housed in one of Siena's finest buildings, there is also a fine art collection, a museum of musical instruments and a manuscript library.

Museo dell'Opera Metropolitana

Piazza del Duomo 8 0577 28 6300 Mar-Oct: 10:30am-7pm daily; Nov-Feb: 10:30am-5:30pm daily; 26 Dec-6 Jan: 10:30am-5:30pm daily 1 Jan, 25 Dec

This museum is built into the unfinished side aisle of the Duomo *(p176)*. Part of it houses sculptures from the exterior of the Duomo that had become eroded. Duccio's double-sided *Maestà*, one of the best Siena school works, has a room to itself. Painted

HIDDEN GEM

Bird's-Eye View

The small balcony of the San Paolo pub *(Vicolo San Paolo 2)*, directly opposite the Torre del Mangia, is the very best place to go for views over the Campo. Come for a drink or panino.

THE PALIO OF SIENA

The Palio is Tuscany's most celebrated festival. It's a bareback horse race, first recorded in 1283, that takes place in the Piazza del Campo each year on 2 July and 16 August at 7pm. The jockeys represent 10 of Siena's 17 *contrade* (districts) and horses are chosen by the drawing of lots. Preceded by days of colourful pageantry and heavy betting, the races themselves last only 90 seconds. Thousands come to watch, and rivalry is intense. The winner is rewarded with a silk *palio* (banner), and the victory celebrations can last for weeks.

in 1308–11, it depicts the Madonna and Child on one side and scenes from the Life of Christ on the other.

Santuario e Casa di Santa Caterina

Costa di Sant'Antonio 6 0577 28 81 75 9:15am-1pm, 3-7:30pm daily

Siena's patron saint, Catherine Benincasa (1347–80), was the daughter of a tradesman. She took the veil as a teenager and became known for her letters and activism on behalf of the church. Her eloquence persuaded Gregory XI to return the seat of the papacy to Rome in 1376, after 67 years of exile in Avignon, France. She died in Rome and was canonized in 1461. Today, her house is surrounded by chapels and cloisters, and is decorated with paintings of her life by artists such as Pietro Sorri and Francesco Vanni, both her contemporaries.

Siena's Palazzo Pubblico, sat on the Piazza del Campo

Santa Maria della Scala

Piazza del Duomo Check website santamariadellascala.com

This former hospital is now a museum housing a collection of paintings and sculpture. In the Sala del Pellegrino, frescoes by Domenico di Bartolo depict hospital scenes from the 1440s.

San Domenico

Piazza San Domenico Daily

This barn-like Gothic church was begun in 1226 and its bell tower was added in 1340. Inside is an exquisite chapel dedicated to St Catherine. This was built in 1460 to store the saint's preserved head, which is now kept in a gilded marble tabernacle on the altar, encircled by frescoes depicting her.

Catherine experienced many visions and received her stigmata in the Cappella delle Volte, at the west end of the church. Here, there is a portrait of her by Andrea Vanni, dated around 1380.

Fortezza Medicea

Viale Maccari Fortezza: daily; theatre: Nov-Apr, performances only

This huge red-brick fortress was built for Cosimo I by Baldassarre Lanci in 1560, following Siena's defeat by the Florentines in the 1554–5 war *(p172)*. The fortress now houses an open-air theatre, and from the entrance bastions there are fine views of the countryside.

EAT

Taverna San Giuseppe

Exceptional food and service, plus an Etruscan wine cellar carved from the rock.

Via Dupré 132 Sun tavernasangiuseppe.it

Grotta Santa Caterina da Bagoga

Charming trattoria run by an ex-Palio jockey.

Via della Galluzza 26 Mon ristorantebagoga.it

Inside San Domenico is an exquisite chapel dedicated to St Catherine, which was built in 1460 to store the saint's preserved head.

⑫

SIENA DUOMO

Piazza del Duomo Pollicino Hours vary, check website
operaduomo.siena.it

Siena's hulking Duomo is a treasure house of late Gothic sculpture, early Renaissance painting and Baroque design. The early architects dressed the cathedral in striking Romanesque stripes, but the form is firmly Gothic. The interior is just as awe-inspiring, from Nicola Pisano's splendid pulpit to the heavily frescoed Piccolomini Library, the work of Pinturicchio and his assistants.

Siena's Duomo (1136–1382) is one of the most spectacular in Italy, and one of the few to have been built south of the Alps in full Gothic style. The mosaic floor is particularly special, with Vasari decreeing it the "largest and most magnificent floor ever made". Many ordinary citizens helped to cart the black-and-white stone used in the church's construction from quarries on the outskirts of the city. In 1339, the Sienese decided to build a new nave to the south, aiming to make their cathedral the biggest in Christendom. This plan came to nothing when plague killed off much of the population soon afterwards. The uncompleted nave now contains a museum of sculpture.

↑ Coffered vaulting inside the dome of Siena Duomo

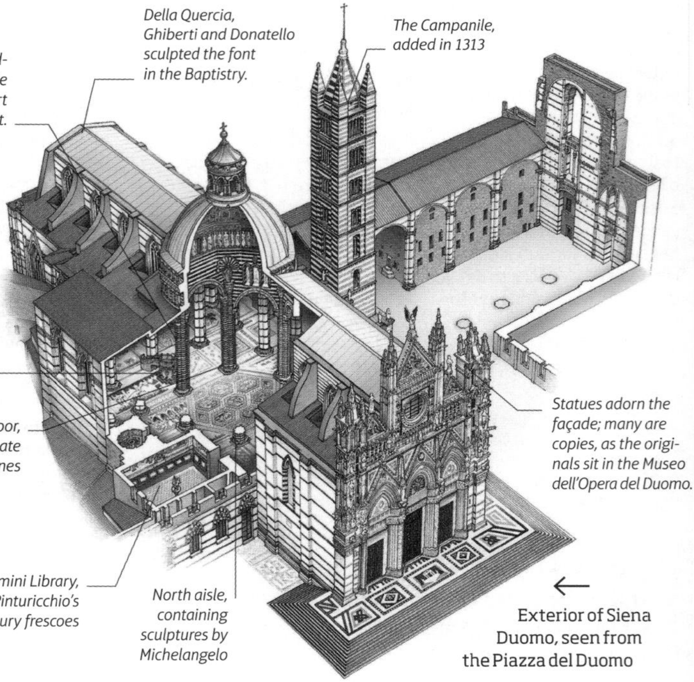

Della Quercia, Ghiberti and Donatello sculpted the font in the Baptistry.

The Campanile, added in 1313

Black-and-white marble pillars support the vault.

Pulpit panels, carved by Nicola Pisano in 1265–8

Inlaid marble floor, covered in intricate and dramatic scenes

Statues adorn the façade; many are copies, as the originals sit in the Museo dell'Opera del Duomo.

Piccolomini Library, filled with Pinturicchio's 16th-century frescoes

North aisle, containing sculptures by Michelangelo

← Exterior of Siena Duomo, seen from the Piazza del Duomo

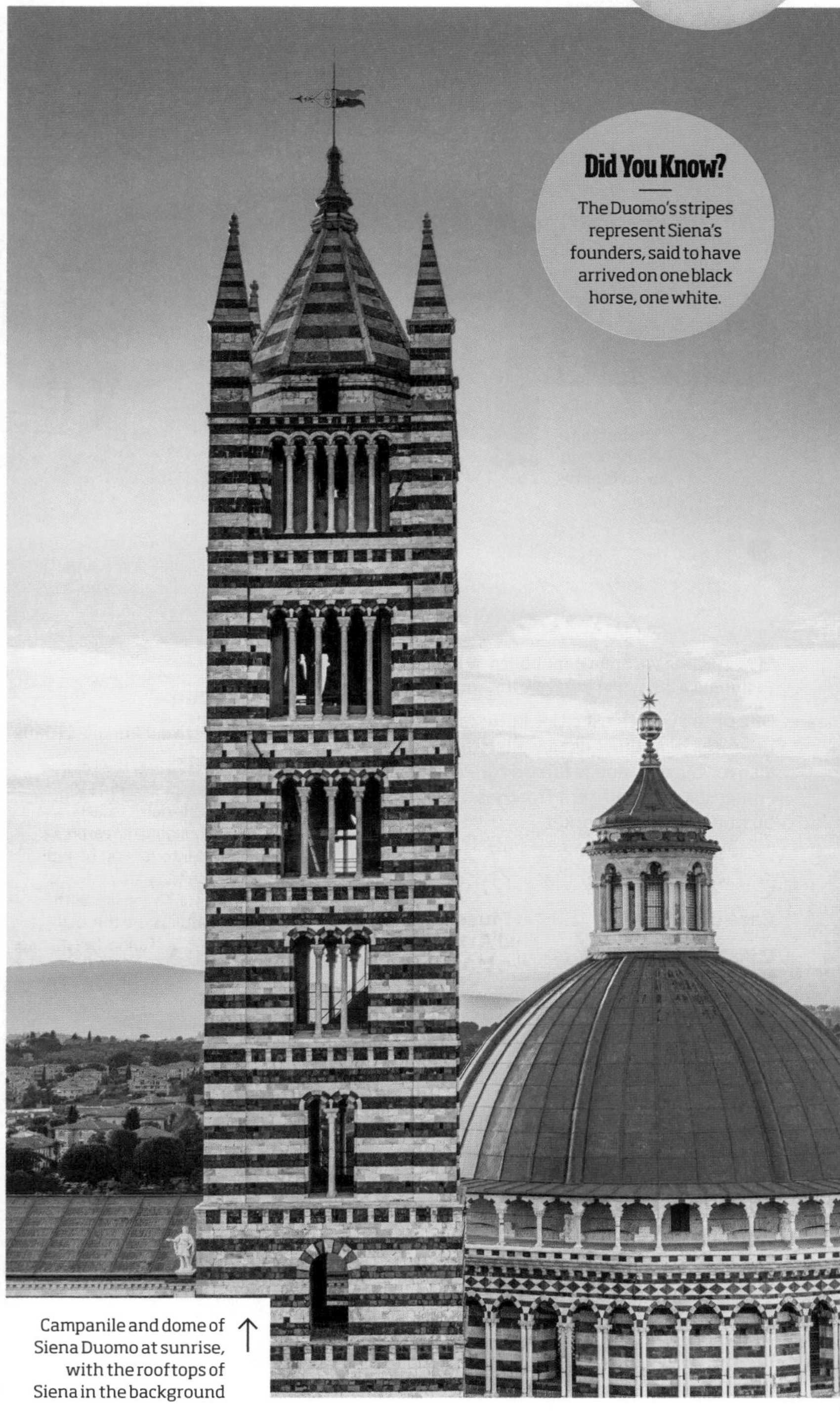

Did You Know?

The Duomo's stripes represent Siena's founders, said to have arrived on one black horse, one white.

Campanile and dome of Siena Duomo at sunrise, with the rooftops of Siena in the background ↑

The bustling antiques market in Piazza Grande

AREZZO

 T4 FS Piazza della Repubblica Piazza della Repubblica 28; www.arezzo.intoscana.it

One of the wealthiest cities in Tuscany, Arezzo produces beautiful gold jewellery for shops all over Europe, and is famed for Piero della Francesca's magnificent frescoes and its bustling antiques market.

① Casa del Vasari

Via XX Settembre 55 0575 354449 8:30am-7:30pm Mon, Wed-Sat, 8:30am-1:30pm Sun

Giorgio Vasari (1512–74) built this house for himself in 1541 and decorated the ceilings and walls with portraits of fellow artists, friends and mentors. A prolific painter and architect, Vasari is most famous for his book, *Lives of the Most Excellent Painters, Sculptors and Architects* (1550). Despite the book's often cavalier attitude to the truth, Vasari's account of many great Renaissance artists has led to him being described as the first art historian.

② Museo Statale d'Arte Medioevale e Moderna

Via di San Lorentino 8 0575 40 90 50 9am-1:30pm, 3-7:30pm Tue, Wed & Sat; 9am-1.30pm Thur; 3-7:30pm Fri & Sun

Housed in the graceful 15th-century Palazzo Bruni, the museum's courtyard contains sculptures dating from the 10th to the 17th century. The collection includes several terracottas by Andrea della Robbia and a superb display of majolica pottery.

③ Duomo

Piazza del Duomo Daily

Begun in 1278, the Duomo was completed in 1510; its façade dates to 1914. A huge building, it features a Gothic interior and beautiful 16th-century stained-glass windows. To the left of the High Altar is the tomb of Guido Tarlati, ruler of Arezzo from 1312 to 1327.

Statue of Ferdinando I de' Medici, which stands on the steps to the Duomo

Did You Know?

The Chimera fountain near the station is a copy of an Etruscan bronze cast here in 380 BC.

Museo Diocesano di Arte Sacra

Piazzetta del Duomo 1 0575 4027268 Apr-Jun: 10am-6pm Wed-Mon; Nov-Mar: 10am-4:30pm Wed-Mon

Among the artifacts removed from the Duomo are three wooden crucifixes, dating from the 12th and the 13th century. The oldest of these was painted by Margaritone di Arezzo in 1264. Also of interest are Bernardo Rossellino,'s terracotta bas-relief of *The Annunciation* (1434), and works by by Vasari and Spinello Aretino.

Piazza Grande

The square is famous for its antiques market. On the west side, the façade of the Palazzo della Fraternità dei Laici is decorated with a relief of the Virgin (1434) by Bernardo Rossellino. The lower half of the building dates from 1377, while the belfry and clock tower date from 1552. The north side of the square features a handsome arcade designed by Vasari in 1573.

Anfiteatro Romano e Museo Archeologico

Via Margaritone 10 0575 222 59 Museum: 8:30am-7:30pm daily; amphitheatre: 8:30am-6pm daily (to 8pm in summer); 1 Jan, 1 May, 25 Dec

To the south of the city centre stands a ruined Roman amphitheatre and the Museo Archeologico. Famous for its extensive collection of Roman Aretine ware, including a piece attributed to the Attic potter Euphronios, the museum has a fascinating display showing how this high-quality, red-glazed pottery was produced and exported throughout the Roman Empire during the 1st century BC.

Pieve di Santa Maria

Corso Italia 7 8:30am-12:30pm, 3-6:30pm daily pievesantamaria.it

Arezzo's main shopping street, Corso Italia, leads uphill to the Pieve di Santa Maria, which has an ornate Romanesque façade. The splendid campanile, the "tower of a hundred holes" was named for the many arches running through it.

Fortezza Medicea e Parco il Prato

Parco il Prato 0575 37 76 78 Summer: 7am-8pm; winter: 7:30am-6:30pm

This imposing 16th-century fortress was built for Cosimo I by Antonio da Sangallo. Partially demolished in the 18th century, only the ramparts remain intact; these offer great views across the Arno valley. The site makes an excellent spot for a picnic.

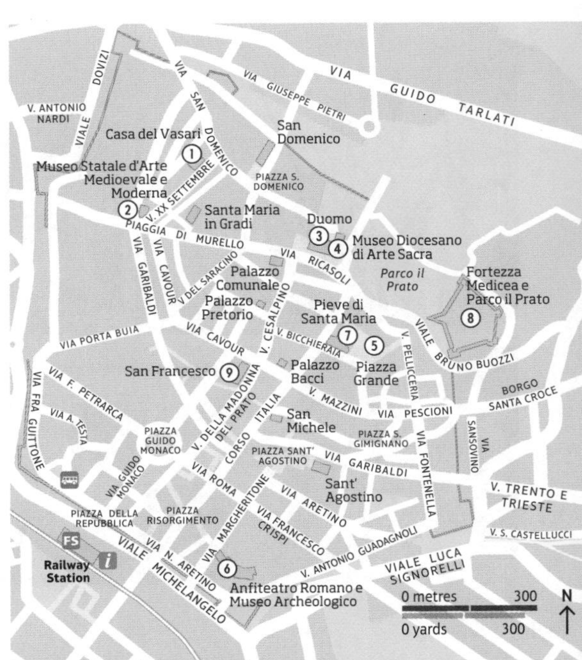

⑨

SAN FRANCESCO

Piazza San Francesco 0575 206 30 Apr–Oct: 9am–7pm Mon–Fri, 9am–6pm Sat, 1–6pm Sun; Nov–Mar: 9am–6pm Mon–Fri, 9am–5:30pm Sat, 1–5:30pm Sun pierodellafrancesca.it

The 13th-century church of San Francesco contains Piero della Francesca's *Legend of the True Cross* (1452–66), one of Italy's greatest fresco cycles. The frescoes, visible once more after a long restoration, show how the Cross was found near Jerusalem by the Empress Helena. Her son, the Emperor Constantine, then adopted it as his battle emblem. Visitors have a limited time in the chapel and advance booking is mandatory.

Della Francesca presents the story of the True Cross in dramatic detail. The narrative begins on the right-hand wall with a scene showing a sprig from the Tree of Knowledge being planted over Adam's grave. The Queen of Sheba then visits Solomon and foresees that a bridge made from the Tree will be used to crucify the world's greatest king. Solomon, assuming he is that king, orders the bridge to be buried. We then see the Annunciation and Christ on the Cross at the centre of the fresco cycle. Centuries later, Constantine has a vision of the Cross and hears a voice saying "in this sign you shall conquer". Constantine goes on to defeat his rival Maxentius, while Judas Kyriakos is tortured into revealing the location of the True Cross. Three crosses are then dug up and Constantine's mother Helena recognizes the True Cross. The Persian king Chosroes is defeated after stealing the True Cross, and it is finally returned to Jerusalem.

↑ Exterior of the Church of San Francesco in Arezzo

1 Constantine adopts the Cross as his battle emblem.

2 The Empress Helena watches the Cross being dug up. The town in the background, symbolizing Jerusalem, is based on 15th-century Arezzo.

3 The Queen of Sheba recognizes the wood of the Cross.

The magnificent interior of San Francesco, with the 13th-century crucifix that forms the focal point of the fresco cycle ↑

Pretty pastel houses in Cortona, with the stunning countryside stretching out behind

CORTONA

T5 Camucia, 5 km (3 miles) SE Piazza Garibaldi Via Nazionale 42; 0575 63 03 52

Cortona is one of the oldest cities in Tuscany. It was founded by the Etruscans, whose work can still be seen in the foundations of the city's massive walls. Cortona was a major seat of power during the medieval period, but declined following its defeat by Naples in 1409, after which it was sold to Florence and lost its autonomy.

Museo Diocesano

Piazza del Duomo 1 0575 628 30 Apr-Oct: 10am-7pm daily; Nov-Mar: 10am-5pm Tue-Sun

Housed in the 16th-century church of Gesù, the museum contains several masterpieces. Chief among these are Fra Angelico's *Annunciation* (1428–30), a *Crucifixion* by Pietro Lorenzetti (c.1280–1348) and a *Deposition* by Luca Signorelli (1441–1523). There is also a Roman sarcophagus featuring Lapiths and Centaurs, which was much admired by Donatello and Brunelleschi.

INSIDER TIP
Eremo le Celle

Walk 3 km (2 miles) from Cortona to see St Francis' cell at the woodland hermitage he is thought to have founded in 1211. The stone monastery fits in perfectly with the natural surroundings.

Duomo

Piazza del Duomo Daily

The present Duomo was designed by Giuliano da Sangallo in the 16th century. Remains of an earlier Romanesque building were incorporated into the west façade. The attractive doorway (1550) was designed by Cristofanello.

Museo dell'Accademia Etrusca

Piazza Signorelli 9 0575 63 72 35 Apr-Oct: 10am-7pm daily; Nov-Mar: 10am-5pm Tue-Sun 1 Jan, 25 Dec

This museum contains some major Etruscan artifacts, including a 4th-century BC bronze chandelier. There are also a number of Egyptian objects. On the west wall of the main hall is a beautiful fresco of Polymnia, the muse of song. It was once believed to date from the 1st or 2nd century, but it is now known to be a skilful 18th-century fake.

Santa Margherita

Piazza Santa Margherita

The Via Crucis, a long uphill lane with gardens on either side leading to this 19th-century church, was laid out as a war memorial in 1947. It is decorated with Futurist mosaics depicting episodes of Christ's Passion by Gino Severini (1883–1966). The church, rebuilt in the Romanesque-Gothic style from 1856 to 1897, has excellent views over the surrounding countryside. A single rose window remains from the original church. A number of Turkish battle standards captured in the 18th century lie near the altar.

↑ The Romanesque-Gothic interior of Santa Margherita church

Santa Maria delle Grazie al Calcinaio

Calcinaio Daily

A 15-minute stroll from the town centre, this remarkable Renaissance church (1485) is one of the few surviving works by Francesco di Giorgio Martini (1439–1502). The building is opened on request – ask at the caretaker's house, beyond a garden to the right of the main entrance.

Parco Archeologico

Località Sodo di Cortona
9am-1pm Fri-Sun
cortonamaec.org

This archaeological just outside Cortona park houses a series of Etruscan tombs, including the Tumulo II del Sodo and the Tanella di Pitagora (once thought to be Pythagoras' tomb). E-bikes are available free of charge.

⑦

Fortezza del Girifalco

Via di Fortezza
10am-6pm Mon-Sun
fortezzadelgirifalco.it

This Medicean fortress, built in its current form in 1561 for Cosimo I, stands at the highest point of Cortona; the view from the ramparts stretches as far as Lake Trasimeno over the regional border in Umbria.

San Niccolò

Via San Niccolò

A secluded church dating from the 15th century, with a charming courtyard garden. The interior has a pair of extraordinary paintings by Luca Signorelli – *Deposition* and *Madonna and Child with Saints* – that sit on either side of the altarpiece. The ornamental ceiling was added in 1768.

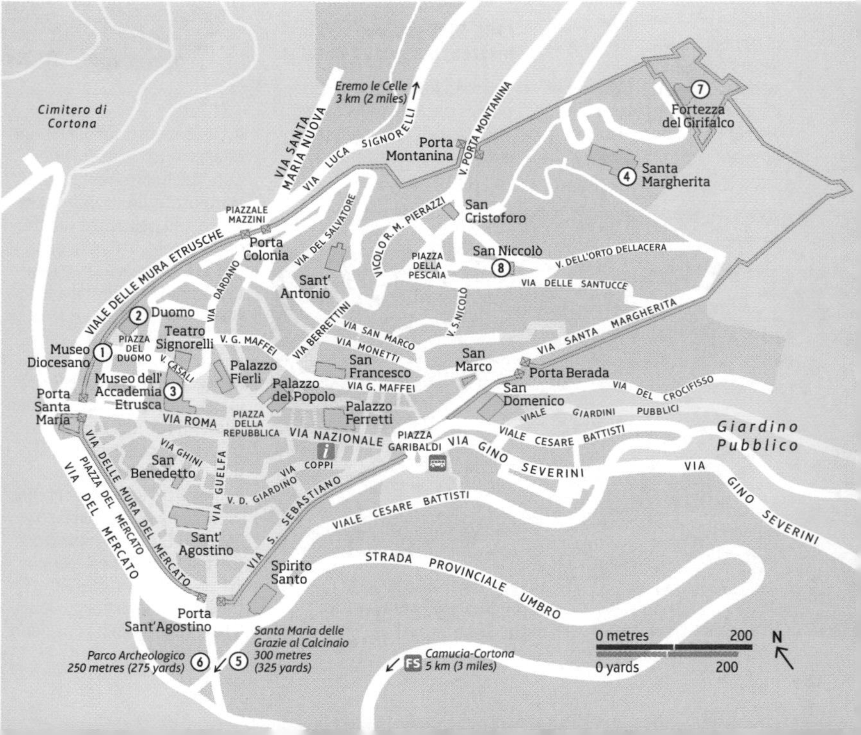

Cimitero di Cortona
Eremo le Celle 3 km (2 miles)
Fortezza del Girifalco ⑦
Santa Margherita ④
Porta Montanina
San Cristoforo
San Niccolò ⑧
Piazzale Mazzini
Porta Colonia
Sant' Antonio
Duomo ②
Teatro Signorelli
Museo Diocesano ①
Piazza del Duomo
Museo dell' Accademia Etrusca ③
Palazzo Fierli
Palazzo del Popolo
San Francesco
Palazzo Ferretti
San Marco
Porta Berada
San Domenico
Porta Santa Maria
Piazza della Repubblica
Piazza Garibaldi
Giardino Pubblico
San Benedetto
Sant' Agostino
Spirito Santo
Porta Sant'Agostino
Viale delle Mura Etrusche
Via Santa Maria Nuova
Via Luca Signorelli
V. Porta Montanina
Via del Salvatore
Vicolo R. M. Pierazzi
Piazza della Pescaia
V. dell'Orto della Cera
Via delle Santucce
Via Dardano
Via Berrettini
Via San Marco
Via Monetti
V. S. Nicolò
Via Santa Margherita
V. G. Maffei
Via G. Maffei
V. Casali
Via Roma
Via Nazionale
Via del Crocifisso
Viale Giardini Pubblici
Viale Cesare Battisti
Via Gino Severini
Via Coppi
Via Ghini
Via Guelfa
V. D. Giardino
Via S. Sebastiano
Via delle Mura del Mercato
Piazza del Mercato
Via del Mercato
Strada Provinciale Umbro
Parco Archeologico 250 metres (275 yards) ⑥
⑤ Santa Maria delle Grazie al Calcinaio 300 metres (325 yards)
Camucia-Cortona 5 km (3 miles)
0 metres 200
0 yards 200
N

EXPERIENCE MORE

Lucignano

S5 Piazza del Tribunale 22; 0575 838 01

The attractive medieval town of Lucignano has many well-preserved 14th-century houses and enjoys sweeping views over the Valdichiana, a fertile area of reclaimed marshland famous for the statuesque white Chianina cattle. The town's street plan is unusual, consisting of a series of four concentric rings encircling the hill upon which the town sits, sheltered by its ancient walls. There are four small piazzas at the centre.

In one, the Collegiata church is fronted by attractive steps, semicircular to reflect the street plan. Completed by Orazio Porta in 1594, it contains some fine gilded wooden angels added in 1706.

The 14th-century Palazzo Comunale houses the **Museo Comunale**. Its highlight is a massive gold reliquary, 2.5 m (8 ft) high, to which numerous artists contributed over the period 1350–1471. Because of its shape, it is known as the Tree of Lucignano. Also of note are two 14th-century paintings by Luca Signorelli: a lunette showing St Francis of Assisi miraculously receiving the stigmata, and a *Madonna and Child*. There are several fine 13th- to 15th-century Siena school paintings and a small painting of the Madonna by Lippo Vanni (1341–75). The vaulted ceiling of the Sala del Tribunale, has frescoes of famous biblical figures and characters from Classical mythology, painted from 1438–65 by various Siena school artists.

In the countryside near Lucignano, the 15th-century Santuario della Madonna delle Querce is attributed to Vasari.

Museo Comunale

Piazza del Tribunale 22 0575 83 80 01 10:30am-1pm, 2:30-6pm Wed-Mon (winter: open Fri-Mon only)

Asciano

S5 Corso Matteotti 78; 0577 71 88 11

The road from Siena to Asciano passes through the strange, undulating Crete landscape, almost bare of vegetation. Asciano itself is medieval, and retains much of its fortified wall. The main street, Corso Matteotti, is lined with smart shops and palazzi. At the top of the street, in Piazza della Basilica, there is a large fountain from 1472. Facing it is the late 13th-century Romanesque Basilica di Sant'Agata.

The **Museo Civico Archeologico e d'Arte Sacra** in the Palazzo Corboli contains late Siena school masterpieces: Duccio's *Madonna and Child* and Ambrogio Lorenzetti's unusual *St Michael the Archangel*. Also on display are local Etruscan finds from the tombs built between the 7th and 4th centuries BC at the Necropoli di Poggio Pinci, 5 km (3 miles) east of Asciano.

WHITE GOLD

One of Italy's most prestigious foodstuffs, the white truffle of Crete Senesi grows around the roots of trees such as oaks, poplars and willows. An annual festival to celebrate the aromatic tuber is held each November in San Giovanni d'Asso, where there is also a dedicated museum, the Museo del Tartufo, in the 13th-century castle cellars. Search out your own truffles with Alessandro of Siena Tartufi on a fun truffle-hunting experience with dogs in the woods near Siena, or visit his cubbyhole shop just off Siena's Piazza del Campo (*sienatartufi.com*).

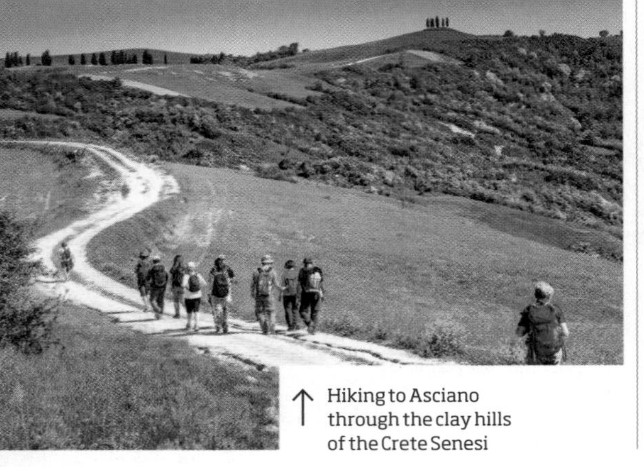

↑ Hiking to Asciano through the clay hills of the Crete Senesi

The soaring ruins of San Galgano abbey, unusual in Tuscany in its Gothic style

About 10 km (6 miles) south of Asciano is **Monte Oliveti Maggiore**. The approach to this abbey is through thick cypresses, with stunning views of eroded cliffs and sheer drops to the valley floor. It was founded in 1313 by the Olivetan order, who were dedicated to restoring the simplicity of Benedictine monastic rule. The 15th-century Baroque rose-pink abbey church has outstanding choir stalls of inlaid wood. Alongside is the Great Cloister, its walls covered by a cycle of frescoes that depict scenes from the life of St Benedict. Begun in 1495 by Luca Signorelli, a pupil of Piero della Francesca, it was finished by Sodoma in 1508 and is considered a masterpiece for the way it combines architectural and naturalistic detail.

Museo Civico Archeologico e d'Arte Sacra
Corso Matteotti 122
0577 71 44 50 Apr-Oct: Wed-Sun; Nov-March: Sat, Sun & hols

Monte Oliveti Maggiore
0577 70 70 18 9:15am-noon, 3:15-5pm daily (to 6pm summer)

San Galgano

R5 (località Chiusdino)
From Siena

The ruined Cistercian abbey is very remote but well worth the journey for the beauty of its woodland surroundings and the majesty of the roof-less building. Begun in 1218, the abbey is Gothic in style, reflecting the French origins of the Cistercian monks who designed and built it. The monks avoided contact with civilization and divided their lives between prayer and labour, clearing the hills of vegetation to graze their sheep. Despite the Cistercian emphasis on poverty, the monks became wealthy from the sale of wool; by the middle of the 14th century, the abbey was corruptly administered and gradually fell into decline. The abbey was eventually dissolved in 1652. Empty for many years, the cloister and other monastic buildings are now being restored for Olivetan nuns. A small shop sells locally produced herbs, wines, olive oils and toiletries.

On a hill above the abbey is the beehive-shaped chapel of Montesiepi, built on the site of St Galgano's hermitage a few years after his death in 1181. St Galgano's sword stands embedded in a stone just inside the door of the circular oratory. The 14th-century stone walls of the side chapel are covered with frescoes showing scenes from Galgano's life by Ambrogio Lorenzetti (1344).

Did You Know?

St Galgano was a soldier who renounced his warrior ways after plunging his sword into a stone.

Did You Know?

The wine growing region of Montalcino supports over 200 producers.

Montalcino

S5 Costa del Municipio 8; 0577 84 93 31; closed Mon

Montalcino's famous Brunello is one of Italy's greatest wines, appreciated the world over. It is made from Sangiovese grapes from the vineyards that surround the appealing hilltop town and there are numerous opportunities to try it here. Dominating from the highest point of town is the Fortezza, built in 1361; there are spectacular views from the impressive ramparts that were added by Cosimo I in the 16th century.

The abbey of **Sant'Antimo** lies about 10 km (6 miles) southeast of Montalcino. Enchantingly beautiful in its setting of olive-clad hills, it is in French Romanesque style, built in creamy travertine stone and alabaster. There is a luminous quality to the stonework of the interior that visibly changes according to the time of day and season. Recordings of plainsong echoing around the walls add to the otherworldly atmosphere. The current community of Augustinian monks sing Gregorian chants at mass, every day except Saturday. They also brew beer and make honey and herbal remedies, on sale in their pharmacy.

Abbazia di Sant'Antimo
D3 Castelnuovo dell' Abate Daily antimo.it

Bagno Vignoni

S5 From Siena
0577 88 73 65

This is a tiny medieval spa village consisting of a handful of houses built around a huge piazza containing an arcaded, stone-lined pool. Constructed by the Medici, the pool is full of hot sulphurous water that bubbles up to the surface from the volcanic rocks deep underground. The pool is no longer open for bathing, but is still well worth a visit to admire the architecture. Sulphur pools in the grounds of the Posta Marcucci hotel and at several other public spas are open for swimming.

Chiusi

T5 Piazza Duomo 1; 0578 22 76 67

Chiusi was one of the most powerful cities in the Etruscan league, reaching the height of its influence in the 7th and 6th centuries BC *(p52)*. There are many Etruscan tombs in the surrounding countryside. The Museo Archeologico is packed with cremation urns, vases decorated with black figures and Bucchero ware, burnished to resemble bronze.

Chiusi's Romanesque Duomo is built from recycled Roman pillars and capitals. The Museo della Cattedrale has an interesting display of

GREAT VIEW
The Val d'Orcia Landscape

All those iconic, quintessentially Tuscan views of gently rolling hills and cypresses featured on postcards and calendars are almost all to be found in the Val d'Orcia. The Madonna di Vitaleta chapel is one favourite among photographers.

→ The Collegiata church in San Quirico d'Orcia, dedicated to a five-year-old martyr

Roman, Lombardic and medieval sculpture. Visits can be arranged here to underground galleries beneath the city, dug by the Etruscans and used as Christian catacombs from the 3rd to the 5th century. Another fascinating tour of subterranean Chiusi's ancient Etruscan tunnels is offered by the **Museo Civico La Città Sotteranea**. The tour ends at an underground lake 30m (100 ft) below ground level.

Museo Civico La Città Sotteranea
Via II Ciminia 2
museisenesi.org

San Quirico d'Orcia

S5 Piazza Chigi 2; 0577 89 97 24

Standing just inside the city walls, San Quirico d'Orcia's pride is the **Collegiata** church, featuring three ornately carved Romanesque portals built onto an 8th-century structure. Begun in 1080, the capitals and lintels of the portals are carved with details of dragons, mermaids and other mythical beasts.

The church commemorates the 3rd-century martyr St Quiricus, who was killed at the age of five by the Romans for the simple act of declaring himself a Christian. Quiricus is depicted in the elaborate altar piece by Sano di Pietro.

Next to the church is the 17th-century Palazzo Chigi, whose frescoed interior has been restored. The Horti Leonini nearby is a 16th-century garden of box hedges. Once a refuge for pilgrims, it is now used as a public sculpture garden during the summer.

Collegiata
Via Dante Alighieri 0577 89 72 36 8am–5pm daily

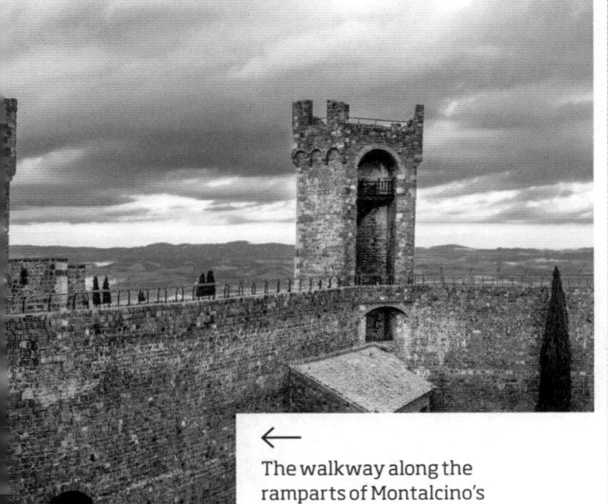

← The walkway along the ramparts of Montalcino's Fortezza, offering great views

TOP 3 MONTALCINO WINERIES

Castello di Banfi
castellobanfi.com
Based around a hilltop castle, this winery runs tours and tastings.

Fattoria dei Barbi
fattoriadeibarbi.it
Cellar tours, a wine museum and a tavern draw the crowds here.

Podere Le Ripi
podereleripi.it
Biodynamic winery with tastings and tours.

The hot springs at Bagno Vignoni

The Madonna di San Biagio church, a Renaissance gem by Giuliano da Sangallo

11 Montepulciano

S5 Piazza Don Minzoni 1; 0578 75 73 41

Montepulciano is built along a narrow limestone ridge and, at 605 m (1,950 ft) above sea level, is one of the highest of Tuscany's hilltop towns. The centre is rich in Renaissance palazzi with a fascinating labyrinth of historic cellars beneath, many still used to age the famous Vino Nobile di Montepulciano, one of Tuscany's top wines.

A long, winding street called Il Corso climbs up into the main square, which crowns the summit of the hill. Among the fine palazzi on Il Corso, Palazzo Bucelli (1648) is particularly noteworthy for its lower façade studded with ancient Etruscan reliefs and funerary urns collected by the 18th-century owner, Pietro Bucelli. Further along Il Corso is the Piazza Michelozzo and the church of Sant'Agostino, built by Michelozzo in 1427; it has an elaborate carved portal featuring the Virgin and Child flanked by St John and St Augustine.

In the Piazza Grande stands the Duomo, designed between 1592 and 1630 by Ippolito Scalza. The façade is unfinished and plain, but the interior is Classical in proportions. It is the setting for an earlier masterpiece from the Siena school, the *Assumption of the Virgin* triptych by Taddeo di Bartolo (1401). Placed over the High Altar, it is rich in jewel-like colours and heavily embossed with gold leaf. Next to the Duomo is the Gothic **Palazzo Comunale**, the town hall. Michelozzo added the 15th-century tower and façade, turning it into a smaller version of Florence's Palazzo Vecchio *(p68)*. Narrow stairs lead to the top of the tower and amazing views. Nearby is the **Museo Civico**, which has an interesting collection of 17th–18th century paintings and sections dedicated to Della Robbia terracottas and local archaeological finds.

Perched on a platform below the city walls, is the beautiful church of **Madonna di San Biagio**. Built of honey and cream-coloured travertine, it is Sangallo's masterpiece. Begun in 1518, the project occupied him until his death in 1534.

In August, there are two festivals in Montepulciano: the Bruscello takes place on the 14th, 15th and 16th, when scenes from the town's turbulent history are re-enacted. For the Bravio delle Botti, on the last Sunday in August, there is a parade through the streets followed by a barrel race held between the town's eight *contradas* (districts) and a banquet.

Palazzo Comunale
Piazza Grande 1 0578 71 73 00 Apr-Oct: 10am-1pm, 2-6pm daily (tower)

Museo Civico
Via Ricci 10 museocivicomontepulciano.it

Madonna di San Biagio
Via di San Biagio 14
8:30am-7pm daily

HIDDEN GEM
The Cellars of Montepulciano

Many of the town's ancient cellars can be visited by the public at restaurants, shops and wine stores, including the historic winemaker Contucci just off the Piazza Grande on Via del Teatro.

12

Pienza

S5 Corso il Rossellino 59; 0578 74 90 71

The centre of Pienza was completely redesigned in Renaissance times by Pope Pius II. Born here in 1405, when it was called Corsignano, Aeneas Sylvius Piccolomini – a leading Humanist scholar and philosopher – was elected pope in 1458. The following year he decided to commission a new centre in Corsignano and rename it Pienza in his own honour. He planned to transform his birthplace into a model Renaissance town, but the grand scheme never progressed beyond the handful of buildings around the Piazza Pio II. The architect Bernardo Rossellino was commissioned to build a Duomo, papal palace and town hall here, which were finished within three years. Subsequently, Rossellino was caught embezzling papal funds, but Pius II forgave him because he was so delighted with his new buildings.

The Duomo, completed by the architect Rossellino in 1459, is now suffering from subsidence at its eastern end. However, the cracks in the walls and floor of the nave do not detract at all from the splendid Classical proportions of this Renaissance church. It is flooded with light from the vast stained-glass windows requested by Pius II; he wanted a *domus vitrea* (literally "a house of glass") that would symbolize the spirit of intellectual enlightenment of the Humanist age.

The **Palazzo Piccolomino** next door to the Duomo was home to Pius II's descendants until 1968. Rossellino's design for the building was influenced by Leon Battista Alberti's Palazzo Rucellai in Florence *(p82)*. The apartments open to the public include Pius II's bedroom and library, which are full of his belongings. At the rear of the palazzo there is an arcaded courtyard and a triple-tiered loggia. The spectacular view across the garden takes in the wooded slopes of Monte Amiata.

On the outskirts of Pienza, on Via del Fonti, is the 11th-century Romanesque parish church of Pieve di Corsignano, in which Pope Pius II was baptized. It has an unusual round tower and a doorway decorated with flower motifs.

Not far from the town is the isolated 16th-century monastery of Sant'Anna in Camprena, with wonderful frescoes painted by Sodoma. It offers accommodation under the *agriturismo* scheme.

PIENZA CHEESE

Pienza is famous for its delicious sheep's cheeses *(right)*. They gain their complexity, say producers proudly, from the wild herbs in the sheep's diet. Many producers are organic, some even treating their flocks with homeopathic remedies. Try some of the variously aged cheeses and other produce at the Taverna del Pecorino *(Via Condotti 1)*.

Palazzo Piccolomini

Piazza Pio II
0578 74 85 03
Tue–Sun Last 2 wks in Nov, Jan–mid-Feb

↓ Floral displays and local delicacies on show in the streets of Pienza

A cobblestoned street in Lucca at dusk

NORTHWEST TUSCANY

The sea has played a key role in the fortunes of this largely coastal area since ancient times, as evidenced by the discovery of 30 Roman vessels near Pisa in 1998. Despite having to rely on an inland port, Pisa became one of Italy's most influential maritime republics, dominating the Western Mediterranean from the 11th century. This lasted until 1406 when the Florentine Medici took over and reduced Pisa's power, making Livorno the region's principal harbour.

Further up the coast, the marble mines at Carrara, first established in Roman times, played an important role in supplying the sculptors of the Renaissance. Michelangelo even spent two years (1518–20) trying to build a road from Serravazza to the coast in order to transport stone for the façade of San Lorenzo in Florence, before eventually abandoning the project. In the early 19th century some of Italy's first seaside resorts were established at Versilia, and Forte dei Marmi continues to be among the most exclusive.

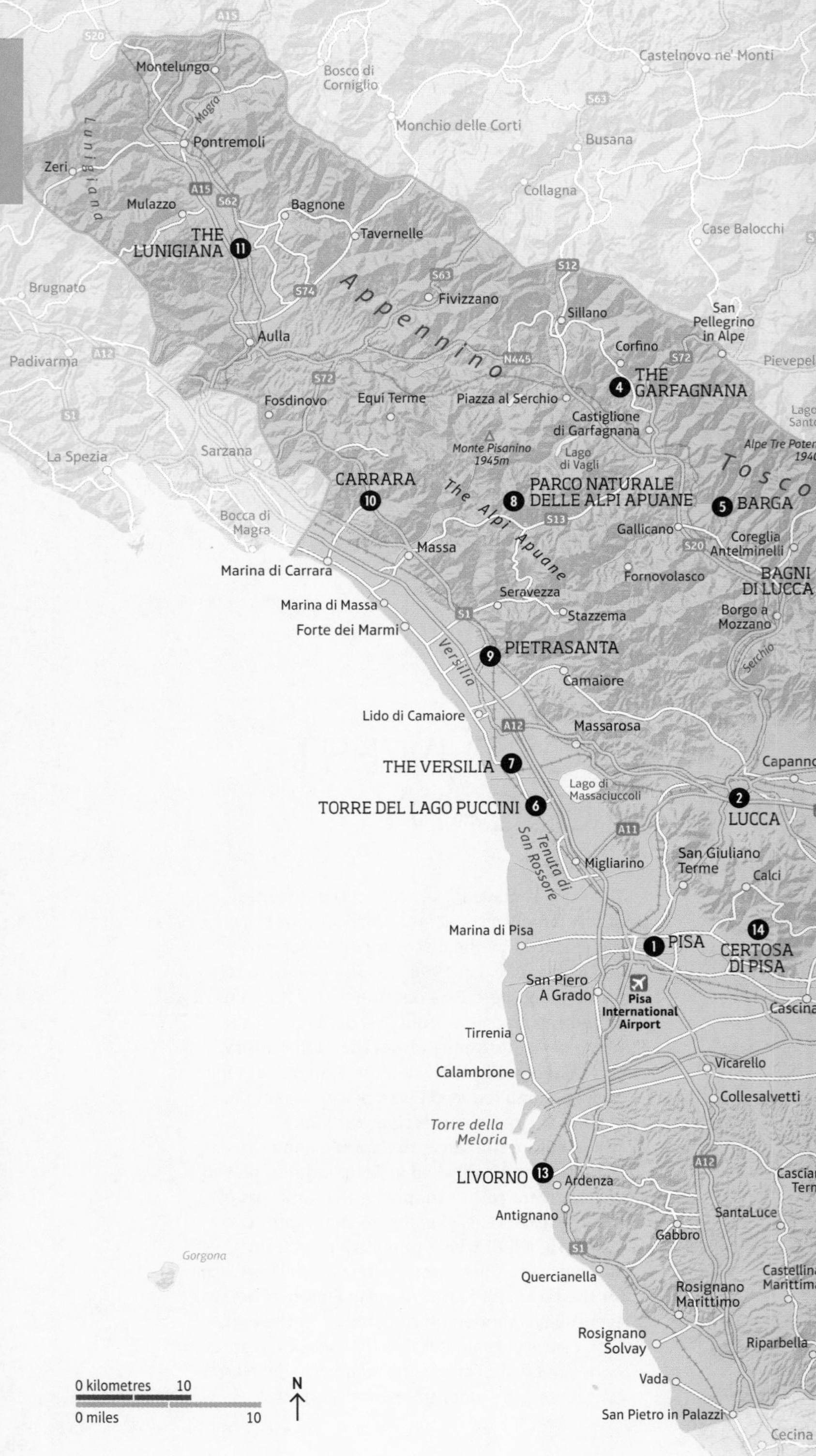

Montelungo
Bosco di Corniglio
Castelnovo ne' Monti
Monchio delle Corti
Busana
Lunigiana
Mogra
Pontremoli
Zeri
Collagna
Mulazzo
Bagnone
Tavernelle
Case Balocchi
THE LUNIGIANA 11
Appennino
Brugnato
Fivizzano
Sillano
San Pellegrino in Alpe
Aulla
Corfino
Padivarma
Pievepela
4 THE GARFAGNANA
Fosdinovo
Equi Terme
Piazza al Serchio
Castiglione di Garfagnana
Lago Santo
Monte Pisanino 1945m
Lago di Vagli
Alpe Tre Potenz 1940r
La Spezia
Sarzana
Tosco
CARRARA 10
PARCO NATURALE DELLE ALPI APUANE 8
5 BARGA
The Alpi Apuane
Bocca di Magra
Gallicano
Coreglia Antelminelli
Massa
Marina di Carrara
Fornovolasco
BAGNI DI LUCCA
Seravezza
Marina di Massa
Stazzema
Borgo a Mozzano
Forte dei Marmi
Serchio
Versilia
9 PIETRASANTA
Camaiore
Lido di Camaiore
Massarosa
THE VERSILIA 7
Capannori
Lago di Massaciuccoli
2 LUCCA
TORRE DEL LAGO PUCCINI 6
Tenuta di San Rossore
Migliarino
San Giuliano Terme
Calci
Marina di Pisa
1 PISA
14 CERTOSA DI PISA
San Piero A Grado
Pisa International Airport
Cascina
Tirrenia
Calambrone
Vicarello
Collesalvetti
Torre della Meloria
LIVORNO 13
Ardenza
Cascian Term
Antignano
SantaLuce
Gabbro
Gorgona
Quercianella
Castellina Marittima
Rosignano Marittimo
Rosignano Solvay
Riparbella
Vada
San Pietro in Palazzi
Cecina
0 kilometres 10
0 miles 10
N

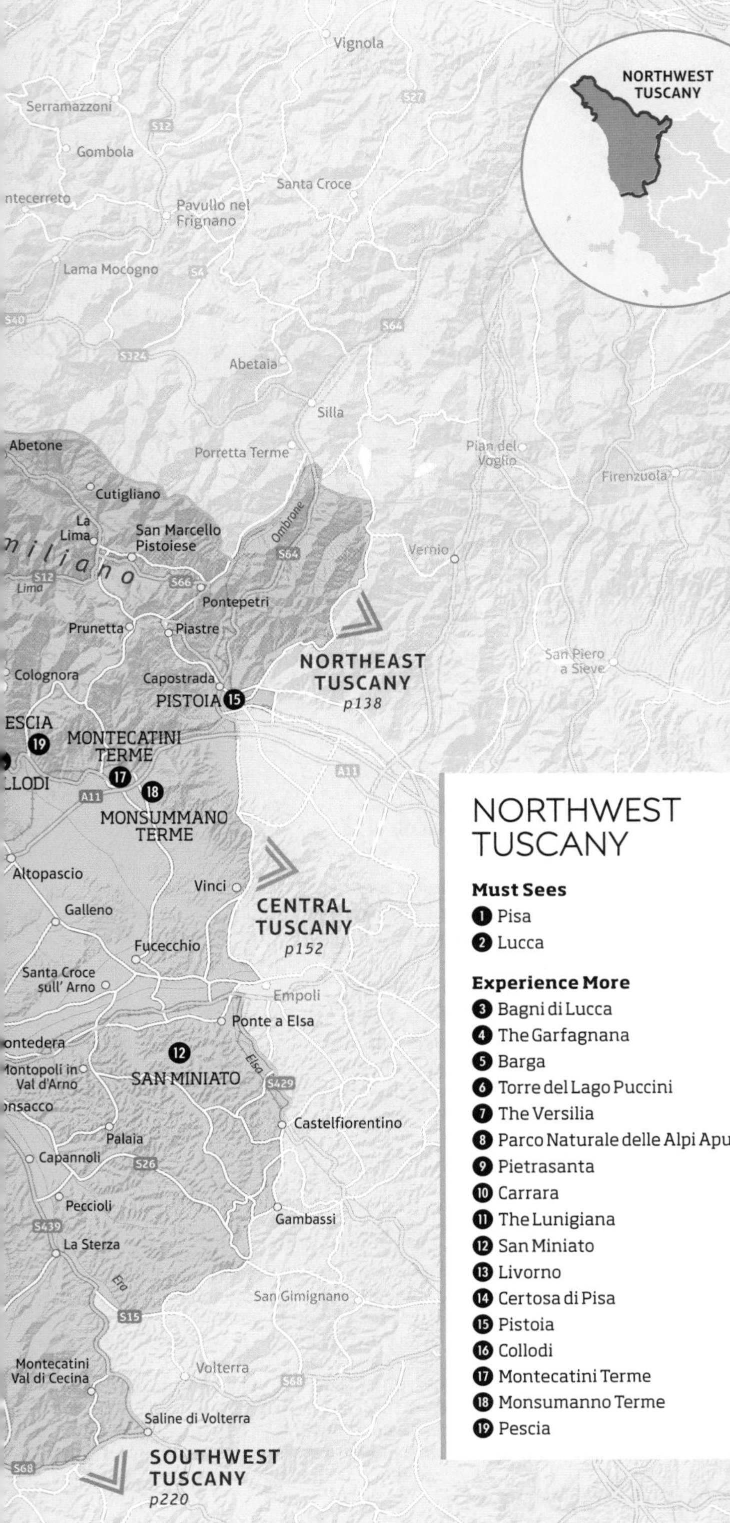

NORTHWEST TUSCANY

Must Sees

1. Pisa
2. Lucca

Experience More

3. Bagni di Lucca
4. The Garfagnana
5. Barga
6. Torre del Lago Puccini
7. The Versilia
8. Parco Naturale delle Alpi Apuane
9. Pietrasanta
10. Carrara
11. The Lunigiana
12. San Miniato
13. Livorno
14. Certosa di Pisa
15. Pistoia
16. Collodi
17. Montecatini Terme
18. Monsumanno Terme
19. Pescia

The historic part of Pisa, with a small bridge across the Arno

❶

PISA

Q3 Galileo Galilei Centrale, Viale Gramsci Piazza Duomo; Piazza Vittorio Emanuele 16; www.pisaunicaterra.it

Now best known for its eponymous leaning tower and elite university, Pisa was a dominant force in the Western Mediterranean from the 11th to the 13th century due to its powerful navy. Trading links with Spain and North Africa led to a cultural revolution, reflected in the splendid buildings of the era: the Duomo, Baptistry and Campanile. Pisa's decline as a maritime power was assured when the Arno began to silt up, and salt marsh now divides the city from the sea.

① Museo Nazionale di San Matteo

Piazzetta San Matteo in Soarta 050 541865 8:30am-7:30pm Tue-Fri 1 Jan, 1 May, 15 Aug, 25 Dec

The medieval convent of San Matteo is located alongside the River Arno. Many exhibits in the museum inside are poorly labelled and the rooms leading off the cloister are unnumbered. Nevertheless, the museum presents a unique opportunity to examine the complete sweep of Pisan and Florentine art from the 12th to the 17th century. Most of the earliest works portray the Virgin and Child; these include Simone Martini's fine polyptych (1321) and a 14th-century statue, the *Madonna del Latte*, attributed to Nino Pisano, another member of the talented family of sculptors. The half-length statue, in gilded marble, shows Christ feeding at his mother's breast. A number of early Renaissance pieces are of interest, particularly Masaccio's *St Paul* (1426), Gentile da Fabriano's radiant 15th-century *Madonna and Child*, and Donatello's reliquary bust of San Rossore (1424–7).

② Piazza dei Cavalieri

The Piazza dei Cavalieri stands at the heart of Pisa's student quarter. The huge building on the north side of the square, covered in exuberant black-and-white *sgraffito* decoration (designs scratched into wet plaster), is the Palazzo dei Cavalieri, housing one of Italy's most prestigious university colleges: the Scuola Normale Superiore. The site was originally occupied by Pisa's medieval town hall, but Cosimo I ordered its destruction when the city fell under

STAY

Palazzo Cini

A stylish hotel with five spacious rooms designed by architect-owner Ivan Cini.

Via Manzoni 12

palazzocinipisa.com

Relais I Miracoli

Unbeatably located; most rooms have views of Pisa's Leaning Tower just across the piazza.

Via Santa Maria 187

relaisimiracoli.it

Royal Victoria

This hotel dates from the 15th century, with antiques and frescoes in each room.

Lungarno Pacinotti 12

royalvictoria.it

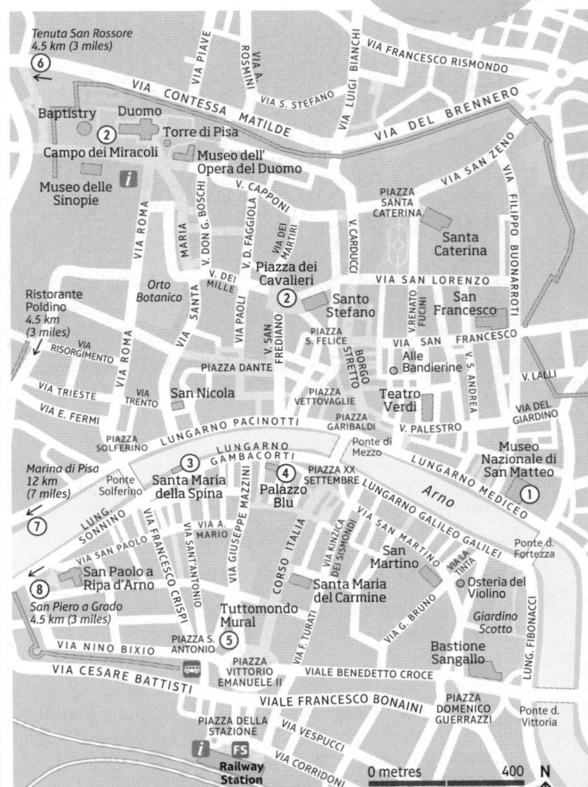

Florentine rule. The council chamber was spared, however, and is now a lecture hall. The present flamboyant building was designed in 1562 by Vasari as the headquarters of the Cavalieri di San Stefano, an order of knights created by Cosimo in 1561. The knights' church, also designed by Vasari, stands next to the Palazzo dei Cavalieri. On the other side of the palazzo is the Palazzo dell'Orologio, incorporating the medieval town jail. Now a library, in 1288 the building was the scene of a most shameful and gruesome episode when Count Ugolino, mayor of Pisa, was imprisoned here with his sons and grandsons. The keys were thrown in the Arno and the prisoners left to starve.

Santa Maria della Spina

Lungarno Gambacorti

055 321 54 46

3-6pm Tue-Sun (times may vary during events or exhibitions)

The roofline of Santa Maria della Spina bristles with spiky Gothic pinnacles, miniature spires and niches sheltering statues of apostles and saints. The church was built to house an unusual relic: a thorn from the Crown of Thorns forced on to Christ's head before His crucifixion. Originally called Santa Maria di Pontenovo, the church's name was changed to Spina, or "thorn", when it acquired this relic in 1333.

GIUGNO PISANO

Throughout June, Pisa celebrates its historical events and traditions in the Giugni Pisano. Alongside countless concerts and exhibitions there are four main celebrations: the Battle, the Regatta, the Luminara and (every four years) the Regatta of the Republics.

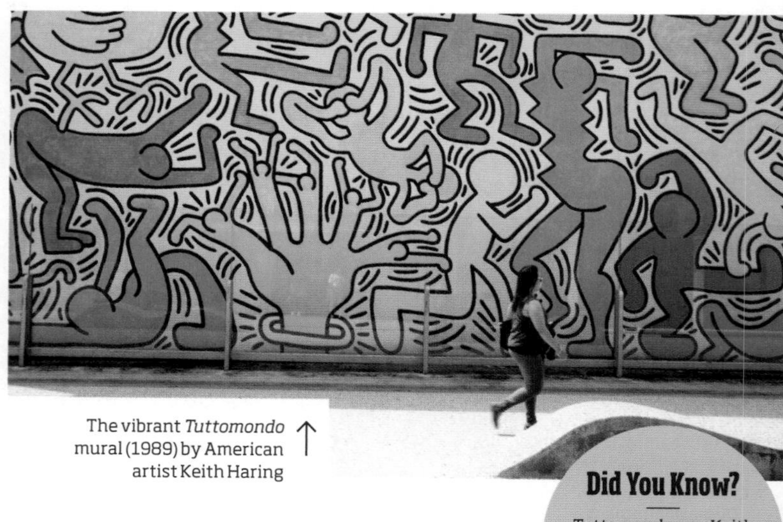

The vibrant *Tuttomondo* mural (1989) by American artist Keith Haring

Did You Know?

Tuttomondo was Keith Haring's last public work; he died just over six months after its completion.

4   

Palazzo Blu

Lungarno Gambacorti 9
10am-7pm Tue-Sun
palazzoblu.it

The striking sky-blue colour of this palazzo, which overlooks the River Arno, dates from the late 18th century, a time when numerous visitors from St Petersburg stayed here. Now a gallery, it regularly hosts world-class temporary exhibitions, while the collection focuses on Pisan art from the 14th to 20th centuries. The beautifully decorated rooms include period furnishings.

Tuttomondo

Via Zandonai

The last of Keith Haring's characteristically colourful murals decorates the back wall of the 14th-century church of Sant'Antonio Abate. The American artist took four days to complete the mural, which features 30 figures in various positions representing peace in the world. The Keith Art Shop Café opposite is an ideal spot to admire the work.

Tenuta San Rossore

Località Cascine Vecchie
6 from Pisa
parcosanrossore.org

The San Rossore estate, just outside Pisa, is at the heart of a vast area of parkland that stretches along the coast from Viareggio to Livorno. Hire a bicycle at the Cascine Vecchie visitor centre, join a horse trek or take a tour by a horse-drawn carriage or road-train. There are scenic picnic spots as well as bars and restaurants on the estate.

Marina di Pisa

On the coast about 12 km (7 miles) west of Pisa, Marina is a former salt marsh. Reclaimed in the 17th century, it is now a modest seaside resort with beach facilities. While the beaches here vary between sand and pebbles, the nearby resorts of Tirrenia (where there is a good nine-hole golf course) and Calambrone have sandy beaches. There is a small marina by the river mouth adjacent to the town,

as well as some evocative traditional fishing huts with suspended nets. The last section of river between Pisa and the sea has several good seafood restaurants.

MUSEO PIAGGIO

Visitors staying in Pisa may want to check out this great museum in Piaggio, just 15 minutes away by train. Vespa scooters have been made in Piaggio since the 1940s, and this collection includes custom and race versions of the iconic motorbikes *(www.museopiaggio.it)*.

San Piero a Grado

Via Vecchia di Marina 5 050 96 00 65 Apr-Oct: 9am-6:30pm daily; Nov-Mar: 9am-5pm daily

San Piero is a handsome 11th-century church built during the reign of Pope John XVIII (1004–9) on the spot where St Peter is believed to have first set foot on Italian soil in AD 42.

According to the Book of Acts (New Testament), he arrived at a set of landing steps by the Arno. The foundations of Roman port buildings have been discovered beneath the present church, which stands where the Arno once flowed into the sea, though silt deposits mean it is now some 6 km (4 miles) from the shore.

Unusually, the church lacks a façade; instead it has semi-circular apses at both the east and west ends. The exterior is decorated with Moorish-style ceramic plates set into the masonry around the eaves – a feature that it shares with the Duomo in San Miniato *(p214)*.

↑ A remote fishing hut in Marina di Pisa

EAT

Ristorante Poldino

Located in the heart of San Rossore; the tasty dishes here are made largely with produce from the estate.

Località Cascine Vecchie 13, Parco San Rossore Mon & Tue poldino.com

Alle Bandierine

Open for dinner only, this family-run restaurant serves delicious spaghetti dishes and excellent seafood.

Via Mercanti 4 ristorantealle bandierine.it

9

CAMPO DEI MIRACOLI

Piazza dei Miracoli 3, 11 Mar & Oct: 9am-7pm daily; Apr-Sep: 8am-8pm (Tower from 9am) daily; Nov-Feb: 9am-6pm daily opapisa.it

Declared a UNESCO World Heritage Site in 1987, this gorgeous square studded with masterpieces of Romanesque architecture was medieval Italy's grandest building project and remains an Italian icon.

Pisa's world-famous Leaning Tower is just one of the splendid religious buildings that rise from the emerald-green lawns of the "Field of Miracles". Lying to the northwest of the city centre, the tower is partnered by the Duomo, begun in 1063, the Baptistry of 1152–1284 and the Campo Santo cemetery, begun in 1278. The Leaning Tower itself was not completed until 1350, when its seven bells were hung. All the buildings feature definite Moorish elements – such as inlaid marble in geometric patterns (arabesques) – with delicate Romanesque colonnading and spiky Gothic niches and pinnacles.

MUSEO DELL'OPERA DEL DUOMO

Housed in the former Chapter House of the cathedral, the museum was opened in 1986. Exhibits, such as the intricately inlaid marble panels, reveal the twin influences of Rome and Islam on Pisan architects in the 12th and 13th centuries. Other pieces include 13th-century statues and sculptures by Nicola and Giovanni Pisano, 15th-18th-century paintings, a fine Roman and Etruscan archaeological collection, and 12th-century ecclesiastical treasures. The museum cloister offers wonderful views of the Leaning Tower.

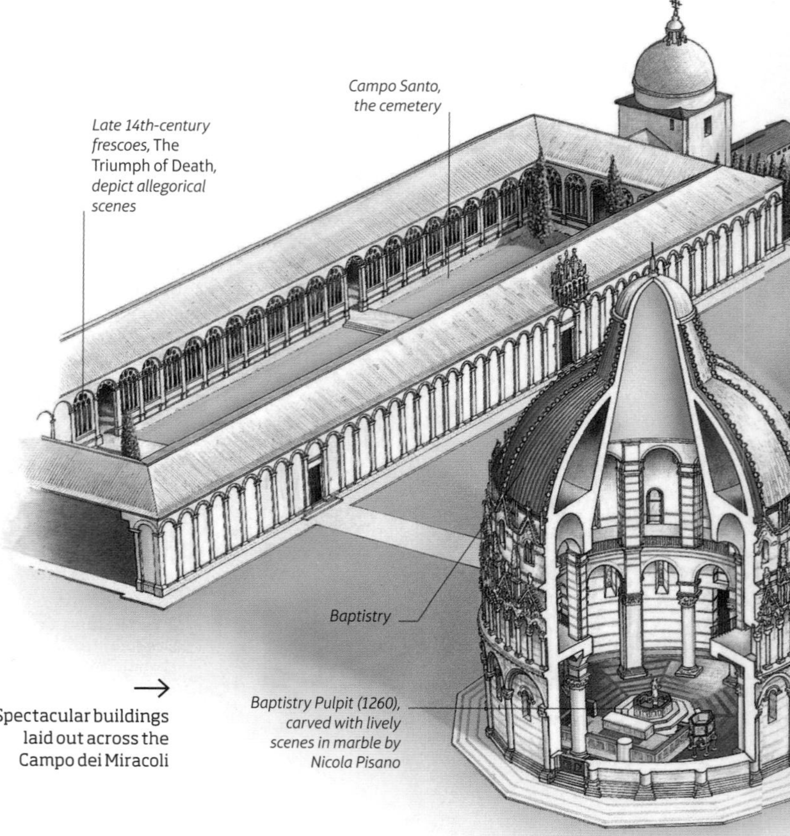

→ Spectacular buildings laid out across the Campo dei Miracoli

1 The Baptistry is the largest in Italy and is topped by a Gothic dome.

2 The Campo Santo cemetery contains recycled Roman sarcophagi and was the burial place of the Pisan upper class.

3 The arches of the Bapistry are dotted with these ornate sculptures.

Did You Know?

The cathedral's south transept doors are replicas; the originals are now in the Museo dell'Opera.

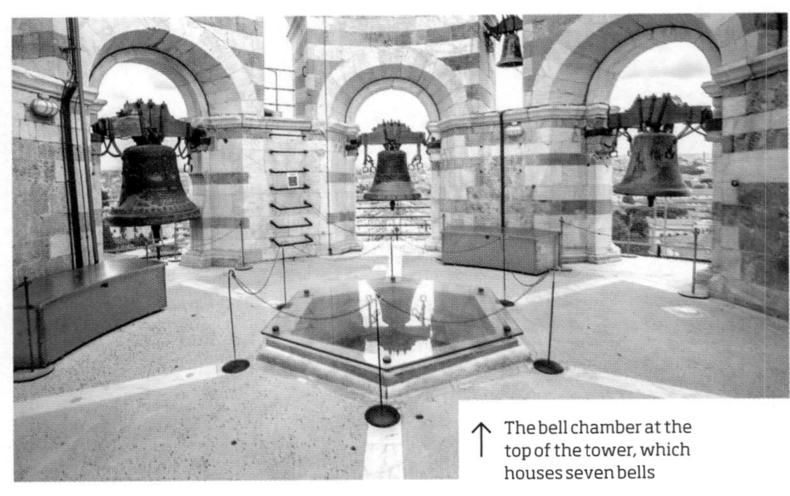

↑ The bell chamber at the top of the tower, which houses seven bells

The Leaning Tower of Pisa

All the buildings of the Campo dei Miracoli lean because of their shallow foundations and the sandy silt subsoil, but none tilts so famously as the Torre Pendente: the Leaning Tower. Begun in 1173, the tower began to tip sideways before the third storey was finished. Despite this, construction continued until its completion in 1350. More than ten years of engineering interventions succeeded in stabilizing the tower in 2008. It should remain secure for at least 200 years.

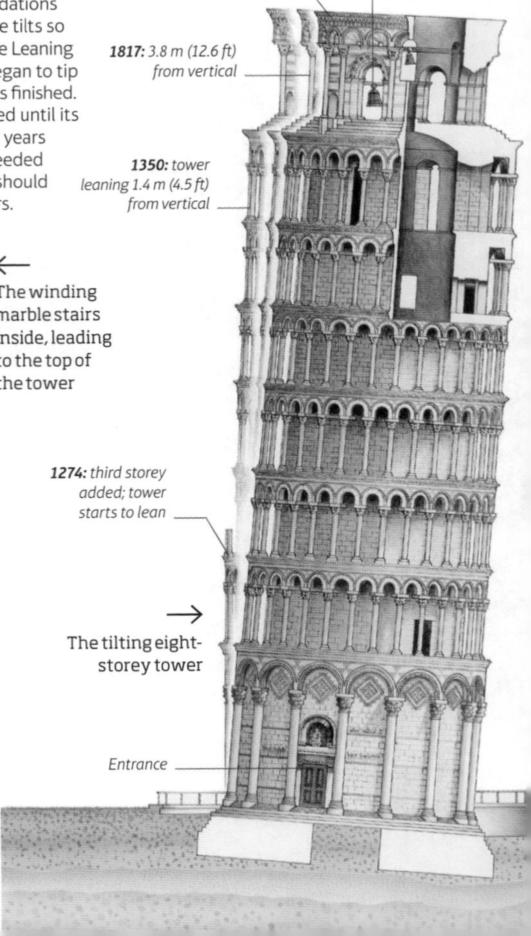

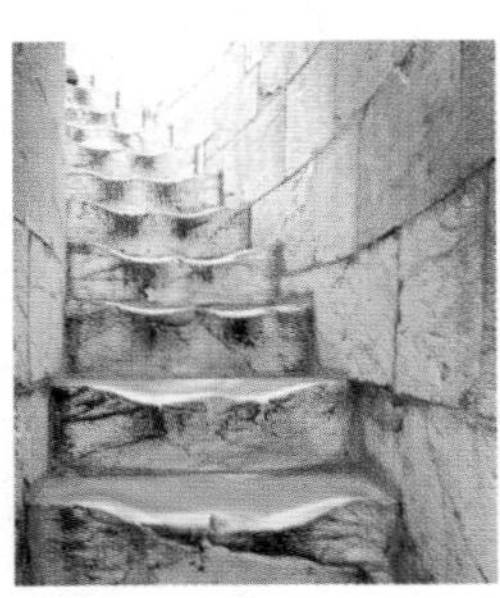

← The winding marble stairs inside, leading to the top of the tower

↑ Ornate detail above the entrance to the Leaning Tower

1993: *5.4 m (17.5 ft) from vertical*

The bells add to the pressure on the tower

1817: *3.8 m (12.6 ft) from vertical*

1350: *tower leaning 1.4 m (4.5 ft) from vertical*

1274: *third storey added; tower starts to lean*

→ The tilting eight-storey tower

Entrance

Did You Know?

The tower's interrupted construction gave the soil time to settle – which prevented it from toppling!

↑ The unmistakable slant of the Leaning Tower of Pisa

↑ Market stalls lining Piazza Anfiteatreo in central Lucca

2

LUCCA

Q3 Piazza Ricasoli Piazzale Verdi Piazza Santa Maria 35; www.luccaturismo.it

Lucca is enclosed by massive red-brick walls, which help give the city its special character by shutting out traffic and the modern world. Built between 1504 and 1645, they are among the best-preserved Renaissance defences in Europe. Within these walls, Lucca is a peaceful city of narrow lanes, with its original ancient Roman street plan preserved intact. Unlike several of Tuscany's hilltop cities, Lucca is flat; many locals use bicycles, which lends the city added charm.

↑ The tree-topped Torre Guinigi, built in the 14th century

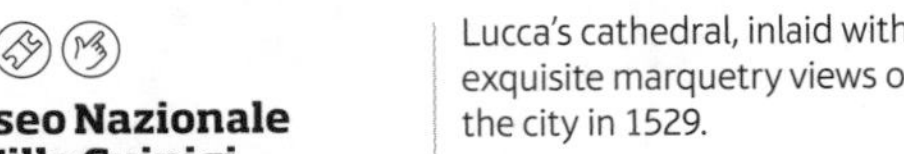

Museo Nazionale di Villa Guinigi

Via della Quarquonia 0583 49 60 33 8:30am-1:30pm Tue-Sat (guided tours at 3:30 or 5:30pm) 1 Jan, 1 May, 25 Dec

This Renaissance villa was built for Paolo Guinigi, who ruled Lucca from 1400 until 1430. The ground floor holds sculpture from Lucca and its surrounds, including fine Romanesque reliefs from the city's churches. The gallery on the floor above displays paintings and choir stalls from Lucca's cathedral, inlaid with exquisite marquetry views of the city in 1529.

Casa Natale di Puccini

Corte San Lorenzo 8 (Via di Poggio) 0583 35 91 54 Apr-Oct: 10am-6pm Wed-Mon; Nov-Mar: 11am-5pm Wed-Mon

The 15th-century house in which Giacomo Puccini (1858–1924) was born contains many interesting artifacts, including portraits of the great composer, costume designs for his operas and the piano he used when composing his last opera, *Turandot*. Puccini died before he was able to finish this, and the composition was completed by Franco Alfano and first performed two years later at La Scala in Milan.

Torre Guinigi

Via Sant'Andrea 45 9:30am-4:30pm daily

Dating from the 1300s, this 44-m- (144-ft-) high tower is one of the many structures built by the Guinigi family.

→ Marble statues in the formal gardens of Palazzo Pfanner

The holm oaks growing at the top of the tower make this a popular attraction.

Via Fillungo

Lucca's principal shopping street winds its way through the heart of the city towards the Anfiteatro Romano. The upper end, towards San Frediano church, has several shops with Art Nouveau ironwork. Halfway down the street, you will find the 13th-century San Cristoforo, which holds exhibitions of work by local artists.

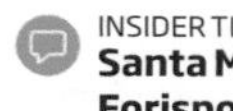

INSIDER TIP

Santa Maria Forisportam

Located beyond the Roman walls of Lucca - *Forisportam* means "outside the gate" - this 12th-century church *(Vicolo Tommasi 1)* contains two great paintings by Guercino.

Palazzo Pfanner

Via degli Asili 33
Apr-Nov: 10am-6pm daily; Dec-Mar: by appt
palazzopfanner.it

The imposing Palazzo Pfanner, built in 1667, has a delightful formal garden to the rear, which can also be viewed from the ramparts. Originally built by the Moriconi family, it was rented and eventually bought outright by Felix Pfanner, an Austrian brewer credited with introducing beer to Lucca. The gardens were laid out in the 18th century, and feature a central avenue lined with Baroque statues of ancient Roman gods and goddesses, which alternate with aromatic lemon trees.

Did You Know?

Scenes from *Portrait of a Lady*, starring John Malkovich and Nicole Kidman, were filmed at Palazzo Pfanner.

Giardino Botanico

Via dell'Orto Botanico 14
0583 44 21 60 10am-5pm daily (to 6pm May & Jun; to 7pm Jul-Sep)
Nov-Mar: Sun

Lucca's delightful botanical garden, tucked into the city walls, was laid out in 1820 – the result of a bequeathal by Marie Louise de Bourbon, Duchess of Lucca. It spans over 2 hectares (5 acres), and has a wide range of Tuscan and international plants.

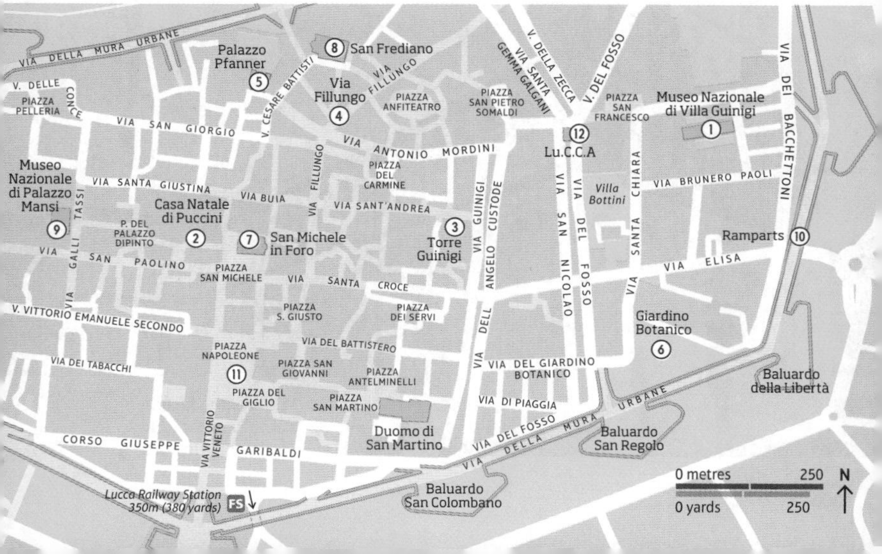

Palazzo Pfanner 5
8 San Frediano
Via Fillungo 4
Museo Nazionale di Villa Guinigi 1
12 Lu.C.C.A
Museo Nazionale di Palazzo Mansi 9
Casa Natale di Puccini 2
7 San Michele in Foro
3 Torre Guinigi
Ramparts 10
Giardino Botanico 6
11
Duomo di San Martino
Baluardo della Libertà
Baluardo San Regolo
Baluardo San Colombano
Lucca Railway Station 350m (380 yards)
0 metres 250
0 yards 250
N

HIDDEN GEM
Montecarlo

This lovely medieval walled village sits midway between Lucca and Montecatini Terme. Here you will find stunning panoramic views, especially from the 14th-century castle, and superb local olive oil and wines.

San Michele in Foro

Piazza San Michele
Daily

As its name suggests, this church stands on the site of the ancient Roman forum. It has a wonderfully rich Pisan-Romanesque façade that competes in splendour with that of San Martino *(p208)*. John Ruskin, the English artist and art historian whose work did so much to revive interest in Italian art during the 19th century, spent many hours here sketching the rich mixture of twisted marble columns and Cosmati work (inlaid marble). The façade is almost barbaric in its exuberance, and the inlaid marble scenes depict wild beasts and huntsmen on horseback, rather than Christian subjects. Only the huge winged figure of St Michael, standing on the pediment and flanked by two angels, marks this out as a church. The splendour of the façade, built between the 11th and 14th centuries, is matched by the arcading of the bell tower. By contrast, the interior has little of interest except for Filippino Lippi's beautiful *Saints Helena, Jerome, Sebastian and Roch* (1457–1504).

San Frediano

Piazza San Frediano
Daily

The striking façade of Lucca's San Frediano church features a colourful 13th-century mosaic, *The Ascension*, by the school of Berlinghieri. Inside, to the right, is a splendid Romanesque font that could easily be mistaken for a fountain, given its size and impressive decoration. The sides are carved with scenes from The Life of Christ and the story of Moses. One dramatic scene shows Moses and his followers dressed in 12th-century armour and looking like Crusaders as they pass through the divided Red Sea with a train of camels.

Amico Aspertini's frescoes (1508–9) in the second chapel in the north aisle tell the story of Lucca's precious relic, the Volto Santo *(p208)*, and give a reasonable impression of what the city looked like in the early 16th century.

Also in the church is a coloured wooden statue of the Virgin, carved by Matteo Civitali, and an altarpiece crafted from a single block of marble by Jacopo

Did You Know?

The "incorruptible" body of St Zita, Lucca's peasant-girl patron saint, is on display in San Frediano.

↑ The striking façade of the Romanesque San Michele in Foro

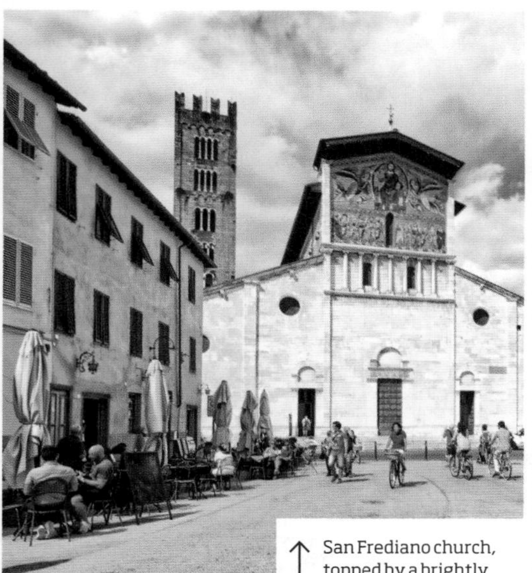

↑ San Frediano church, topped by a brightly patterned mosaic

della Quercia in the Cappella Trenta. It is carved in the shape of a polyptych, with five Gothic-spired niches.

9  

Museo Nazionale di Palazzo Mansi

Via Galli Tassi 43
0583 555 70
8:30am-7pm Tue-Sat

Lucca's picture gallery is in the impressive 17th-century Palazzo Mansi, with paintings and furnishings of the same period, typical of the time when Mannerism was being superseded by Baroque and Rococo art. There are also works by Bronzino, Pontormo, Sodoma, Andrea del Sarto, Tintoretto and Salvatore Rosa.

Ramparts

A promenade runs along the top of the city walls, built in 1504–1645, of which a complete circuit measures 4 km (2 miles). Marie Louise de Bourbon made the ramparts into a public park in the early 19th century, with a double avenue of trees. It makes for a delightful walk, with fine views of Lucca. There are occasional guided tours of the chambers and passages inside one of the bastions. For more information on the tours, which it is necessary to book in advance, contact Compagnia Balestrieri Lucca on 338 237 1277.

Piazza Napoleone and Piazza del Giglio

Piazza Napoleone was laid out in 1806 when Lucca was under the imposed rule of Elisa Baciocchi, Napoleon's sister. The statue in the square is of her successor, Marie Louise de Bourbon. She faces the massive Palazzo Ducale, with its elegant colonnade, built by Ammannati in 1578. Behind her is the Piazza del Giglio, with the Teatro del Giglio (1817) on the south side of the square. The theatre is renowned for its productions of operas by Lucca native Giacomo Puccini.

Lu.C.C.A

Via della Fratta 36
10am-7pm Tue-Sun
1 Jan, 24, 25 & 31 Dec
luccamuseum.com

The exhibitions are always interesting at this innovative contemporary gallery, and many include interactive displays that make it popular for family visits. There is a bookshop and a good café on site – though foodies may prefer to head straight for L'Imbuto, the gallery's superb Michelin-starred restaurant.

THE HISTORY OF LUCCA

The city was founded by the Romans, and Caesar, Pompey and Crassus cemented their First Triumvirate here. According to legend, St Peter's disciple Paulinus brought Christianity to Lucca. Largely ruled by local lords - except during one 14th-century stint under Pisa - Lucca remained proudly independent of Florence until Napoleon gave the city to his sister Elisa in 1805.

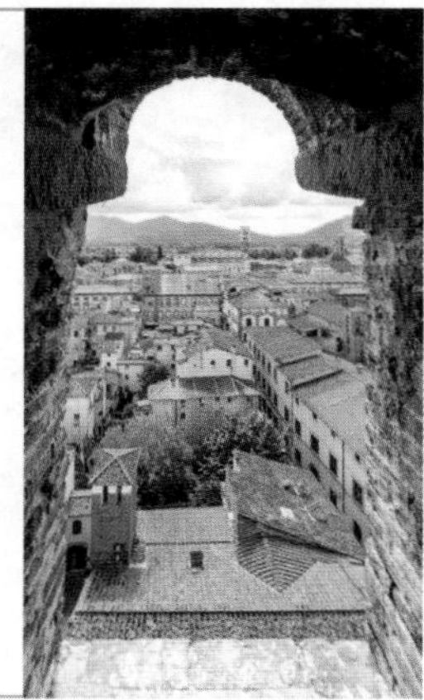

13

SAN MARTINO

Piazza San Martino Museum & bell tower: 10am-6pm daily (7pm in summer); cathedral: check website for timings
museocattedralelucca.it

Slotted beside a brick bishop's palace, this Romanesque cathedral rises dramatically from San Martino square. Inside, the *Volto Santo* remains a major draw for pilgrims.

Lucca's extraordinary cathedral, with its façade abutting incongruously on to the campanile, is dedicated to St Martin. He is the Roman soldier depicted on the façade dividing his cloak with a sword to share it with a needy beggar. This and other scenes from the life of the saint form part of the complex decorations covering the 13th-century façade. There are also reliefs depicting *The Labours of the Months* and intricate panels of inlaid coloured marble showing hunting scenes, peacocks and flowers.

Did You Know?

Early pilgrims believed that Nicodemus, who witnessed the Crucifixion, carved the *Volto Santo.*

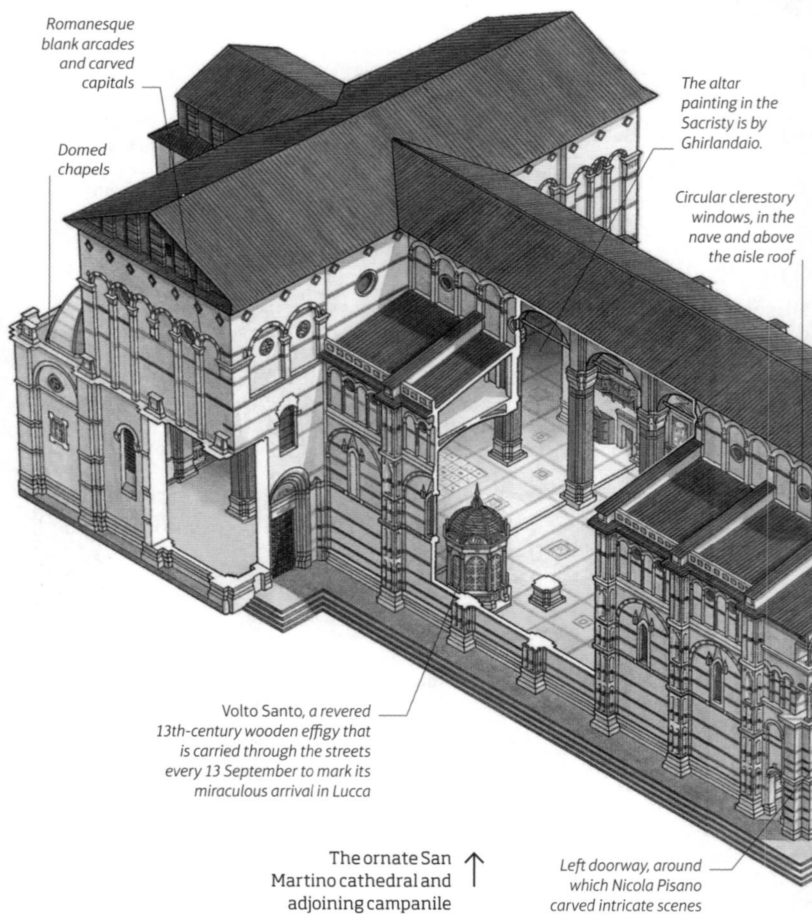

The ornate San Martino cathedral and adjoining campanile ↑

1 San Martino's somewhat mismatched exterior dates back to 1261, when the cathedral was joined to the pre-existing campanile and the latter's top two towers were added to suit the cathedral's façade.

2 The sculpture at the front of the church shows St Martin famously sharing his cloak with a beggar.

3 The interior of San Martino features impressive pillared arches.

1

3

2

MUSEO DELLA CATTEDRALE

Housed in the 14th-century former archbishop's palace, this museum displays the treasures of San Martino. These include the 11th-century carved stone head of a king from the original façade and a 14th-century sculpture of Count Fazio, who contributed to the cost of constructing the cathedral. There is also a rare 12th-century Limoges enamel casket, which possibly held a relic of St Thomas à Becket. The *Croce di Pisani* made by Vincenzo di Michele in 1411 is a masterpiece.

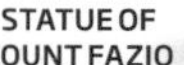
STATUE OF COUNT FAZIO

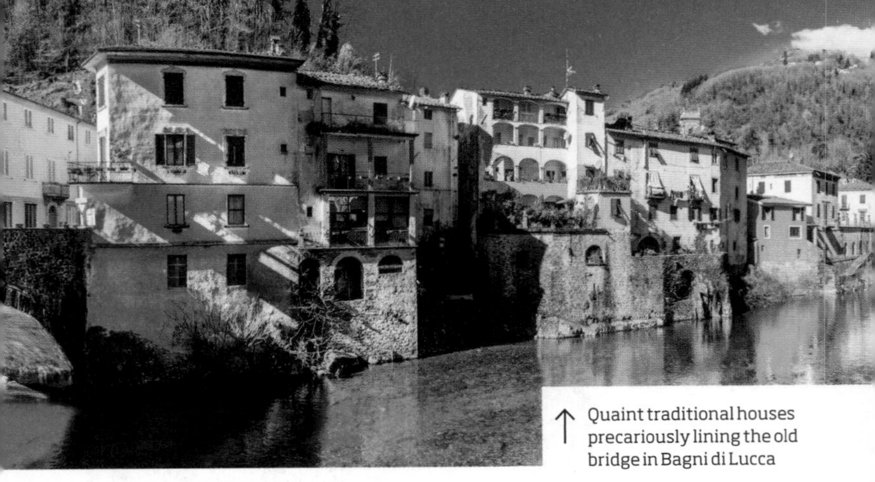

↑ Quaint traditional houses precariously lining the old bridge in Bagni di Lucca

EXPERIENCE MORE

Bagni di Lucca

Q2 Via del Casino; 0583 80 57 45

Visitors come to Bagni di Lucca for its lime-sulphate springs. In the 19th century, it was one of Europe's most fashionable spa towns *(p218)*: the Casino, built in 1837, was the first to be licensed in Europe. Also from that time are the Neo-Gothic English Church, the elegant Palazzo del Circolo dei Forestieri restaurant and the Cimitero Anglicano (Protestant Cemetery). Bagni di Lucca makes a good base for exploring the surrounding hills, cloaked in chestnut woods. You can walk to Montefegatesi, a hamlet surrounded by the peaks of the Alpi Apuane, and then continue to Orrido di Botri, a dramatic gorge.

The Ponte della Maddalena is a hump-backed bridge across the river Serchio, just north of the village of Borgo a Mozzano. It is called Ponte del Diavolo (Devil's Bridge) because, according to local legend, the Devil offered to build the bridge in return for possession of the first soul to cross it; the canny villagers agreed and, when it was finished, sent a dog across.

INSIDER TIP
Wild Hot Springs

If you're on a budget, you can bathe for free in the centuries-old thermal waters at Equi Terme, in the heart of the Lunigiana *(p213)*. In southern Tuscany, there are stunning natural spa pools at Saturnia *(p230)*.

The Garfagnana

Q2 FS Castelnuovo di Garfagnana Via Cavalieri di Vittorio Veneto, Castelnuovo di Garfagnana; 0583 64 10 07

This mountainous region, which contains the Parco Naturale delle Alpi Apuane *(p212)*, can be explored from its unofficial "capital", Castelnuovo di Garfagnana, with its fortified old town and castle and bustling Thursday market. The tourist information centre and the office of the Garfagnano Ambiente e Sviluppo on Piazza dell'Erbe can both supply plenty of inspiration for things to do and see.

From Castelnuovo, a scenic drive takes you to the Alpe Tre Potenze. You can return via San Pellegrino in Alpe, with its **Museo Etnografico**, and also visit **Parco dell' Orecchiella**, a nature park, and its Orto Botanico Pánia di Corfino, featuring a collection of local alpine plants.

Did You Know?

Many residents of Barga emigrated to Glasgow in the 1800s and the town now has close Scottish ties.

Museo Etnografico

Via del Voltone 15, San Pellegrino in Alpe 0583 64 90 72 Sep-Jun: Tue-Sun; Jul & Aug: daily

Parco dell'Orecchiella

Centro Visitatori, Orecchiella 0583 61 90 02 Park: Jun-Sep: daily, Apr, May & Oct: Sun; Orto Botanico Pánia di Corfino: Jul-Aug: daily, May-Jun & Sep: Sun

5

Barga

Q2

Barga is the most attractive of the towns that line the Serchio valley, leading northwards from Lucca. The little walled town, with its steep streets paved with stone, is the setting for a highly regarded opera festival held in July and August.

Barga's Duomo stands on a grassy terrace at the highest point in the town. There are glorious views from here of the gleaming whitemarble and limestone peaks of the Alpi Apuane.

The 11th-century Duomo is dedicated to San Cristoforo (St Christopher). The exterior is decorated with interesting Romanesque carvings of interlaced knots, wild beasts and knights in armour. Over the north portal, a frieze thought to be a scene from a folk tale depicts a banquet.

Inside, a huge wooden statue of St Christopher dates to the 12th century, and there is a gilded tabernacle guarded by two charming terracotta angels by Luca della Robbia.

Most impressive of all is the massive marble pulpit, standing fully 5 m (16.5 ft) tall, supported by pillars that, in turn, rest on the back of man-eating lions. The work of Guido Bigarelli of Como, it dates from the early 13th century. The lively sculptures on the upper part depict the Evangelists, the Three Magi, the Annunciation, the Nativity and the Baptism of Christ.

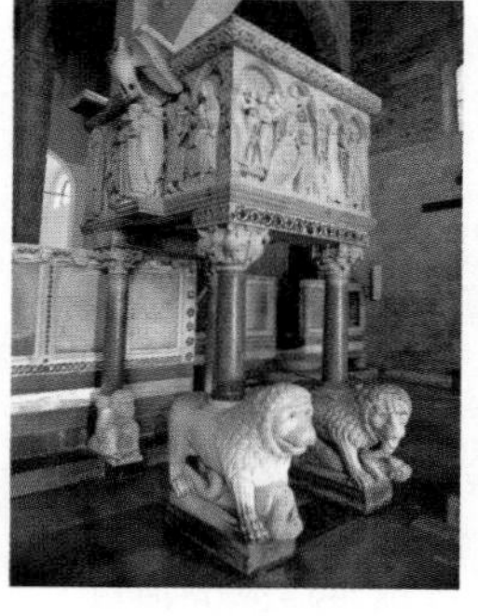

↑ Lions guarding the main portal and pulpit of Barga's Duomo

Torre del Lago Puccini

Q3 Viale Kennedy 2; 0584 35 98 93

The composer Giacomo Puccini (1858–1924) lived here, beside Lago di Massaciuccoli, so he could indulge his passion for shooting waterfowl. He and his wife are buried in the **Museo Villa Puccini**, in the mausoleum between the piano room and the gun room where he kept his rifle ("my second favourite instrument"). The operas are performed in the open-air theatre in summer *(p51)*. The reed-fringed lake is now a nature reserve.

Museo Villa Puccini

Piazzale Belvedere Puccini 266 0584 34 14 45; 0584 35 93 22 (Teatro Opera Puccini)
Tue-Sun Nov, 25 Dec
giacomopuccini.it

The Versilia

Q3 Viareggio Viale Carducci 10, Viareggio; www.luccatourist.it

The Versilia, sometimes called the Tuscan Riviera because of the many beach resorts that line this 30-km (18-mile) strip, stretches from Marina di Carrara in the north down to Marina di Torre del Lago Puccini. In the 1820s, towns such as Massa, Pietra Santa and Camaiore developed marinas and lidos along the part of the coast they controlled. These inland towns are linked by roads to their coastal twins. Here, villas and hotels with fine walled gardens line the streets, with the mountains of the Alpi Apuane as a backdrop.

The beaches are divided into numerous bathing establishments run by hotels or private operators, who charge for use of the beach and its facilities. Forte dei Marmi is perhaps the most beautiful of these resorts; much favoured by wealthy Florentines and Milanese, it's packed with high-fashion boutiques. Equally popular is Viareggio, famous for its elegant "Liberty style" (Art Nouveau) villas and hotels, built in the 1920s after the original boardwalk and wooden chalets of the resort went up in flames in 1917. A fine example is the Gran Caffé Margherita, designed by Galileo Chini. Viareggio's carnival *(p50)*, held on Sundays from Febrary to Lent and on Shrove Tuesday, is famous throughout Italy.

← Monument to Puccini at Torre del Lago Puccini

8

Parco Naturale delle Alpi Apuane

Q2 Castelnuovo di Garfagnana Piazza Delle Erbe 1, Castelnuovo di Garfagnana; 0583 64 42 42

The Parco Naturale delle Alpi Apuane, northwest of Castelnuovo di Garfagnana, was designated a nature reserve in 1985. It is an area where spectacular jagged peaks and wooded valleys are crisscrossed by hiking trails and scenic mountain roads. Monte Pisanino is the highest peak in the area, at 1,945 m (6,320 ft). It towers above Lago di Vagli, an artificial lake covering the drowned village of Fabbrica. Nearby are Vagli di Sotto and Vagli di Sopra, ancient villages with rugged stone houses. To the south, in the valley of the Turrite Secca, a spectacular mountain road leads to Seravezza, passing through a white-walled tunnel called the Galleria del Cipollaio. Northwest, at Arni, are the Marmitte dei Giganti (Giants' Cooking Pots), great hollows left by the glaciers of the Ice Age.

Southeast, at Calomini, is a 12th-century rock-cut hermitage, home to a Capuchin monk; just a few minutes away at Fornovolasco is the Grotta del Vento (Cave of the Wind), famed for its extraordinary rock formations. To the east, past Barga at Coreglia Antelminelli, is the **Museo della Figurina di Gesso**, devoted to the history of locally made plaster figurines once sold all over Europe.

INSIDER TIP
Lardo di Colonnata

This must-try delicious pork speciality has been made in the pretty village of Colonnata in the Alpi Apuane since AD 1000. It is aged in marble vats with a mixture of salt, garlic, pepper and rosemary for at least six months.

Museo della Figurina di Gesso

Via del Mangano 17, Coreglia Antelminelli 0583 780 82 9am-1pm Mon-Fri, 10am-1pm Sat & Sun

9

Pietrasanta

Q2 Piazza Statuto

This medieval town has long been a draw for sculptors from all over the world, thanks to the white marble quarried from the Alpi Apuane mountains that form the town's backdrop. More recently, artistic metal-casting foundries have been established here alongside the many marble workshops, and numerous famous artists come to work both in stone and bronze.

The **Museo dei Bozzetti**, in a former monastery, contains a fascinating collection of maquettes and scale models that have been used in preparation for artworks, including César's famous thumb sculpture. The town's Piazza Duomo is dominated by the 13th-century Duomo di San Martino, with its splendid 14th-century façade. The adjacent brick campanile was to have been covered in marble but its real draw is the spectacular helical staircase inside by Donato Benti, the Florentine sculptor and architect believed to have been Michelangelo's agent.

Did You Know?

The first customer at the marble quarry on Monte Altissimo in the Apuan Alps was Michelangelo.

→ Hikers passing farm buildings and mountain lodges in the Alpi Apuane

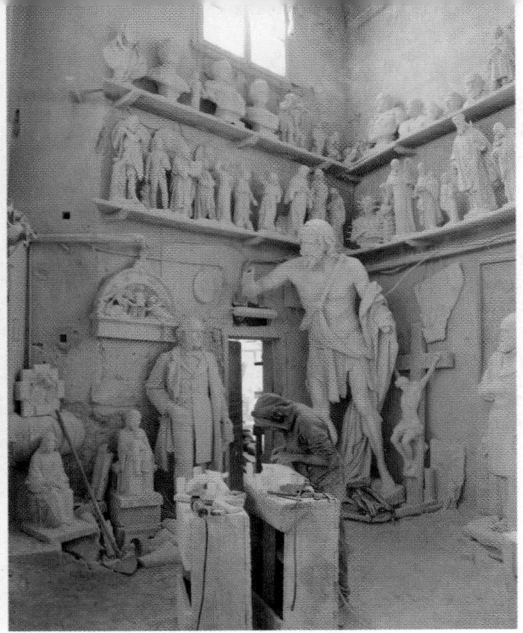

←
Plaster casts lining Studi Nicoli, one of Carrara's many marble workshops

A footpath and cycleway leads from the town to the nearby seaside resort of Marina di Pietrasanta and continues through the pines of the extensive Parco della Versiliana to Forte dei Marmi.

Museo dei Bozzetti
Via Sant'Agostino 1
museodeibozzetti.it

Carrara

P2 Piazza Cesare Battisti 1; 0585 64 14 22

Carrara is world famous for its white marble. The 300 or so quarries near the town date to Roman times, making this the oldest industrial site in continuous use in the world. In Carrara itself, there are myriad showrooms and workshops where the marble is sawn into sheets or sculpted into statues and ornaments. Many of the workshops welcome visitors. You can also discover more about the techniques of crafting marble at the **Museo Civico del Marmo**. Perhaps unsurprisingly, Carrara's **Duomo** uses the local marble to full effect: it covers its Pisan-Romanesque façade, which features a rose window. In the same square is the house where Michelangelo used to stay on his visits to buy marble for his sculptures. The façade is marked by a plaque and by carvings of the sculptor's tools.

Tour buses from Carrara regularly visit the quarries at Colonnata and at Fantiscritti, where a museum displays marble-quarrying techniques. By car, follow the numerous signs for the "Cave di Marmo".

Museo Civico del Marmo
Viale XX Settembre
0585 84 57 46 May-Sep: 9:30am-1pm, 3-6pm Mon-Sat; Oct-Apr: 9am-12:30pm, 2:30-5pm Mon-Sat

Duomo
Piazza del Duomo Daily

11

The Lunigiana

P1 Aulla Via Salucci 5, Aulla; 0187 42 14 39

The Lunigiana (Land of the Moon) area is named after the port of Luni – so called because of the moon-like luminescence of the marble shipped from here in Roman times. This is good walking country, with pretty villages and many statuesque castles, including Fosdinovo, Aulla and Verrucola, just outside Fivizzano. This was the main town of the Lunigiana during Florentine rule; the Piazza Medicea has some splendid Renaissance palazzi and an elegant fountain (1683), and a small museum devoted to the history of printing, which began here in 1471.

PIETRASANTA'S CONTEMPORARY SCULPTURES

Over 70 modern sculptures by international artists decorate piazzas, gardens and other locations throughout Pietrasanta. Among them are works by Fernando Botero (born 1932) and Igor Mitoraj (1944–2014), both of whom had studios here.

Eros Alato con Mano by Igor Mitoraj

Did You Know?

A prestigious white truffle grown in the San Miniato hills is celebrated in a festival each November.

12

San Miniato

R3 🚌 ℹ Piazza del Popolo 1; 0571 427 45

Straddling the crest of one of the region's highest hills, San Miniato manages to remain aloof from the industrial conurbation of the Arno valley. There are many fine historic buildings here, including the 13th-century Rocca (castle) built for Frederick II (1194–1250), the German Holy Roman Emperor.

The town played a major part in Frederick's Italian military campaigns. He dreamed of rebuilding the ancient Roman Empire that lay divided between papal and imperial authority. To this end, he conquered large areas of Italy. His battles fuelled fierce local struggles between the imperial Ghibellines and the papal Guelphs. Local people still refer to the town as San Miniato al Tedesco (of the German).

In the Piazza del Duomo, only the red-brick façade survives from the original 12th-century cathedral. The majolica plates set within it show evidence of trade with Spain or North Africa. They seem to represent the North Star and the constellations of Ursus Major and Minor: key reference points for early navigators.

The campanile, the Torre di Matilda, is named in honour of the great Countess Matilda, born in Livorno in 1046.

INSIDER TIP

Livorno by Boat

See the most attractive parts of historic Livorno from a different viewpoint with a boat tour through the pretty network of canals that were established in the 17th century *(www.livornoinbattello.it)*.

Livorno

Q4 FS 🚌 ⛴ ℹ Piazza Cavour 6; 0586 20 46 11

The fact that Livorno is now a bustling city (it is Italy's second-busiest container port) is thanks to Cosimo I. In 1571, he chose Livorno, then a tiny fishing village, as the site for Tuscany's new port after Pisa's harbour silted up. From 1607 to 1621 the English marine engineer Sir Robert Dudley built the great sea wall that protects the harbour. In 1608, Livorno was declared a free port, open to all traders, regardless of religion or race. People fleeing wars or religious persecution, including Jews, Protestants and Greeks, settled here and contributed greatly to the city's success.

When the architect Buontalenti planned the new city of Livorno in 1576, he envisaged the huge Piazza Grande at the heart of a network of wide avenues. The square's original appearance has, however, been lost. This is partly due to controversial postwar rebuilding, which cut the square into two halves: the present Piazza Grande to the south and the Largo Municipio to the north. In the former is the Duomo, a prominent victim of Livorno's wartime bombing. Formerly a 16th-century cathedral by Pieroni and Cantagallina, it was rebuilt in 1959, retaining only the original entrance portico, with its Doric arcades. These have been attributed to Inigo Jones, who served his apprenticeship under the architect Buontalenti. Jones later used an almost identical design for the

←

The first rays of the rising sun, caught by the campanile of San Miniato

arcades of his Covent Garden piazza in London.

The Piazza Micheli contains Livorno's best-known monument: the *Monumento dei Quattro Mori*. Bandini's bronze figure of Duke Ferdinand I dates from 1595; Pietro Tacca's four Moorish slaves, also cast in bronze, were not added until 1626. Naked and manacled, the dejected slaves are a stark reminder that Livorno once had a thriving slave market. From the Piazza Micheli there are views of the Fortezza Nuovo. Standing on the sea in a strategic position on the Medici port, this 16th-century fortress was built by Antonio da Sangallo the Elder to incorporate an existing medieval structure, including a square tower (the oldest part) and the tall, round Mastio di Matilde, which dates from the mid-13th century. The complex is often used for concerts and other events.

The Fortezza lies within an area known as Venezia Nuovo, or "New Venice", laid out in the 17th century along a series of canals. Although it only covers a few blocks, this is one of the city's most scenic areas.

VIA FRANCIGENA

This ancient pilgrim's route from Canterbury in England to Rome passes through San Miniato and can be followed on foot, bike or horseback. The 15 stages, making up a total of 380 km (236 miles), are clearly signposted. There is an app (*www.viefrancigene.org*) and a good network of accommodation options (*www.viafrancigenatoscana.org*).

South of the Fortezza Nuova, Piazza XX Settembre is renowned for its bustling "American Market" whose name derives from the large amounts of American army surplus that was sold here after World War II. A US army base, Camp Darby, still operates to the north of Livorno.

The perfect end to a day of sightseeing around the city is a sunset stroll on the Terrazza Mascagni. This vast, elegant terrace over the sea was built in the 1920s, and restored in the 1990s. The colonnades of the balustrade, chessboard paving and graceful gazebo make it a place of great charm.

14 Certosa di Pisa

Q3 (località Calci) From Pisa 050 93 84 30 8:30am-6:30pm Tue-Sat; 8:30am-12:30pm Sun (admission half past the hour)

This Carthusian monastery was founded in 1366 and rebuilt during the 18th century. The splendid church is lavishly decorated, and some buildings form the University of Pisa's **Museo di Storia Naturale**. Exhibits include 16th-century anatomical wax models. The unfinished campanile sits alongside and the church is backed by olive groves and the towering presence of Monte Serra. At 917 m (3,000 ft) above sea level, it is the highest of the Monti Pisani, which form a stunning backdrop to the village of Calci.

Museo di Storia Naturale

Certosa di Pisa 050 221 29 70 Jun-mid-Sep: 10am-8pm daily; mid-Sep-May: 9am-7pm daily Public hols

←

Colour-washed buildings and the octagonal Santa Caterina in Venezia Nuovo, Livorno

Pistoia

R2 Palazzo dei Vescovi, Piazza del Duomo 4; 0573 216 22

Assassination in Pistoia's narrow alleyways was commonplace. The favoured weapon was a tiny but deadly dagger called a pistole, made by the city's ironworkers, who also specialized in surgical instruments.

The citizens of Pistoia acquired a reputation for viciousness and intrigue in the 13th century. The cause was a feud between two of the city's rival factions, the Neri and Bianchi (Blacks and Whites), that spread to involve other cities. Assassination in Pistoia's narrow alleyways was commonplace. The favoured weapon was a tiny but deadly dagger called a pistole, made by the city's ironworkers, who also specialized in surgical instruments. Pistoia still thrives on metalworking: everything from buses to mattress springs is made here.

Piazza del Duomo, the main square in the historic centre, is dominated by the **Cattedrale di San Zeno** and its bulky campanile, originally built in the 12th century as a watchtower in the city walls. The interior is rich in funerary monuments, including the tomb of poet Cino da Pistoia, in the south aisle. He is shown in a relief (1337) lecturing to a class of young boys.

Nearby is the Cappella di San Jacobo, its remarkable silver altar decorated with more than 600 statues and reliefs, all added between 1287 and 1456. Nearly every silversmith of note in Tuscany contributed to the extra-ordinarily rich design, including Brunelleschi. On the opposite side of the square is the Palazzo del Comune (town hall), which has the **Museo Civico** upstairs. Exhibits range from medieval altar paintings to the work of 20th-century Pistoian artists, architects and sculptors. Also in the square is the beautifully restored. In the basement of this bishop's palace you can see the excavated remains of Roman buildings. Upstairs is the Museo della Cattedrale,

INSIDER TIP
Pistoia Blues Festival

This major event not only features blues but top rock, soul and jazz artists, who play to enthusiastic crowds in Piazza del Duomo *(pistoiablues.com)*.

→ Pistoia's Duomo, with its substantial bell tower and octagonal Baptistry (1359)

→ The tranquil interior of the Museo Civico

which has some fine reliquaries, crucifixes and chalices made by local goldsmiths between the 13th and15th centuries. Visits are by guided tour only.

The church of **Sant'Andrea** is reached by walking through Piazza della Sala, the site of Pistoia's lively open-air market. Inside is Giovanni Pisano's pulpit (completed in 1301), considered by some to be his masterpiece, even more accomplished than the pulpit he later made for Pisa's Duomo. It is decorated with reliefs depicting scenes from the Life of Christ.

On Piazza Giovanni XXIII, the Ospedale del Ceppo is a former hospital and orphanage, founded in 1277. It was named after the *ceppo*, or hollowed-out tree trunk, that was used in medieval times to collect donations for its work. The striking façade of the main building features coloured and glazed terracotta panels (1514–25) by Giovanni della Robbia illustrating the Seven Works of Corporeal Mercy. The portico is by Michelozzo.

South of the Piazza del Duomo, the work of Marino Marini (1901–80), Pistoia's most famous 20th-century artist, is housed in the **Centro Marino Marini** museum in the Palazzo del Tau. On display are drawings and casts, which trace the development of his style. Marini specialized in sculpting primitive forms in bronze and clay. His subjects included a horse and rider *(p108)*, and Pomona, the ancient Roman goddess of fertility. Nearby on the same street is the **Capella del Tau**. This chapel owes its name to the letter T (*tau* in Greek), which appeared on the cloaks of the monks who built it and symbolized a crutch. Inside the chapel there are frescoes of the creation and the life of St Anthony Abbot, who founded the order, which is dedicated to tending the sick and crippled.

Just north of the Cappella del Tau, on Via Cavour, is the 12th-century church of San Giovanni Fuorcivitas ("St John outside the city", since the church once stood beyond the city walls). Its north flank is strikingly clad in banded marble and there is a Romanesque relief of *The Last Supper* over the portal. Inside is Giovanni Pisano's holy water basin, carved in marble with figures of the Virtues, and an equally masterly pulpit by Guglielmo da Pisa, carved in 1270 with New Testament scenes. Both works are among the finest of this period, when artists were reviving the art of carving.

Cattedrale di San Zeno
Piazza del Duomo 0573 250 95 8am-12:30pm, 3:30-7pm daily

Museo Civico
Palazzo del Comune, Piazza del Duomo 0573 37 12 96 10am-2pm Tue-Fri, 10am-6pm Sat, Sun & hols

Palazzo dei Vescovi
Piazza del Duomo 0573 36 92 72 10:15am-4pm Tue, Thu, Fri; 10:15am-6pm Sat-Sun Mon, Wed

Sant'Andrea
Via Sant'Andrea 21 0573 219 12 8am-12:30pm, 3-6:30pm daily

Centro Marino Marini
Palazzo del Tau, Corso Silvano Fedi 30 11am-6pm Tue-Sat, 2:30-7:30pm Sun fondazionemarino marini.it

Cappella del Tau
Corso Silvano Fedi 70 0573 322 04 8:15am-1:30pm Mon-Sat

Collodi

Q3 Piazza Collodi; 0572 42 96 60

There are two main sights in this town: the **Villa Garzoni**, with its theatrical terraced gardens tumbling down the hillside and, for children, the **Pinocchio Park**.

The author of *The Adventures of Pinocchio* (1881), Carlo Lorenzini, was born in Florence, but his uncle was custodian of the Villa Garzoni and Lorenzini frequently stayed here as a child. Fond memories led him to use Collodi as his pen name, and, in 1956, the town decided to repay the compliment by setting up the theme park. The park consists of gardens featuring mosaics and sculptural tableaux based on the adventures of the puppet, plus a maze, playground, exhibition centre and children's restaurant.

Villa Garzoni
Via Vittorio Veneto 1
0572 42 95 90 (Garden only) daily; times vary

Pinocchio Park
Via san Gennaro 3
9am-sunset daily
pinocchio.it

TAKING THE WATERS

Spa culture at Tuscany's hot springs has a long history. The Romans built bath complexes where army veterans who settled in towns such as Florence and Siena could relax. St Catherine of Siena (1347-80), who suffered from scrofula, and Lorenzo de' Medici (1449-92), who was arthritic, both sought relief in the sulphurous waters at Bagno Vignoni *(p186)*. However, Tuscan spas really came into their own as high-society destinations in the early 19th century, when Bagni di Lucca became one of the most fashionable spas in Europe, frequented by emperors and kings.

← The interior of the Neo-Classical Terme Tettuccio

Montecatini Terme

R3 Viale Verdi 66; 0572 77 22 44

Of all Tuscany's many spa towns, Montecatini Terme, with its beautiful formal gardens and distinguished spas, is the most interesting. Terme Leopoldine (1926), built in the style of a Classical temple, is named after Grand Duke Leopoldo I, who first encouraged the development of the town in the 18th century. The most splendid spa is the Neo-Classical Terme Tettuccio (1925–8), with its circular, marble-lined pools, fountains and lovely Art Nouveau tiles depicting languorous nymphs. Terme Torretta, named after its mock-medieval tower, is noted for its tea-time concerts, while Terme Tamerici has beautifully tended gardens. Visitors can obtain day tickets to the spas to drink the waters and relax in the reading, writing and music rooms. More information is available from the Direzione delle Terme, at Viale Verdi 41.

A popular excursion from Montecatini Terme is to take the funicular railway up to the ancient fortified village of Montecatini Alto. In its quiet main piazza, there are antique shops and well-regarded restaurants with outdoor tables. From the Rocca (castle), there are sweeping views over the mountainous countryside. Nearby, at Ponte Buggianese, in San Michele church, you can see modern frescoes by the Florentine artist Pietro Annigoni (1910–88) on the theme of Christ's Passion.

↓ The magnificent Terme Tettuccio in Montecatini Terme

18

Monsumanno Terme

R3 · Viale Verdi 66/68; 0572 772244

Much loved by the Medici family, Monsummano grew around the Santuario di Santa Maria della Fontenuova (1602–5) built for Ferdinando I. The church is surrounded on three sides by a portico, where a series of lunettes (1630–33) by Giovanni da San Giovanni tell the legend of a shepherdess who found her lost sheep here thanks to an apparition of the Madonna. Ferdinando I also commissioned the Osteria dei Pellegrini lodgings for pilgrims, which now hosts the local history museum, the **Museo della Città e del Territorio**. Just outside the town at Villa Renatico Martini, the **Museo di Arte Contemporanea e del Novecento** has an interesting collection of 20th–21st-century art. Monsummano is also famous for its spa waters: at the **Grotta Giusti** resort there is an atmospheric natural cave with hot underground waters.

Nearby, the tiny hilltop village of Monsumanno Alto has fabulous views and castle ruins, while the views from the appealing village of Montevettolini, a 16th-century Medici hunting base, are even finer.

Museo della Città e del Territorio

Piazza Ferdinando Martini · 9am-1pm Mon-Fri & 3:30-5:30pm Tue & Thu (4-6pm in summer) · museoterritorio.it

Museo di Arte Contemporanea e del Novecento

Via Gragnano 349 · 9:30am-12:30pm Wed & Sat-Sun, 3:30pm-6:30pm Thu-Mon (4-7pm in summer) · macn.it

Grotta Giusti

Via della Grotta Giusti · 9am-7pm daily · grottagiustispa.com

↑ Part of the Grotta Giusti spa establishment, Monsumanno Terme

Pescia

Q3 · Via Fratelli Rosselli 2 (0572 49 09 19)

Pescia's wholesale flower market is one of Italy's biggest, and there are some interesting sights in the city.

In the church of San Francesco are frescoes on *The Life of St Francis* (1235), by Bonaventura Berlinghieri. The artist knew St Francis and it is claimed that the frescoes are an accurate portrait of the saint. The Duomo, remodelled in Baroque style by Antonio Ferri in 1693, has a massive campanile that was given its onion-dome "cap" in 1771.

There is a small collection of religious paintings and illuminated manuscripts in the **Museo Civico**, and the **Museo Archeologico della Valdinievole** displays finds from nearby Valdinievole, the pretty "Vale of Mist".

Museo Civico

Palazzo Galeotti, Piazza Santo Stefano 1 · 0572 47 79 44 · For restoration

Museo Archeologico della Valdinievole

Piazza Leonardo da Vinci 1 · 0572 47 75 33 · For restoration

Boats in the Porto Santo Stefano in Maremma

SOUTHWEST TUSCANY

This corner of the region was first inhabited by the ancient Etruscans, who were attracted by the prolific mineral deposits; the iron, in particular, drew the Etruscans to Elba in the 8th century BC. On the Costa degli Etruschi, Populonia (today an archaeological site) held an important position as one of 12 Dodecapoli (city-states). Both the Etruscans and the Romans drained the swamps of the Maremma to create richly fertile farming land, but it returned to wilderness after the collapse of the Roman Empire and the area saw little development for hundreds of years. In the 19th century Elba became home to Napoleon during his exile (1814–15); while there, the emperor ran the island efficiently, rationalizing the military, and the economic and social infrastructure. The marshland of the Maremma was reclaimed permanently around this time, and Monte Argentario – once an island – was firmly linked to the mainland by a dyke built across the Orbetello lagoon in 1842. Bolgheri, one of Italy's most prestigious wine-making areas, rose to prominence in the 1970s as the producer of several Supertuscans.

SOUTHWEST TUSCANY
NORTHWEST TUSCANY
p192
Casciana Terme
Santa Luce
Volterra
Era
San Pietro in Palazzi
Cecina
Marina di Cecina
La California
Colline Metallifere
Pomarance
Forte di Bibbona
Bolgheri
Serrazzano
San Guido
Terme di Bagnolo
Marina di Castagneto-Carducci
Donoratico
Monteverdi Marittimo
Cornia
Castagneto Carducci
Sassetta
San Vincenzo
Monte Calvo 648m
COSTA DEGLI ETRUSCHI
Campiglia Marittima
Suvereto
MASSA MARITTIMA
THE MAREMMA
Golfo di Baratti
Venturina
Populonia
Valpiana
Marina di Salivoli
Piombino
Prato Ranieri
Follonica
Gavorrano
Canale di Piombino
Golfo di Follonica
Scarlino
Capo Vita
Isola Palmaiola
ELBA
Cavo
Rio Marina
Marciana Marina
Portoferraio
Punta Ala
Poggio Ballone 630m
Marciana
Procchio
San Martino
Riva del Sole
Pomonte
Lacona
Castiglione della Pescaia
Marina di Campo
Capoliveri
Punta di Fetováia
Punta dei Ripalti
Pianosa
TUSCAN ARCHIPELAGO
0 kilometres 10
0 miles 10
N
Giglio Porto

SOUTHWEST TUSCANY

Must See

1. The Tuscan Archipelago
2. Elba

Experience More

3. Costa degli Etruschi
4. Massa Marittima
5. The Maremma
6. Saturnia
7. Sovana
8. Pitigliano
9. Orbetello
10. Monte Argentario
11. Capalbio

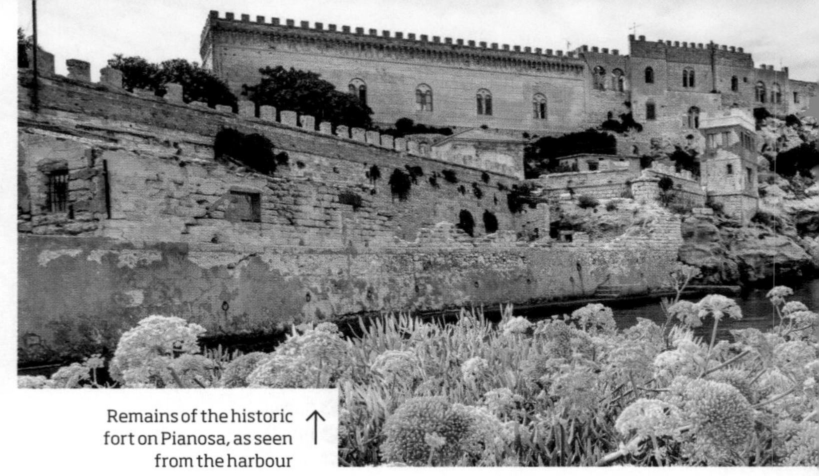

Remains of the historic fort on Pianosa, as seen from the harbour

THE TUSCAN ARCHIPELAGO

P5 Isola di Capraia; 0586 905235 Via Provinciale 9, Isola del Giglio; www.islepark.gov.it

The six small islands that – together with the larger Elba *(p226)* – make up Tuscany's archipelago are idyllic natural paradises; restricted access to several only adds to their appeal as unspoiled havens. Terrain among the islands varies wildly from flat to mountainous, though all allow for sensational walking and watersports.

1 

Gorgona

The northernmost island on the archipelago, Gorgona is also the smallest, measuring just 2 sq km (1 sq mile). Beautiful and wild, it has a hilly interior almost entirely covered in dense scrub, pretty coves and a rugged coastline nested by seabirds. There are two attractive fortresses – one built by the Medici and the other by the Pisans – and a tiny fishing village that dates from the 1700s. The island has hosted a detention centre since 1869 and only accompanied visits are permitted (with a maximum of 75 visitors per day).

2 

Pianosa

Flat Pianosa was rich in agriculture in ancient times. Historic remains include traces of Roman baths at Cala Giovanna, two forts, and catacombs below the village. Access to much of the island is restricted to tours, which include mountain bike, kayak and snorkelling excursions.

3  

Capraia

Rocky Capraia measures 19 sq km (7 sq miles) and rises to nearly 500 m (1,640 ft) above sea level. It's the only island of the archipelago to have volcanic origins, visible in the reddish terrain at the Cala Rossa bay. The cluster of buildings around the port is connected to a second village by the island's only road, which slopes down from Forte San Giorgio, one of a series of 16th-century fortifications built during Genoese rule. There are a range of walks, from a 20-minute stroll to a seven-hour hike. Boat trips are available, plus there is a good choice of hotels and restaurants here.

Montecristo

The looming granite mass of this island inspired Alexandre Dumas' famous 1844 work

INSIDER TIP
Island Activities

The archipelago is a top diving destination thanks to clear, unpolluted waters rich in shipwrecks and marine life. There is superb walking too; explore during the Tuscany Walking Festival *(www.tuscanywalkingfestival.it)*.

The Count of Montecristo. The island was originally named Mons Christi by monks who first arrived in the 5th century, fleeing persecution; the monastery was abandoned in 1553 following pirate attacks. As a protected nature reserve, access to the island is strictly limited, with a lengthy waiting list. There is a community of wild goats, but the only human inhabitants are the reserve wardens.

---

⑤   

Giglio

With an area of 21 sq km (8 sq miles), Giglio is the largest island of the archipelago besides Elba. There is a good network of footpaths and some spectacular diving locations along the coast. Campese, the most modern of the island's three villages, has a long sandy beach that is popular with families and surfers. Ferries arrive at Giglio Porto, a pretty harbour with a 16th-century watchtower, shops, hotels and eateries. The island is best known for its medieval hilltop village of Giglio Castello, which has a 12th-century Pisan castle, and its fruity white, Ansonica, which is celebrated with a wine festival in the last weekend of September.

↑ The pastel-coloured buildings of Giglio's attractive harbour

⑥

Giannutri

This small, half-moon shaped island stretches only 5 km (3 miles) long and 500 m (1,640 ft) wide, and is home to the remarkable remains of an ancient Roman villa. Built between 90 and 100 AD, Villa Domizia was fronted by a large terrace with steps down to the sea, with associated structures including a cistern, baths, a harbour and fish works. The island has a rugged coastline with a series of caves and two pebbly beaches; it's freely accessible in parts while other areas can be seen with a guide.

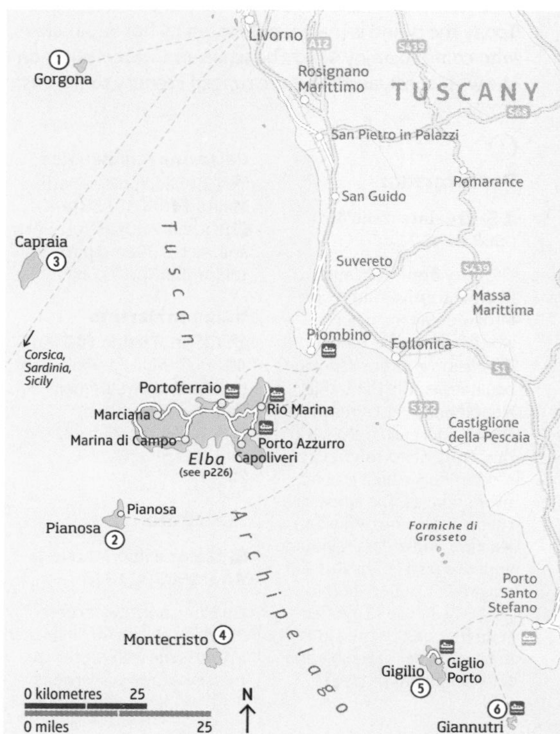

↑ Rio Marina harbour, with a lighthouse guarding the curve of the bay

2

ELBA

P6 Elba Airport Piombino Marittima infoelba.com

Elba's most famous resident was Napoleon, who spent nine months in exile here after the fall of Paris in 1814. Today the island is mainly populated by holiday-makers, who come to enjoy sandy beaches and watersports on the west coast, and the more rugged scenery to the east.

①

Portoferraio

 **Calata Italia 43; 0565 29 46 71**

The ferry from mainland Piombino arrives into Portoferraio, Elba's main port, which has a pretty harbour. The main sights are Napoleon's two houses. The **Palazzina Napoleonica** (also known as the Villa dei Mulini) stands in the centre of Portoferraio, a modest house built around two windmills. The emperor's country residence, **Villa San Martino**, had a Classical façade imposed on it by the Russian emigré Prince Demidoff in 1851. The house's Egyptian-style frescoes, painted in 1814, are a reminder of Napoleon's Nile campaigns of 1798–9.

Palazzina Napoleonica
Villa Napoleonica dei Mulini 0565 91 58 46 8:30am-7:30pm Mon-Sat in summer; 8:30am-1pm in winter (to 1pm Sun & public hols)

Villa San Martino
San Martino 0565 91 46 88 9am-7pm Tue-Sun (to 1pm Sun) in summer, 9am-4pm in winter

②

Marciana

 **Municipio, Marciana Alta; 0565 90 12 15**

On Elba's northwest coast is Marciana Marina, while further inland is the well-preserved medieval town of Marciana Alta. Here the **Museo Civico Archeologico** houses exhibits from Etruscan ships wrecked off Elba. There is also a cable car, which you can take up Monte Capanne, Elba's highest peak at 1,019 m (3,300 ft). Marciana makes a good base for exploring the island's western half.

Museo Civico Archeologico
Via del Pretorio 66, Marciana Alta 348 703 9374 Apr-Sep: daily

③

Rio Marina

 **Lungomare G Marconi 2, Gli Spiazzi; 0565 96 20 04**

This intriguing village grew up around its harbour, which was built specifically to transport the iron ore that

Did You Know?

Elba and the other islands are home to Audouin's gull - the world's rarest species of seagull.

was mined nearby. There are still open-cast mines that extract the ores that attracted the Etruscans to Elba, and the **Museo dei Minerali** explains the geology of the island and the history of its local mining traditions.

Museo dei Minerali
Palazzo Comunale
0565 96 20 88 Apr-mid-Oct: daily; mid-Oct-Mar: by appt

Porto Azzurro

Via Cerboni 3

This pretty fishing village and popular seaside resort was founded in 1603 by Philip III of Spain, who intended to make it a strategic defensive centre. The imposing Forte Longone (now a prison) dominates the town from on high. On the seafront, Piazza Matteotti is the hub of local life, with concerts and events organized here in summer. The 17th-century Madonna di Monserrato, which was built to recall the Spanish church of Monserrat, is located just outside Porto Azzurro. There is also a variety of beaches, including Terranera beach, which has black sand due to the local mineral pyrite.

Capoliveri

Viale Australia 1; 10:30am-12:30pm daily

This appealing medieval hilltop village has sea views on both sides of the Monte Calamita promontory. The presence of large quantities of magnetite – which sends compasses haywire – on Monte Calamita has resulted in numerous legends regarding shipwrecks caused by the pull of the mineral. Visitors can tour the local mines, which once played a major role in the traditional life here, as well as enjoy the wealth of local beaches. The promontory is also home to the scenic Capoliveri Bike Park, which has over 100 km (60 miles) of trails of varying degrees of difficulty.

NAPOLEON ON ELBA

Napoleon himself chose Elba as the location for his exile. He was assigned sovereignty of the island under the 1814 Treaty of Fontainebleau, and was a popular and efficient ruler. His main residence in Portoferraio, the Palazzina Napoleonica, enjoys a panoramic position overlooking the coast and today houses a multimedia exhibition about its most famous owner.

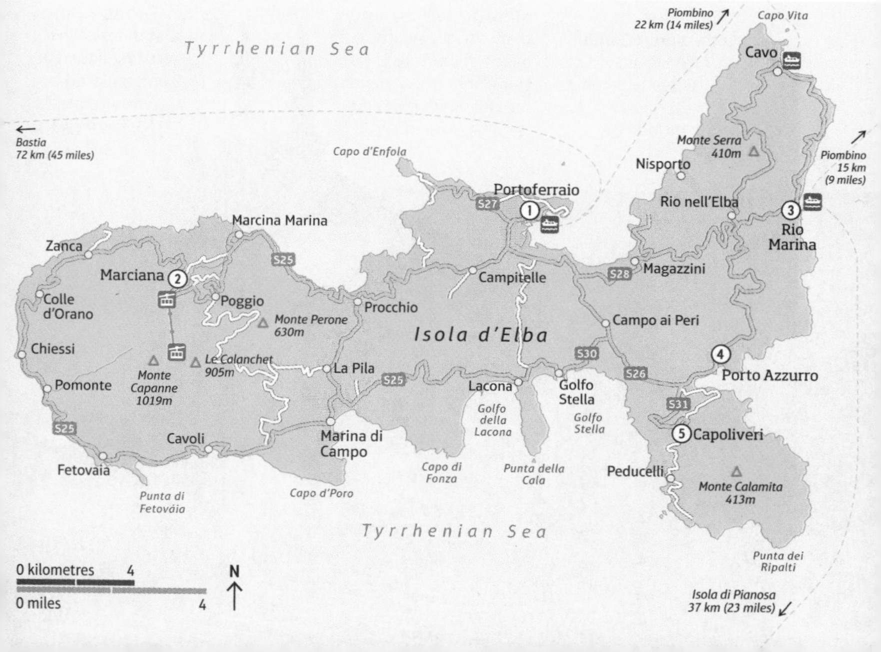

Tyrrhenian Sea
Piombino 22 km (14 miles)
Capo Vita
Cavo
Bastia 72 km (45 miles)
Capo d'Enfola
Monte Serra 410m
Nisporto
Piombino 15 km (9 miles)
Portoferraio
Rio nell'Elba
Rio Marina
Marcina Marina
Zanca
Marciana
Magazzini
Campitelle
Colle d'Orano
Poggio
Procchio
Monte Perone 630m
Campo ai Peri
Isola d'Elba
Chiessi
Le Calanchet 905m
La Pila
Monte Capanne 1019m
Pomonte
Lacona
Golfo Stella
Porto Azzurro
Golfo della Lacona
Golfo Stella
Cavoli
Marina di Campo
Capoliveri
Fetovaia
Capo di Fonza
Punta della Cala
Peducelli
Monte Calamita 413m
Punta di Fetovàia
Capo d'Poro
Tyrrhenian Sea
0 kilometres 4
0 miles 4
N
Punta dei Ripalti
Isola di Pianosa 37 km (23 miles)

EXPERIENCE MORE

Costa degli Etruschi

Q4-5 Livorno Piazza Barontini 26, Cecina visitcostadegli etruschi.com

The stunning stretch of coastline between Livorno and Piombino is known as Costa degli Etruschi due to the many traces of Etruscan settlements, particularly at the vast Parco Archeologico di Baratti e Populonia on the Baratti Gulf, where there are also remains of a Roman acropolis and an 11th-century Benedictine monastery.

This is a largely undeveloped area, rich in glorious vegetation and beautiful beaches with black or pale sand and rocky bays. There is a pleasing range of interesting villages and small towns, both on the coast and dotting the hills just inland. The views of Elba are spectacular from much of the area, including the tiny walled village of Popolonia Alta, where there are sections of fresco attributed to Il Sodoma in the 15th-century Santa Croce church.

Other highlights of the area include the well-preserved medieval villages of Suvereto and Montescudaio and the prestigious resort of Castiglioncello, with reddish cliffs and pretty bays that have inspired both painters and writers. The attractive hill town of Castagneto Carducci and the nearby village of Bolgheri, both built around medieval castles owned by the noble Della Gherardesca family, are famous for their fine wines, and there is a multi-sensory wine museum, **MUSEM**, at the Casone di Ugolino estate with its 15th-century farm.

MUSEM

Via Casone di Ugolino 24, Castagneto Carducci
10am-8pm Tue-Sun
casoneugolino.com

Massa Marittima

R5 Amatur, Via Todini 3-5 (0566 90 27 56)

The hill town of Massa Marittima is a surprising jewel with a prosperous history, thanks to the nearby mines of the Colline Metallifere where metal ores (copper, silver and lead) have been extracted since Etruscan times. The medieval Città Vecchia centres on the unusual, star-shaped Piazza Garibaldi, where the main monuments are located. They include the Romanesque Duomo, dedicated to St Cerbone, a 6th-century saint whose story is told in stone above the door, and the 13th-century Palazzo Podestà, which hosts the **Museo Archeologico**. Built in 1228, the **Torre del Candeliere** was reduced in height and linked to the 14th-century Fortezza Senese at a later date, while a bell was first added in 1413 and replaced by the current one in 1760. The views

↑ The marshy Maremma, where morning mists are a common phenomenon

from the top are magnificent. Other worthwhile sights in the town are the **Museo della Miniera** (Museum of Mining), parts of which are located within a former mine shaft. The Fonte dell'Abbondanza on Via Ximenes is a large three-arched structure where local residents once came for their water. One of the original frescoes has recently been brought to light: *l'Albero della Fecondità*, in which two women pull each other's hair as they fight over the phallic fruit they are picking from a tree.

Museo Archeologico
Palazzo del Podestà, Piazza Garibaldi 0566 90 22 89 Tue-Sun

Torre del Candeliere
Piazza Matteotti
Tue-Sun

Museo della Miniera
Via Corridoni
0566 90 22 89 Tue-Sun

The Duomo in Massa Marittima's Piazza Guiseppe Garibaldi

The Maremma

R6 Livorno/Grosseto
FS

The ancient Etruscans were the first to inhabit the marshes of the Maremma, followed by the Romans, but after the collapse of the Roman Empire the area was virtually uninhabited until the 18th century. Although reclaimed land is now farmed here, the appearance and character of the Maremma is of a vast and largely wild area of natural beauty thanks to the **Parco Naturale della Maremma**, a protected nature reserve that stretches for 25 km (15 miles) along the coast. The Alberese visitor centre is the main entry point for the reserve, which has a good network of foot and cycle paths, as well as a beach, a series of look-out towers and a 12th-century Cistercian abbey.

Grosseto, the main town of the Maremma, has a late 13th-century Duomo with a striking black-and-white façade and well-preserved 16th-century walls. Its Museo Archeologico e d'Arte della Maremma has Etruscan and Roman artifacts, many from the ancient sites of Roselle and Vetulonia, just inland from Castiglione della Pescaia. This historic fishing village is now an attractive seaside resort while the more exclusive Punta Ala is popular with yacht owners and golfers.

Did You Know?

Bandits once roamed the Maremma; the most famous was Domenico Tiburzi, the "Robin Hood of Tuscany".

Parco Naturale della Maremma
Centro Visite Alberese, Via Bersagliere 7/9 8:30am-8pm daily
parco-maremma.it

SUPERTUSCANS

When Tuscany's winemakers started breaking away from the strict regulations governing Chianti and experimenting with different blends, adding grapes such as Cabernet Sauvignon to their Sangiovese, the resulting wines could only be labelled "table wine" despite their indisputable quality. To set them apart from the rest, top-of-the-range wines like Tignanello, Ornellaia and Sassicaia are now referred to as the Supertuscans.

Saturnia

S6 Via Mazzini 4; 0564 60 12 80

Saturnia is famous for its hot springs (37° C/98.6° F), which according to legend are the result of lightning sent by Saturn to calm mankind's warring ways. The waters can be enjoyed for free in a lovely natural context at the rock pools of Cascate del Mulino, which is on the Gorello river just outside Saturnia. It is possible to bathe in the warm sulphur water here at any time, all year round.

The **Terme di Saturnia**, on the other hand, is a resort hotel that provides excellent spa facilities, health treatments and even a golf course.

The ancient centre of Saturnia has several Roman remains, including the Porta Romana gate, while the striking medieval castle (not open to the public) was largely rebuilt in the early 20th century.

Near Saturnia, local administrative centre Manciano has wide-open views to all sides from its hilltop position, a 15th-century tower and the **Museo di Preistoria e Protostoria**, which recounts the history of the area from the Palaeolithic era to the Bronze Age, with multimedia displays to bring the ancient finds to life. The town also has a beautiful church dedicated to St George. Also nearby, the stunning walled medieval town of Montemerano stands on a hill covered in olive trees. The town wall is still largely intact and entry to Montemerano is through three gates. At the centre of the town is the Piazza del Castello, a charming square enclosed by historic stone houses and wild flowers exploding with colour.

Terme di Saturnia
termedisaturnia.it

Museo di Preistoria e Protostoria
Via Corsini 5, Manciano
Jun-Sep: 10:30am-1pm & 4:30-8pm; Oct-May: 10am-1:30pm & 3-6pm Fri-Sun (closed Fri Jan-Mar)

Sovana

S6

Sovana sits on a ridge high above the Lente valley. Its main street is lined with cafés, restaurants and shops. The 13th-century Romanesque Rocca Aldobrandesca fortress (closed to the public), named after the Teutonic family that ruled in the area until 1608, is now in ruins.

The frescoes of the late 15th-century Siena school in the medieval church of **Santa Maria** were discovered under the whitewashed walls. The main altar is sheltered by a 9th-century canopy that was originally in the Romanesque **Duomo**. This 12th-century building incorporates sculpture from earlier churches built on the same site.

The Etruscans dug tombs nearby in the soft limestone cliffs bordering the river Lente. The most complete set of **Necropoli Etrusca** can be found in a valley just to the west of Sovana.

Santa Maria
Piazza del Pretorio
Daily

Duomo
Piazza del Pretorio
Daily in summer; Sat & Sun only in winter

Necropoli Etrusca
Poggio di Sopra Ripa
0564 61 40 74 Feb-Nov: 10am-7pm daily; Dec-Jan: 9am-5pm Sat & Sun

←

Enjoying the thermal waters of Saturnia in natural rock pools

Pitigliano

S6 Piazza Garibaldi 51; 0564 61 71 11

Pitigliano looks spectacular perched on a plateau, high above cliffs carved out by the river Lente. The houses seem to grow out of the cliffs, which are riddled with caves cut out of soft limestone. The caves have been used for centuries to store wine and olive oil.

A maze of tiny medieval streets passes through the Jewish ghetto, formed when Jews fleeing from Catholic persecution in Rome took refuge here in the 17th century, when Pitigliano was a frontier town between the Grand Duchy of Tuscany and the Papal States. The town's offer of protection earned it the nickname "little Jerusalem".

The splendid interior of the sturdy, fortress-like Palazzo Orsini in the town centre, the oldest parts of which date from the 13th century, hosts the **Museo Palazzo Orsini**, which includes a wooden statue carved by Jacopo della Quercia alongside ancient manuscripts, religious paintings and gold and silver items. There is also a small exhibition of work by the artist Francesco Zuccarelli, who was born in Pitigliano in 1702. One of his first commissions, following his apprenticeship in Rome and then Florence, was a pair of chapel altarpieces that can be seen in the medieval **Duomo**, whose huge bell tower supports a bell that weighs 3 tonnes. The **Museo Civico Archeologico** contains a range of finds from ancient local settlements.

INSIDER TIP

Etruscan Footpaths

Bordering Tuscany, Lazio and Umbria, the area known as Tuscia is rich in Etruscan remains. Just outside Pitigliano is the Vie Cave, ancient footpaths carved into the rock face. An afternoon's walk along these pathways is recommended.

Museo Palazzo Orsini

Piazza della Fortezza Orsini 10am-1pm, 3-7pm (to 5pm in winter) Tue-Fri (daily in Aug) palazzo-orsini-pitigliano.it

Duomo

Piazza San Gregorio
Daily

Museo Civico Archeologico

Piazza della Fortezza Orsini 59 0564 61 40 67
Call to check times

Did You Know?

The Palazzo Orsini in Pitigliano has its water supply brought in by an aqueduct built in 1545.

→

A picture-perfect narrow street in the old town of Pitigliano

9

Orbetello

R7 FS 🚌 i Piazza della Repubblica 1; 0564 86 04 47

The town of Orbetello perches on a spit of land jutting into a sheltered lagoon, which at its tip is connected by a causeway to the promontory of Monte Argentario.

Sections of ancient Etruscan wall are still visible flanking the canal that links the two halves of the lagoon. The town walls were built during Spanish rule (15th–16th century), as was the **Polveriera Guzman** (1692), a former arsenal now home to the Museo Archeologico. The façade of the Duomo, built in the 13th century but altered over the centuries, has a splendid rose window. The **Ex-Caserma Umberto I** displays the Frontone di Talamone, a fragmented ancient Etruscan terracotta temple decoration with incredibly fine sculpting.

The WWF-protected **Oasi di Orbetello** nature reserve is a paradise for bird-watchers, thanks to its location on migratory routes, while a windmill, the last of nine built here in the 15th century, adds a scenic touch.

Near Orbetello, the ancient Roman colony of Cosa (founded 173 BC) has some fascinating remains including complex plumbing work, as well as spectacular sea views. The **Museo di Cosa,** containing relics from the ancient settlement, is close by.

Did You Know?

From late winter and early spring, flocks of migrating flamingoes can be seen in the Orbetello lagoon.

The WWF-protected Oasi di Orbetello nature reserve is a paradise for bird-watchers, thanks to its location on migratory routes.

Polveriera Guzman

Viale Mura di Levante 7
Closed for restoration

Ex-Caserma Umberto I

Piazza Repubblica 1
9:30am-1pm (9am-12:30pm Oct-Mar) & 4-8pm (to 7pm Sep-Jun) daily

Oasi di Orbetello

SS Aurelia 148 km, Località Ceriolo III, Albinia Sep-May: 9:30am-3:30pm Sat-Sun (last entry 1:30pm) wwf.it

Museo di Cosa

 Via delle Ginestre 35, Ansedonia 0564 88 14 21
9am-7pm daily

10

Monte Argentario

R7 🚌 i Piazzale Sant'Andrea, Porto Santo Stéfano; 0564 81 42 08
monteargentario.info

Monte Argentario was an island until the early 18th century, when the shallow waters separating it from the mainland began to silt up. Two sandy spits of land, known as *tomboli*, were created, enclosing the Orbetello lagoon. The two harbour towns of Porto Ercole and Porto Santo Stéfano are favoured by wealthy yacht owners. There

WATERSPORTS AND WALKING

Monte Argentario is full of opportunities for sports lovers. The peninsula is crossed by a good network of footpaths with routes suitable for all levels. Watersports are highly popular; there are excellent facilities for yachters and boats of all kinds can be rented. The biggest year-round draw is diving; the numerous dive centres also provide lessons.

are good fish restaurants in both, and from the Strada Panoramica there are views of rocky coves, cliffs and bays.

The many fortifications that dot the landscape date mostly from the 16th century; one of the most spectacular is the star-shaped **Forte Stella**, near Porto Ercole. A boat trip is a great way to see the peninsula and there are plenty on offer.

Forte Stella

Daily; Apr–Jun, Sep: 10:30am–12:30pm & 4–6pm (6–8pm Sep); Jul–Aug: 5–9pm

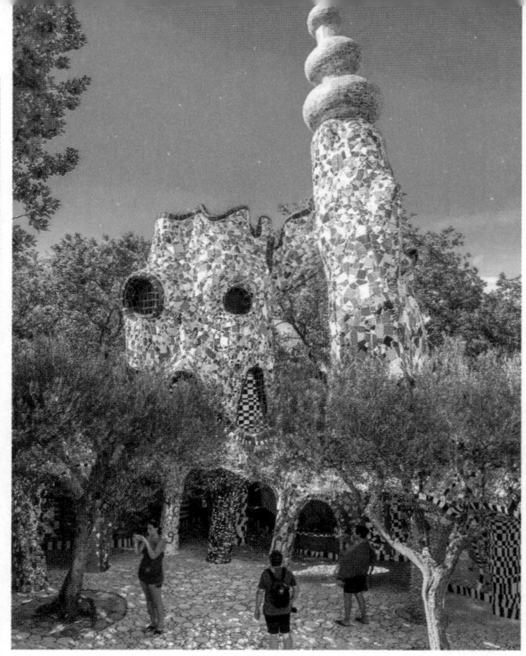

↑ The weird and wonderful sculptures of the Giardino dei Tarocchi, Capalbio

11

Capalbio

S7

Like Porto Ercole, Capalbio is popular with wealthy Italians and its beaches and restaurants are busy in summer. Behind them rises a charming medieval hilltop village dominated by a 12th-century castle with stunning views over the coastline and countryside from the well-preserved surrounding walls. The church of San Nicola has some charming 14th–15th century frescoes.

At Pescia Fiorentina, southeast of Capalbio, is a modern sculpture garden created by the late French artist Niki de Saint-Phalle between 1978 and 2002. The **Giardino dei Tarocchi** was inspired by the figures of the Tarot; the bigger pieces each represent one card from the Tarot pack. Among the sculptures is *The Tower*, a glittering three-storey edifice made out of broken mirrors. The garden can be visited by group tour only.

Giardino dei Tarocchi

Garavicchio, Pescia Fiorentina

giardinodeitarocchi.it

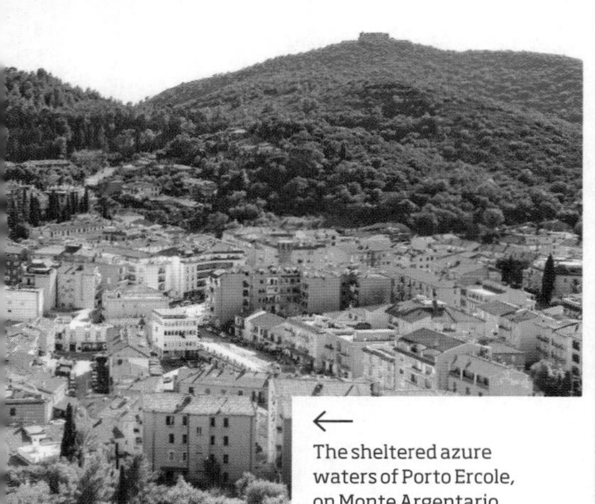

← The sheltered azure waters of Porto Ercole, on Monte Argentario

NEED TO KNOW

A classic cypress-lined road in Val d'Orcia

BEFORE YOU GO

Forward planning is essential to any successful trip. Be prepared for all eventualities by considering the following points before you travel.

ELECTRICITY SUPPLY

Power sockets are type F and L, fitting two- and three-pronged plugs. Standard voltage is 220–230v.

Passports and Visas

EU nationals and citizens of the UK, US, Canada, Australia and New Zealand do not need visas for stays of up to three months. Consult your nearest Italian embassy or check the Polizia di Stato website if you are travelling from outside these areas.

Polizia di Stato
W poliziadistato.it

Travel Safety Advice

Visitors can get up-to-date travel safety information from the **UK Foreign and Commonwealth Office**, the **US State Department** and the **Australian Department of Foreign Affairs and Trade**.

Australia
W smartraveller.gov.au
UK
W gov.uk/foreign-travel-advice
US
W travel.state.gov

Customs Information

An individual is permitted to carry the following within the EU for personal use:

Tobacco products 800 cigarettes, 400 cigarillos, 200 cigars or 1 kg of smoking tobacco.
Alcohol 10 litres of alcoholic beverages above 22 per cent strength, 20 litres of alcoholic beverages below 22 per cent strength, 90 litres of wine (60 litres of which can be sparkling wine) and 110 litres of beer.
Cash If you plan to enter or leave the EU with €10,000 or more in cash (or the equivalent in other currencies) you must declare it to the customs authorities.

If travelling from outside the EU, limits vary, so check restrictions before departing.

Insurance

It is wise to take out an insurance policy covering theft, loss of belongings, medical problems, cancellation and delays.

EU citizens are eligible for free emergency medical care in Italy provided they have a valid **EHIC** (European Health Insurance Card); the same applies to Australian citizens with a Medicare card. Visitors from outside the EU must arrange their own private medical insurance.

EHIC
W gov.uk/european-health-insurance-card

Vaccinations

No vaccinations are needed for Italy, but mosquito repellent is useful in summer.

Money

Major credit and debit cards are accepted widely and contactless payments are becoming increasingly common. Minimum amounts are often required for card transactions however, so carry cash for smaller payments. ATMs *(bancomat)* are available outside most banks, which are plentiful in the larger towns and cities though less so in smaller villages.

Booking Accommodation

Florence and Tuscany offer a huge variety of accommodation. During peak season lodgings fill up and prices become inflated, so book in advance.

All accommodation providers are obliged to add a tourist tax to rates. This varies from €1 to €5 per night, for a maximum of 7 nights; under 12s are exempt. Always check if the tourist tax is included in quoted rates.

Under Italian law, hotels are required to register guests at police headquarters and issue a receipt of payment *(ricevuta fiscale)*.

Travellers with Specific Needs

Many of Tuscany's old town centres have cobbled streets, steep slopes, steps or narrow pavements, presenting difficulties for visitors with reduced mobility. Historic buildings often lack lifts or ramps, but larger hotels, restaurants and bars are obliged to have accessible, well-equipped bedrooms and bathrooms.

Both Florence and Pisa airports *(p238)* provide special assistance, which should be reserved at least 48 hours in advance.

RFI provides assistance at railway stations; details are available on their website and at the Sala Blu point at Florence's Santa Maria Novella station.

Travelability organizes personalized holidays with special assistance for travellers with disabilities throughout Tuscany.

RFI
W rfi.it
Travelability
W travel-ability.com

Language

At least a modest level of English is spoken widely in Florence and in most of Tuscany.

Closures

Lunchtime Churches and smaller shops shut for two or three hours, around 12:30–3:30pm.
Monday Many museums close all day.
Sunday Churches and cathedrals do not allow tourists to visit during Mass but those wishing to participate are of course welcome. Public transport runs a reduced service and most shops have reduced opening hours.
Public holidays Shops either close early or for the whole day; museums and public transport adopt Sunday hours.
Restaurants Many restaurants and bars close for one day during the week (usually Monday, Tuesday or Wednesday).

PUBLIC HOLIDAYS

1 Jan	New Year's Day
6 Jan	Epiphany
Mar/Apr	Easter Sunday
Mar/Apr	Easter Monday
25 Apr	Liberation Day
1 May	Labour Day
2 Jun	Republic Day
15 Aug	Ferragosto
1 Nov	All Saints' Day
8 Dec	Immaculate Conception
25 Dec	Christmas Day
26 Dec	St Stephen's Day

GETTING AROUND

Whether you are visiting for a short city break or rural country retreat, discover how best to reach your destination and travel like a local.

AT A GLANCE

PUBLIC TRANSPORT COSTS

MAIN CITIES

€1.50

70 mins transfers incl bus and tram

OTHER TOWNS

€1.20

70 mins transfers incl bus and tram

TICKET ON BOARD

€2.50

70 mins transfers incl bus and tram

TOP TIP

Avoid on-the-spot fines - be sure to stamp your ticket to validate your journey.

SPEED LIMIT

MOTORWAY

130 **km/h** (80mph)

DUAL CARRIAGEWAYS

110 **km/h** (70mph)

SECONDARY ROAD

90 **km/h** (50mph)

URBAN AREAS

50 **km/h** (30mph)

Arriving by Air

International and domestic flights arrive at Pisa and Florence. Pisa's Galileo Galilei airport is the biggest international airport in Tuscany and has multiple connections to the UK and to most European countries. Galileo Galilei is located just 1 km (half a mile) from the centre of Pisa; the **PisaMover** transit service (operated by Trenitalia) takes only 5 or 6 minutes from the airport to Pisa Centrale station, from where it is about an hour by train to Florence, 30 minutes to Lucca or 2 hours to Siena.

Florence's Amerigo Vespucci airport is smaller and offers direct flights only to major European capitals and business cities. It is situated about 4 km (2 miles) from the city centre. Transfers are operated by **Volainbus**, a 20-minute shuttle that connects every half hour to Autostazione, Florence's main bus station.

PisaMover
W pisa-mover.com
Volainbus
W ataf.net

Train Travel

International Train Travel

Regular trains connect Italy to the main towns and cities in France, Switzerland, Austria and Eastern Europe, and journeys should be reserved in advance. You can buy tickets and passes for multiple international journeys via **Eurail** or **Interrail**; however, you may still need to pay an additional reservation fee depending on which rail service you travel with. Always check that your pass is valid before boarding.

Eurail
W eurail.com
Interrail
W interrail.eu

Regional Trains

Trenitalia is the main operator in Italy; tickets can be bought online and e-tickets are accepted. Tickets for journeys on standard trains (Regionale) within Tuscany can also be bought at tobacconists and lottery outlets.

GETTING TO AND FROM THE AIRPORT

Airport	Transport	Price	Journey time
Pisa	People Mover shuttle (PisaMover)	€2.70 (€5.40 return)	5 mins
	Taxi	€9	10 mins
Florence	Bus (Volainbus)	€6 (€10 return)	20 mins
	Taxi	€22	20 mins

RAIL JOURNEY PLANNER

Showing Tuscany's key train routes, this map is a handy reference for rail travel in the region. Journey times are listed below.

Florence to Arezzo	50-100 mins
Florence to Lucca	80-100 mins
Florence to Pisa	65-85 mins
Florence to Siena	90-110 mins
Siena to Grosseto	80-90 mins

High-speed rail services (*alta velocità* or AV) are provided from Florence and Pisa to cities outside the region by **Trenitalia**; private company **Italo Treno** also offers high-speed services from Florence only. High-speed trains need reservations with allocated seating. For the cheapest prices, book between 90 and 120 days in advance. Note that of Florence's ten railway stations, Santa Maria Novella is its central hub.

Train tickets must be validated before boarding by stamping them in machines at the entrance to platforms. Fines are applied if you are found with an unvalidated ticket; if for any reason you are unable to validate a ticket before boarding go immediately to the ticket inspector.

Trenitalia
W trenitalia.com
Italo Treno
W italotreno.it

Public Transport

Most Tuscan towns and cities provide efficient local bus services (plus trams in Florence), but the more rural areas are often poorly served, especially on Sundays and public holidays when there is a reduced timetable.

Buses and Trams

Tickets should be bought in advance and are available from dedicated kiosks, newsagents and tobacconists as well as some bars; ten-journey tickets can be bought at a reduced rate (€14/€11). All tickets must be validated at the time of boarding; validation machines can be found inside the bus or tram. Tickets are also available on board from the driver but cost more (€2.50).

Ticket prices have been standardized within Tuscany since July 2018, with one rate for the ten provincial capitals (€1.50) and another for elsewhere (€1.20); local transport tickets for one town are not valid in another.

Long-Distance Bus Travel

Long-distance buses are the best way to reach many destinations within Tuscany, particularly the more hilly or mountainous areas of the region not served by railways or where stations are at a distance from the historic centre.

Autolinee Toscane connects Mugello and northeastern Tuscany with Florence and Arezzo, while the north and much of the west (including Elba) is served by **CTT Nord**; **Tiemme** operates throughout the southern half of the region.

Long-distance services within Italy, including numerous Tuscan destinations, are provided by **Autolinee Baltour**. **Flixbus** runs a low-cost bus service to Italian and European destinations.

Autolinee Toscane
W autolineetoscane.it
CTT Nord
W cttnord.it
Tiemme
W tiemmespa.it
Autolinee Baltour
W baltour.it
Flixbus
W flixbus.it

Guided Bus Tours

City Sightseeing runs hop-on hop-off tours of Florence and Livorno with audioguides in a variety of languages.

City Sightseeing
W city-sightseeing.it

Taxis

Official registered taxis in Italy are white and can be found in strategic locations around all Tuscan cities; it is illegal for taxis to stop in the street if hailed. Unofficial taxis should be avoided, as should drivers who come into stations or airports offering their services; official taxi drivers do not do this.

Tariffs are displayed inside taxis and a meter should be visible and running during the entire journey, except for fixed-tariff journeys, such as from Florence or Pisa airport to the city centre. Supplements are added for luggage and journeys at night. If you are planning a long journey by taxi it's a good idea to ask for an estimate before leaving. There is a long list of estimated fees for out-of-town destinations from Pisa on the **Cotapi** official taxi website.

Many taxis do not accept credit card payments so if you wish to pay by card, specify this when calling or ask if the service is available before leaving. Those in groups of more than three people or those with disabilities or transporting lots of luggage should specify this information when booking, to ensure that a suitable vehicle is sent.

Taxis in Italy aren't particularly cheap but the obvious benefits of door-to-door travel and free access to limited traffic zones makes them a useful option.

Cotapi, Pisa
W cotapi.it

Driving

A road trip through Tuscany is the best way to see the more remote and rural parts of the region and gives you the freedom to choose when and where to go without having to rely on public transport routes and timings. However, it can also be a hair-raising experience at times. Italians have a reputation for driving erratically, so make sure you are familiar with the rules of the road *(see right)*.

Driving to Florence and Tuscany

Florence and Tuscany are easily reached from other European countries via the International European Road Network that connects major roads across national borders within Europe. Once in Italy, the A1 motorway *(autostrada)* runs from north to south from Milan to Naples, passing through Florence and Tuscany, while the A12, intended to link Genoa to Rome along Italy's west coast, currently ends just south of Livorno before reappearing in Lazio for the last section to Rome. The A11 links Florence to Pisa via Prato, Pistoia and Lucca.

Tolls are payable on motorways in Tuscany and in most of Italy; drivers must take a ticket from an automatic machine on entering the motorway and this is used to calculate the toll automatically at the exit. To avoid queuing to leave the motorway, pay by credit card and choose one of the lanes designated for card payments or invest in a prepaid Viacard, available at one of the Punto Blu offices near many motorway exits. Avoid the dedicated Telepass lanes, which are for Telepass account holders with the relevant electronic reader.

If you wish to avoid toll roads, there is almost always an alternative route signposted. Note that in Italy road signs for motorways are green, whereas toll-free main roads have blue signs. The **ACI** (Autombile Club d'Italia) website has a section in English with useful information for visiting motorists.

ACI
W aci.it

Car Rental

To rent a car in Italy you must be over 18 and have a valid EU driving licence or International Driving Permit. Most rental companies require you to have held a licence for at least one year, some have a minimum age of 21 and most apply young driver surcharges for under 25s. You also need to have a credit card as guarantee for the rental.

Driving in Florence and Tuscany

Many of the region's cities, towns and villages have well-preserved historic centres that are only accessible to residents' vehicles; other cars entering the limited traffic zone (*zona a traffico limitato*, or ZTL) are subject to fines. If you're staying at a hotel in the centre, ask in advance about access; this is usually possible, at least for depositing and collecting bags, but you will need to advise staff of your registration number to avoid incurring fines.

It's a good idea to park outside the centre and explore on foot, even where there isn't a limited traffic zone, as the narrow and often steep streets of many places can be challenging to drive through.

Parking spaces marked with blue lines are subject to payment and there should be a meter nearby; yellow lines signal restrictions such as parking for residents or the disabled only, or for loading and unloading (a sign will detail the specifics), while white lines indicate free parking.

Rules of the Road

Drive on the right, use the left lane only for passing, and give way to traffic from the right. Seat belts are required for all passengers in the front and back, and heavy fines are levied for using a mobile phone while driving.

During the day dipped headlights are compulsory when driving on motorways, dual carriageways and on all out-of-town roads. A red warning triangle and fluorescent vest must be carried at all times, for use in the event of an emergency. Between mid-November and mid-April it is obligatory to carry winter tyres or snow-chains on all vehicles except motorcycles.

If you have an accident or breakdown, switch on your hazard warning lights and place a warning triangle 50 m (55 yd) behind your vehicle. In the event of a breakdown, call the ACI freephone emergency line (803-116 from an Italian phone; 800-116800 from a non-Italian mobile phone) or the emergency services (112 or 113).

The legal drink-drive limit is strictly enforced *(p242)*. If you are drinking alcohol, use public transport or take a taxi.

Hitchhiking

Hitchhiking *(autostop)* is illegal on motorways, and is not commonplace in large cities such as Florence. In more rural areas it is an uncommon but not unheard of transport method for travellers on a budget. Always consider your own safety before entering an unknown vehicle.

Cycle and Scooter Hire

Tuscany has more *strade bianche* – gravel-surfaced "white roads" – than any other Italian region, and they are perfect for exploring the countryside by bike. **Florence by Bike** and numerous other agencies rent out city bikes, race bikes, mountain bikes and e-bikes, and most hotels can organize this, sometimes with special rates. Bike-sharing schemes also operate in most of Tuscany's major cities. The **Piste Ciclabili** website has an interactive map of cycle paths throughout Italy.

Scooters are another great way to see more of the countryside and they can be hired at numerous places around the region, especially in the Chianti area and in Florence. An ordinary driving licence is sufficient for vehicles up to 125cc in Italy; helmets are obligatory.

Florence by Bike
W florencebybike.it
Piste Ciclabili
W piste-ciclabili.com

Ferries

Toremar is the main ferry company for Elba and the islands of the archipelago, operating from the ports of Livorno (to Gorgona and Capraia), Piombino (to Portoferraio, Cavo and Rio Marina on Elba and to Pianosa) and Porto Santo Stefano (to Capraia and Giannutri). Hydrofoil services are also available for Cavo and Portoferraio on Elba. Advance booking is advisable, particularly in summer and when travelling with a vehicle. Get to the port an hour early if taking a car.

Toremar
W toremar.it

PRACTICAL INFORMATION

A little local know-how goes a long way in Florence and Tuscany. Here you can find all the essential advice and information you will need during your stay.

AT A GLANCE

EMERGENCY NUMBERS

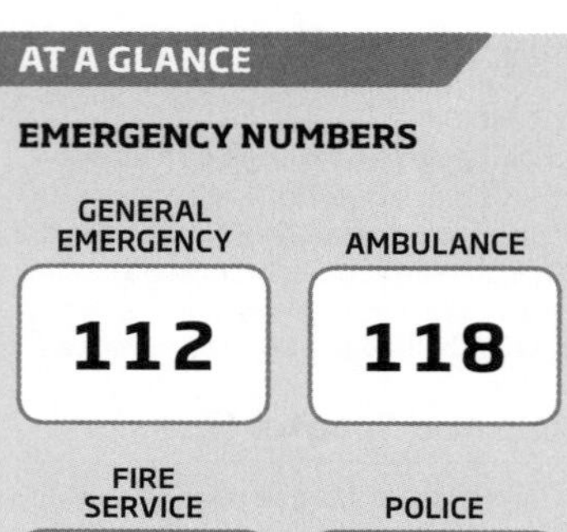

TIME ZONE

CET/CEST: Central European Summer Time (CEST) runs from the last Sun in Mar to the last Sun in Oct

TAP WATER

Unless otherwise stated, tap water in Florence and Tuscany is safe to drink.

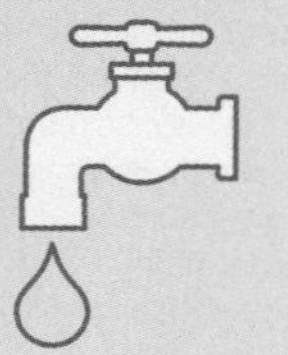

TIPPING

Waiter	Not expected
Hotel Porter	€1 a bag
Housekeeping	€1 a day
Concierge	€1-2
Taxi Driver	Not expected

Personal Security

Though rare, pickpocketing and bag-snatching can happen, especially around busy tourist sights and on crowded buses. Take the usual precautions to keep valuables and other belongings safe and beware of leaving items unattended, especially on beaches.

If you have anything stolen, report the crime within 24 hours at the nearest police station (Polizia or Carabinieri), taking ID with you. Make sure that you get a copy of the crime report *(denuncia)* if you need to make an insurance claim.

Contact your embassy if you have your passport stolen, or in the event of a serious crime or accident.

Health

Seek medicinal supplies and advice for minor ailments at pharmacies *(farmacia)*. You can find details of the nearest 24-hour service on all pharmacy doors.

Emergency medical care in Italy is free for all EU and Australian citizens. If you have an EHIC card *(p237)* or Australian Medicare card, be sure to present this as soon as possible. You may have to pay for treatment and reclaim the money later.

For visitors coming from outside the EU and Australia, payment of hospital and other medical expenses is the patient's responsibility. It is therefore important to arrange comprehensive medical insurance before travelling.

Smoking, Alcohol and Drugs

Smoking is banned in enclosed public places. Possession of narcotics is prohibited and could result in a prison sentence.

Italy has a strict limit of 0.5mg BAC (blood alcohol content) for drivers. This means that you cannot drink more than one small beer or a small glass of wine if you plan to drive. For drivers with less than three years' driving experience the limit is 0.

ID

By law you must carry identification with you at all times in Italy. A photocopy of your passport photo page (and visa if applicable) should suffice. If you are stopped by the police you may be asked to present the original document within 12 hours.

Local Customs

You can be fined for dropping litter and sitting on steps outside certain monuments and it is an offence to climb into public fountains.

Illegal street traders operate in many of Tuscany's city centres; avoid making any purchases from them as you could be fined by the local police.

It is also illegal to take sand, shells and stones from beaches (except during authorized trips, such as the mineral-hunting experiences organized on Elba).

Visiting Churches and Cathedrals

Entrance to many churches is free, although there are admission fees for the more famous monuments and in others you may be charged a small fee to see a certain area, such as a chapel, cloister or underground ruins.

Strict dress codes apply: cover your torso and upper arms, and ensure shorts and skirts cover your knees.

Mobile Phones and Wi-Fi

Wi-Fi is generally widely available, and cafés, bars, restaurants and some cultural venues will usually allow you to use their Wi-Fi on the condition that you make a purchase. Some city centres have free Wi-Fi hotspots; ask at tourist offices or hotels for information or install the WiFi°Italia°It app *(see right)*.

Visitors travelling to Italy with EU tariffs can now use their devices abroad without being subject to the high roaming charges of the past. Users will be charged the same rates for data, voice calls and SMS services as they would pay at home. Note that usage within the EU may or may not be included in your contract, so be sure to check before you depart.

Post

Stamps *(francobolli)* are sold at tobacconists (*tabacchi* – look for a blue sign with a white T). Although the Italian state post can be slow, the private postal services with yellow letterboxes at souvenir stalls and shops in popular tourist destinations cost more and usually take longer.

Taxes and Refunds

VAT (IVA) is usually 22%. Under certain conditions, non-EU citizens can claim a refund. Either claim the rebate before you buy (show your passport to the shop assistant and complete a form), or claim it later by presenting a customs officer with your receipts as you leave. Stamped receipts will be sent back to the vendor to issue a refund. Information is available from international tax-free shopping organisations such as **Global Blue**.

Global Blue
W globalblue.com

Discount Cards

In Florence, the Firenzecard provides entry to many museums and sites and is valid for 72 hours from its first use. The Firenzecard+ also covers public transport and can be used for discounts at affiliated restaurants and shops.

In other cities cumulative tickets are sometimes available for a selection of sights.

Firenzecard
W firenzecard.it

WEBSITES AND APPS

ENIT
Check out Italy's national tourist board website at www.italia.it

Visit Tuscany
The official tourism website for Tuscany, at www.visittuscany.com

The Tuscany Region Travel Planner
muoversintoscana.regione.toscana.it/navigator.aspx

WiFi°Italia°It
Connect to free Wi-Fi hotspots throughoutTuscany and Italy

INDEX

Page numbers in **bold** refer to main entries.

D

E

F

G

H

PHRASE BOOK

IN EMERGENCY

Help!	**Aiuto!**	*eye-**yoo**-toh*
Stop!	**Ferma!**	*fair-**mah***
Call a doctor	**Chiama un medico**	*kee-**ah**-mah oon **meh**-dee-koh*
Call an ambulance	**Chiama un' ambulanza**	*kee-**ah**-mah oon am-boo-**lan**-tsa*
Call the police	**Chiama la polizia**	*kee-**ah**-mah lah pol-ee-**tsee**-ah*
Call the fire brigade	**Chiama i pompieri**	*kee-**ah**-mah ee pom-pee-**air**-ee*
Where is the telephone?	**Dov'è il telefono?**	*dov-**eh**eel teh-**leh**-foh-noh?*
The nearest hospital?	**L'ospedale più vicino?**	*loss-peh-**dah**-leh pee-oovee-**chee**-noh?*

COMMUNICATION ESSENTIALS

Yes/No	**Si/No**	***see/noh***
Please	**Per favore**	*pair fah-**vor**-eh*
Thank you	**Grazie**	***grah**-tsee-eh*
Excuse me	**Mi scusi**	*mee **skoo**-zee*
Hello	**Buon giorno**	*bwon **jor**-noh*
Goodbye	**Arrivederci**	*ah-ree-veh-**dair**-chee*
Good evening	**Buona sera**	***bwon**-ah **sair**-ah*
morning	**la mattina**	*lah mah-**tee**-nah*
afternoon	**il pomeriggio**	*eel poh-meh-**ree**-joh*
evening	**la sera**	*lah **sair**-ah*
yesterday	**ieri**	*ee-**air**-ee*
today	**oggi**	***oh**-jee*
tomorrow	**domani**	*doh-**mah**-nee*
here	**qui**	***kwee***
there	**la**	***lah***
What?	**Quale?**	***kwah**-leh?*
When?	**Quando?**	***kwan**-doh?*
Why?	**Perchè?**	*pair-**keh**?*
Where?	**Dove?**	***doh**-veh*

USEFUL PHRASES

How are you?	**Come sta?**	***koh**-meh stah?*
Very well, thank you.	**Molto bene, grazie.**	***moll**-toh **beh**-neh **grah**-tsee-eh*
Pleased to meet you.	**Piacere di conoscerla.**	*pee-ah-**chair**-eh dee coh-**noh**-shair-lah*
See you soon.	**A più tardi.**	*ah pee-**oo tar**-dee*
That's fine.	**Va bene.**	*va **beh**-neh*
Where is/are ...?	**Dov'è/Dove sono...?**	*dov-**eh**/doveh **soh**noh?*
How long does it take to get to ...?	**Quanto tempo ci vuole per andare a ...?**	***kwan**-toh **tem**-poh chee voo-**oh**-leh pair an-**dar**-eh ah...?*
How do I get to ...?	**Come faccio per arrivare a ...?**	*koh-meh **fah**-choh pair arri-**var**-eh ah...?*
Do you speak English?	**Parla inglese?**	***par**-lah een-**gleh**-zeh?*
I don't understand.	**Non capisco.**	*non ka-**pee**-skoh*
Could you speak more slowly, please?	**Può parlare più lentamente, per favore?**	*pwoh par-**lah**-reh pee-**oo** len-ta-**men**-teh pair fah-**vor**-eh?*
I'm sorry.	**Mi dispiace.**	*mee dee-spee-**ah**-cheh*

USEFUL WORDS

big	**grande**	***gran**-deh*
small	**piccolo**	***pee**-koh-loh*
hot	**caldo**	***kal**-doh*
cold	**freddo**	***fred**-doh*
good	**buono**	***bwoh**-noh*
bad	**cattivo**	*kat-**tee**-voh*
enough	**basta**	***bas**-tah*
well	**bene**	***beh**-neh*
open	**aperto**	*ah-**pair**-toh*
closed	**chiuso**	*kee-**oo**-zoh*
left	**a sinistra**	*ah see-**nee**-strah*
right	**a destra**	*ah **dess**-trah*
straight on	**sempre dritto**	***sem**-preh **dree**-toh*
near	**vicino**	*vee-**chee**-noh*
far	**lontano**	*lon-**tah**-noh*
up	**su**	***soo***
down	**giù**	***joo***
early	**presto**	***press**-toh*
late	**tardi**	***tar**-dee*
entrance	**entrata**	*en-**trah**-tah*
exit	**uscita**	*oo-**shee**-ta*
toilet	**il gabinetto**	*eel gah-bee-**net**-toh*
free, unoccupied	**libero**	***lee**-bair-oh*
free, no charge	**gratuito**	*grah-**too**-ee-toh*

MAKING A TELEPHONE CALL

I'd like to place a long-distance call.	**Vorrei fare una interurbana.**	*vor-**ray far**-eh oona in-tair-oor-**bah**-nah.*
I'd like to make a reverse-charge call.	**Vorrei fare una telefonata a carico del destinatario.**	*vor-**ray far**-eh oona teh-leh-fon-**ah**-tah ah **kar**-ee-koh dell dess- tee-nah-**tar**-ree-oh.*
I'll try again later.	**Ritelefono più tardi.**	*ree-teh-**leh**-foh-noh pee-oo **tar**-dee.*
Can I leave a message?	**Posso lasciare un messaggio?**	***poss**-oh lash-**ah**-reh oon mess-**sah**-joh?*
Hold on	**Un attimo, per favore**	*oon **ah**-tee-moh, pair fah-**vor**-eh*
Could you speak up a little please?	**Può parlare più forte, per favore?**	*pwoh par-**lah**-reh pee-**oo for**-teh, pair fah-**vor**-eh?*
local call	**la telefonata locale**	*lah teh-leh-fon-**ah**-ta loh-**kah**-leh*

SHOPPING

How much does this cost?	**Quant'è, per favore?**	*kwan-**teh**, pair fah-**vor**-eh?*
I would like ...	**Vorrei ...**	*vor-**ray**...*
Do you have ...?	**Avete ...?**	*ah-**veh**-teh...?*
I'm just looking.	**Sto soltanto guardando.**	*stoh sol-**tan**-toh gwar-**dan**-doh*
Do you take credit cards?	**Accettate carte di credito?**	*ah-chet-**tah**-teh **kar**-teh dee **creh**-dee-toh?*
What time do you open/close?	**A che ora apre/ chiude?**	*ah keh **or**-ah **ah**-preh/kee-**oo**-deh?*
this one	**questo**	***kweh**-stoh*
that one	**quello**	***kwell**-oh*
expensive	**caro**	***kar**-oh*
cheap	**a buon prezzo**	*ah bwon **pret**-soh*
size, clothes	**la taglia**	*lah **tah**-lee-ah*
size, shoes	**il numero**	*eel **noo**-mair-oh*
white	**bianco**	*bee-**ang**-koh*
black	**nero**	***neh**-roh*
red	**rosso**	***ross**-oh*
yellow	**giallo**	***jal**-loh*
green	**verde**	***vair**-deh*
blue	**blu**	*bloo*
brown	**marrone**	*mar-**roh**-neh*

TYPES OF SHOP

antique dealer	**l'antiquario**	*lan-tee-**kwah**-ree-oh*
bakery	**la panetteria**	*lah pah-net-tair-**ree**-ah*
bank	**la banca**	*lah **bang**-kah*
bookshop	**la libreria**	*lah lee-breh-**ree**-ah*
butcher's	**la macelleria**	*lah mah-chell-eh-**ree**-ah*
cake shop	**la pasticceria**	*lah pas-tee-chair-**ee**-ah*
chemist's	**la farmacia**	*lah far-mah-**chee**-ah*
department store	**il grande magazzino**	*eel **gran**-deh mag-gad-**zee**-noh*
delicatessen	**la salumeria**	*lah sah-loo-meh-**ree**-ah*
fishmonger's	**la pescheria**	*lah pess-keh-**ree**-ah*
florist	**il fioraio**	*eel fee-or-**eye**-oh*
greengrocer	**il fruttivendolo**	*eel froo-tee-**ven**-doh-loh*
grocery	**alimentari**	*ah-lee-men-**tah**-ree*
hairdresser	**il parrucchiere**	*eel par-oo-kee-**air**-eh*
ice cream parlour	**la gelateria**	*lah jel-lah-tair-**ree**-ah*
market	**il mercato**	*eel mair-**kah**-toh*
news-stand	**l'edicola**	*leh-**dee**-koh-lah*
post office	**l'ufficio postale**	*loo-**fee**-choh pos-**tah**-leh*
shoe shop	**il negozio di scarpe**	*eel neh-**goh**-tsioh dee **skar**-peh*
supermarket	**il supermercato**	*eel su-pair-mair-**kah**-toh*
tobacconist	**il tabaccaio**	*eel tah-bak-**eye**-oh*
travel agency	**l'agenzia di viaggi**	*lah-jen-**tsee**-ah dee vee-**ad**-jee*

SIGHTSEEING

art gallery	**la pinacoteca**	*lah peena-koh-**teh**-kah*
bus stop	**la fermata dell'autobus**	*lah fair-**mah**-tah dell **ow**-toh-booss*
church	**la chiesa**	*lah kee-**eh**-zah*
	la basilica	*lah bah-**seel**-i-kah*
garden	**il giardino**	*eel jar-**dee**-no*
library	**la biblioteca**	*lah beeb-lee-oh-**teh**-kah*
museum	**il museo**	*eel moo-**zeh**-oh*
railway station	**la stazione**	*lah stah-tsee-**oh**-neh*

tourist information	**l'ufficio turistico**	*loo-**fee**-choh too-**ree**-stee-koh*
closed for the public holiday	**chiuso per la festa**	*kee-**oo**-zoh pair lah **fess**-tah*

STAYING IN A HOTEL

Do you have any vacant rooms?	**Avete camere libere?**	*ah-**veh**-teh **kah**-mair-eh **lee**-bair-eh?*
double room	**una camera doppia**	*oona **kah**-mair-ah **doh**-pee-ah*
with double bed	**con letto matrimoniale**	*kon **let**-toh mah-tree-moh-nee-**ah**-leh*
twin room	**una camera con due letti**	*oona **kah**-mair-ah kon **doo**-eh **let**-tee*
single room	**una camera singola**	*oona **kah**-mair-ah **sing**-goh-lah*
room with a bath, shower	**una camera con bagno, con doccia**	*oona **kah**-mair-ah kon **ban**-yoh, kon **dot**-chah*
porter	**il facchino**	*eel fah-**kee**-noh*
key	**la chiave**	*lah kee-**ah**-veh*
I have a reservation.	**Ho fatto una prenotazione.**	*oh **fat**-toh oona preh-noh-tah-tsee-**oh**-neh*

EATING OUT

Have you got a table for ...?	**Avete un tavolo per ...?**	*ah-**veh**-teh oon **tah**-voh-loh pair ...?*
I'd like to reserve a table.	**Vorrei riservare un tavolo.**	*vor-**ray** ree-sair-**vah**-reh oon **tah**-voh-loh*
breakfast	**colazione**	*koh-lah-tsee-**oh**-neh*
lunch	**pranzo**	***pran**-tsoh*
dinner	**cena**	***cheh**-nah*
The bill, please.	**Il conto, per favore.**	*eel **kon**-toh pair fah-**vor**-eh*
I am a vegetarian.	**Sono vegetariano/a.**	***soh**-noh **veh**-jeh-tar-ee-**ah**-noh/nah*
waitress	**cameriera**	*kah-mair-ee-**air**-ah*
waiter	**cameriere**	*kah-mair-ee-**air**-eh*
fixed price menu	**il menù a prezzo fisso**	*eel meh-**noo** ah **pret**-soh **fee**-soh*
dish of the day	**piatto del giorno**	*pee-**ah**-toh dell **jor**-no*
starter	**antipasto**	*an-tee-**pass**-toh*
first course	**il primo**	*eel **pree**-moh*
main course	**il secondo**	*eel seh-**kon**-doh*
vegetables	**il contorno**	*eel kon-**tor**-noh*
dessert	**il dolce**	*eel **doll**-che*
cover charge	**il coperto**	*eel koh-**pair**-toh*
wine list	**la lista dei vini**	*lah **lee**-stah day **vee**-nee*
rare	**al sangue**	*al **sang**-gweh*
medium	**a puntino**	*a poon-**tee**-noh*
well done	**ben cotto**	*ben **kot**-toh*
glass	**il bicchiere**	*eel bee-kee-**air**-eh*
bottle	**la bottiglia**	*lah bot-**teel**-yah*
knife	**il coltello**	*eel kol-**tell**-oh*
fork	**la forchetta**	*lah for-**ket**-tah*
spoon	**il cucchiaio**	*eel koo-kee-**eye**-oh*

MENU DECODER

apple	**la mela**	*lah **meh**-lah*
artichoke	**il carciofo**	*eel kar-**choff**-oh*
aubergine	**la melanzana**	*lah meh-lan-**tsah**-nah*
baked	**al forno**	*al **for**-noh*
beans	**i fagioli**	*ee fah-**joh**-lee*
beef	**il manzo**	*eel **man**-tsoh*
beer	**la birra**	*lah **beer**-rah*
boiled	**lesso**	***less**-oh*
bread	**il pane**	*eel **pah**-neh*
broth	**il brodo**	*eel **broh**-doh*
butter	**il burro**	*eel **boor**-oh*
cake	**la torta**	*lah **tor**-tah*
cheese	**il formaggio**	*eel for-**mad**-joh*
chicken	**il pollo**	*eel **poll**-oh*
chips	**patatine fritte**	*pah-tah-**teen**-eh **free**-teh*
baby clams	**le vongole**	*leh **von**-goh-leh*
coffee	**il caffè**	*eel kah-**feh***
courgettes	**gli zucchini**	*lyee dzoo-**kee**-nee*
dry	**secco**	***sek**-koh*
duck	**l'anatra**	***lah**-nah-trah*
egg	**l'uovo**	*loo-**oh**-voh*
fish	**il pesce**	*eel **pesh**-eh*
fresh fruit	**frutta fresca**	***froo**-tah **fress**-kah*
garlic	**l'aglio**	***lahl**-yoh*
grapes	**l'uva**	***loo**-vah*
grilled	**alla griglia**	*ah-lah **greel**-yah*
ham cooked/cured	**il prosciutto cotto/crudo**	*eel pro-**shoo**-toh **kot**-toh/**kroo**-doh*
ice cream	**il gelato**	*eel jel-**lah**-toh*
lamb	**l'abbacchio**	*lah-**back**-kee-oh*
lobster	**l'aragosta**	*lah-rah-**goss**-tah*
meat	**la carne**	*la **kar**-neh*
milk	**il latte**	*eel **laht**-teh*
mineral water fizzy/still	**l'acqua minerale gasata/naturale**	***lah**-kwah mee-nair-**ah**-leh gah-**zah**-tah/nah-too-**rah**-leh*
mushrooms	**i funghi**	*ee **foon**-gee*
oil	**l'olio**	***loll**-yoh*
olive	**l'oliva**	*loh-**lee**-vah*
onion	**la cipolla**	*lah chee-**poll**-ah*
orange	**l'arancia**	*lah-**ran**-chah*
orange/lemon juice	**succo d'arancia/di limone**	***soo**-koh dah-**ran**-chah/dee lee-**moh**-neh*
peach	**la pesca**	*lah **pess**-kah*
pepper	**il pepe**	*eel **peh**-peh*
pork	**carne di maiale**	***kar**-neh dee mah-**yah**-leh*
potatoes	**le patate**	*leh pah-**tah**-teh*
prawns	**i gamberi**	*ee **gam**-bair-ee*
rice	**il riso**	*eel **ree**-zoh*
roast	**arrosto**	*ar-**ross**-toh*
roll	**il panino**	*eel pah-**nee**-noh*
salad	**l'insalata**	*leen-sah-**lah**-tah*
salt	**il sale**	*eel **sah**-leh*
sausage	**la salsiccia**	*lah sal-**see**-chah*
seafood	**frutti di mare**	***froo**-tee dee **mah**-reh*
soup	**la zuppa, la minestra**	*lah **tsoo**-pah, lah mee-**ness**-trah*
steak	**la bistecca**	*lah bee-**stek**-kah*
strawberries	**le fragole**	*leh **frah**-goh-leh*
sugar	**lo zucchero**	*loh **zoo**-kair-oh*
tea	**il tè**	*eel **teh***
herb tea	**la tisana**	*lah tee-**zah**-nah*
tomato	**il pomodoro**	*eel poh-moh-**dor**-oh*
tuna	**il tonno**	*eel **ton**-noh*
veal	**il vitello**	*eel vee-**tell**-oh*
vegetables	**i legumi**	*ee leh-**goo**-mee*
vinegar	**l'aceto**	*lah-**cheh**-toh*
water	**l'acqua**	***lah**-kwah*
red wine	**vino rosso**	***vee**-noh **ross**-oh*
white wine	**vino bianco**	***vee**-noh bee-**ang**-koh*

NUMBERS

1	**uno**	***oo**-noh*
2	**due**	***doo**-eh*
3	**tre**	*treh*
4	**quattro**	***kwat**-roh*
5	**cinque**	***ching**-kweh*
6	**sei**	***say**-ee*
7	**sette**	***set**-teh*
8	**otto**	***ot**-toh*
9	**nove**	***noh**-veh*
10	**dieci**	*dee-**eh**-chee*
11	**undici**	***oon**-dee-chee*
12	**dodici**	***doh**-dee-chee*
13	**tredici**	***treh**-dee-chee*
14	**quattordici**	*kwat-**tor**-dee-chee*
15	**quindici**	***kwin**-dee-chee*
16	**sedici**	***say**-dee-chee*
17	**diciassette**	*dee-chah-**set**-teh*
18	**diciotto**	*dee-**chot**-toh*
19	**diciannove**	*dee-chah-**noh**-veh*
20	**venti**	***ven**-tee*
30	**trenta**	***tren**-tah*
40	**quaranta**	*kwah-**ran**-tah*
50	**cinquanta**	*ching-**kwan**-tah*
60	**sessanta**	*sess-**an**-tah*
70	**settanta**	*set-**tan**-tah*
80	**ottanta**	*ot-**tan**-tah*
90	**novanta**	*noh-**van**-tah*
100	**cento**	***chen**-toh*
1,000	**mille**	***mee**-leh*
2,000	**duemila**	***doo**-eh **mee**-lah*
5,000	**cinquemila**	***ching**-kweh **mee**-lah*
1,000,000	**un milione**	*oon meel-**yoh**-neh*

TIME

one minute	**un minuto**	*oon mee-**noo**-toh*
one hour	**un'ora**	*oon **or**-ah*
half an hour	**mezz'ora**	*medz-**or**-ah*
a day	**un giorno**	*oon **jor**-noh*
a week	**una settimana**	*oona set-tee-**mah**-nah*
Monday	**lunedì**	*loo-neh-**dee***
Tuesday	**martedì**	*mar-teh-**dee***
Wednesday	**mercoledì**	*mair-koh-leh-**dee***
Thursday	**giovedì**	*joh-veh-**dee***
Friday	**venerdì**	*ven-air-**dee***
Saturday	**sabato**	***sah**-bah-toh*
Sunday	**domenica**	*doh-**meh**-nee-kah*

ACKNOWLEDGMENTS

The publisher would like to thank the following for their kind permission to reproduce their photographs:

Key: a-above; b-below/bottom; c-centre; f-far; l-left; r-right; t-top

123RF.com: Alkanc 75tl; Michele Bighignoli 95cb; Stefan Ember 75tr; gonewiththewind 207tl; jakobradlgruber 8cl; Brian Kinney 95bl; Malgorzata Kistryn 54cr; Erik Lattwein 11t; Christian Mueller 16cl; Anna Pakutina 104cr; Tosca Weijers 157tr, 158br; Wojciech Wyszkowski 231br.

4Corners: Pietro Canali 68-9b; Roland Gerth 156cl; Maurizio Rellini 47b, 143crb; Luca Da Ros 137, 220.

Agriturismo il Giardino, didactic farm: 29tr.

akg-images: Mondadori Portfolio / Remo Bardazzi 209br.

Alamy Stock Photo: AB Forces News Collection 28-9b; age fotostock 131br; ahc 198-9b; Arco Images GmbH © ADAGP, Paris and DACS, London 41br; 225tr; Vito Arcomano 191tr; Mario Llorca / Awakening 50crb; Azoor Photo 91cr; Frank Bienewald 37t; David Burton 44bl; Josse Christophel 55cb; Classic Image 91tr; Clearview 95crb; colaimages 55bc; David Collingwood 13t, 71clb; 115br; Cultura Creative (RF) 30bl; Ian Dagnall 102bl; DanitaDelimont.com / Gilles Delisle / Jaynes Gallery 24-5t; Adam Eastland 72bl, 92-3b, 110clb, 123bc; Elbardamu 25b; escapetheofficejob 209tr; Peter Forsberg 20bl; freeartist 186-7b, 210t; Eddy Galeotti 90-1, 142bl; Manfred Glueck 22cla; GoneWithTheWind 145t; Rik Hamilton 121, 122b; Brian Harris 48bl, 150tl; Hemis 33crb, 41cl, 123cra, 148-9t, 211tc; Rolf Hicker Photography 160t; Ted Horowitz 12clb; IanDagnall Computing 54-5t; imageBROKER 35cl, 148bl, 199cra, 230-1t; Independent Photo Agency Srl 43cl; 93tr; INTERFOTO 53tl; isogood 126-7; Paul Mayall Italy 46br; Jam World Images 167tl; John Kellerman 67tc, 80b, 85tl, 108br; Gunter Kirsch 174b; KODAKovic Fashion 146t; Joana Kruse 215bl; morten larsen 178br; Brian Lawrence 25cla; LianeM 157cra; Melvyn Longhurst 54tl, 115tl; LOOK Die Bildagentur der Fotografen GmbH 22-3ca, 40-1t, 213tl; David Lyons 20t; Dennis MacDonald 70-1t; MARKA 16cra, 47cra; Francisco Martinez 214t; mauritius images GmbH 39c; Emanuele Mazzoni 39br; Peter Moulton 112tl; MuseoPics - Paul Williams 66cr; Novarc Images 8-9b; Odyssey-Images 54br; PAINTING 72-3b; Gianni Pasquini 51tl; Peter Adams Photography Ltd 191b; PhotoBliss 178t; PhotosIndia.com LLC 53cla; PjrTravel 147br; Gillian Price 212b; Alex Ramsay 111bl; Realy Easy Star / Roberto Carnevali 144b, / Claudio Pagliarani © Niki de Saint Phalle Charitable Art Foundation / ADAGP, Paris and DACS, London 2018 233tr, / Lara Pessina 167br, / Toni Spagone 151tr; REDA &CO srl 51cr, 51clb, 161tr, 219tr; robertharding 30-1t, 145br; rudi1976 10ca; Scenics & Science 227tr; Wolfgang Schauf © ADAGP, Paris and DACS, London 2018 213br; SFM ITALY A 40br; StevanZZ 12t, 27br; Stockimo /uyennguyen 19tr; Wojciech Stróżyk 23tr, 181; SuperStock 113tl; Andriana Syvanych 33bl; The Picture Art Collection 97bl; The Picture Pantry 29cl; Domenico Tondini 31bl; TravelCollection 163tr; Paolo Trovò 198t; Universal Images Group North America LLC 52crb; kavalenkava volha 129t; Sebastian Wasek 26cla; Westend61 GmbH 28tl; Philip Wolmuth 55cra.

AWL Images: Marco Bottigelli 234-5; ClickAlps 19tl; Hemis 157tc, Tim Mannakee 32-3t; Mark Sykes 16br, 120cr, 202bl.

Bridgeman Images: Basilica San Francesco, Arezzo, Tuscany, Italy 180bc.

Canyon Park: 36-7b.

Depositphotos Inc: CAHKT 202t; Scrisman 52cb; Vrabelpeter1 93tc; wjarek 163br.

Dreamstime.com: Abxyz 104bl; Adisa 82-3b; Annamavritta 48-9t; Mila Atkovska 84bl; Frank Bach 183cla; Michal Bednarek 156-7b; Gordon

Bell 70bl; Boggy 110-1t; Botond 12-3b; Marco Ciannarella 182t; Wessel Cirkel 50clb; Sorin Colac 6-7; Maciej Czekajewski 190tl; Danciaba 143bl; Donyanedomam 22-3t; Eddygaleotti 53clb; Efired 75cr; Elbardamux 51tr; Ermess 4; Fisfra 26b; Prochasson Frederic 203; Filip Fuxa 164-5t; Georgiakari 50cl; Giuseppemasci 122-3t; Iryna1 136, 192; Wieslaw Jarek 201tr; Jborzicchi 50cra; Dragan Jovanovic 211br; Sergii Kolesnyk 78-9; Laszlo Konya 162bl; Horst Lieber 206b; Igiancarlo Liguori 68cra; Lianem 143clb; Vaclav Mach 27cl; Madrabothair 18tr, 96t; Marcovarro 107br; Aliaksandr Mazurkevich 218clb; Mineria6 24br, 72-3t; Minnystock 18-9ca, 37cl, 74-5b; Minoandriani 69tc; Martin Molcan 172-3t; Luciano Mortula 20crb, 27t; Roberto Nencini 38bl, 184br, 215cra, 224-5t; Nicknickko 125tl, 125tr; Corina Daniela Obertas 180cr; Małgorzata Paulina Pakuła 34br; Anna Pakutina 90cl, 93cla, 105, 112-3bc, 126cr, 176cra; Gianni Pasquini 50cr; Photofires 53crb; Photogolfer 90clb, 107tr; Photopips 185br; Rigmanyi 204t; M. Rohana 175tr; Romanotino 13cr; Scaliger 8clb; Shaiith 2-3, 201tl; Cellai Stefano 56-7, 60br, 61tl, 86-7, 98-9, 217tr; Aleksandr Stepanov 10clb; Stevanzz 49cb, 177, 226t, 228-9t; Timedreamer 104crb; Raluca Tudor 11crb, 202clb; Tupungato 77bl, 109t; Denisa Vlaicu 166b; Vvoevale 76-7t; Wallaceweeks 120b; Michael Warwick 37br; Wave Break Media Ltd 13br; Xbrchx 54cb; Alessandro Zappalorto 42br; Zatletic 201cra; Zummolo2014 50cla, 124.

Enoteca Pinchiorri: Gianni Ugolini 31cr.

Getty Images: AFP / Joseph Barrak 43br; Alinari Archives, Florence / Fratelli Alinari 55tr; Ayhan Altun 69tr, 131tl; Atlantide Phototravel 61cb, 102bc, 116-7,158-9t; Corbis /Stefano Bianchetti 53tr, / Leemage 160br, 92bl, / Summerfield Press 73bc; De Agostini Picture Library - DEA 26tr, 53bc, / G. Dagli Orti 52bc, 52t, / G. Nimatallah 35br, / S. Vannini 107cra; Sofie Delauw 11br; Danita Delimont 135bl, 168; EyeEm / Andrea Vittorio Castelli 132-3; Heritage Images 123cl; Jon Hicks 51br; Jean-Pierre Lescourret 8cla; Laura Lezza 20cr; Maremagnum 102cb, 128bl, 197crb, 228b; Roberto Moiola 227cl; Numbersix 216-7b; Sabino Parente 60cl, 62-3; Mondadori Portfolio 73cra, 126clb, 126crb, 126bl; by Andrea Pucci 29br; Francesco Prandoni / Redferns 42-3t; Ernesto S. Ruscio 45b; I just try to tell my emotions and take you around the world 134c, 138.

Courtesy of Gucci: 69cra.

iStockphoto.com: Eileen_10 71crb; Adisa 47cr; altmodern 207br; Borchee 66t; dp1974 44ca; faber1893 188-9; frankix 187tr, 205tr; georgeclerk 32bl; Hibiscus81 218-9b; Jag_cz 18tl; JordiRamisa 38-9t; NickNick_ko 36tl; ledmark31 107tl; marozne 94-5t; Ominojarre 49br; Ossiridian 185t; ROMAOSLO 150-1b; ronnybas 10-1b; SerrNovik 16t; starmaro 120cra; StevanZZ 22tl, 232-3b; TerryJ 46-7t, 82tl; Daniel Tomlinson 135t, 152; TommasoT 142-3t; tupungato 204cra; Matteo Viviani 44-5t; VladZymovin 196t; Zummolo 209c.

© Keith Haring Foundation: 198t.

Museo Galileo, Florence: 81br.

Museo Marino Marini Firenze: Studio Lorenzo Michelini 83tc.

Palazzo Strozzi: 81tl.

Rex by Shutterstock: AGF / Stefano Dalle Luche 51cl; EPA-EFE / Maurizio Degl Innocenti 71bl.

Robert Harding Picture Library: John Woodworth © ADAGP, Paris and DACS, London 2018 125cra.

Photo Scala, Florence: 180cl, 180clb, 180cb, 180bl; courtesy of the Ministero Beni e Att. Culturali 104cb; courtesy of the Ministero Beni e Att. Culturali e del Turismo 92tr.

SuperStock: age fotostock / Clickalps SRLs 34-5t, / Jose Peral 209c; agf photo 75cla; Silvio Fiore 91cb; fototeca gilardi 91br.

Front flap
123RF.com: Erik Lattwein cra; **Alamy Stock Photo:** Rik Hamilton cla; **AWL Images**: Tim Mannakee cb; **iStockphoto.com:** JordiRamisa br, StevanZZ tc, ROMAOSLO bl.

Sheet Map Cover
Dreamstime.com: Veronika G.

Cover
Front and spine: **Dreamstime.com:** Veronika Galkina.
Back: **Alamy Stock Photo:** The Picture Pantry c; **Dreamstime.com:** Veronika Galkina bc, Stevanzz tr; Getty Images: Danita Delimont cla.

For further information see: www.dkimages.com

The information in this DK Eyewitness Travel Guide is checked regularly.
Every effort has been made to ensure that this book is as up-to-date as possible at the time of going to press. Some details, however, such as telephone numbers, opening hours, prices, gallery hanging arrangements and travel information, are liable to change. The publishers cannot accept responsibility for any consequences arising from the use of this book, nor for any material on third party websites, and cannot guarantee that any website address in this book will be a suitable source of travel information. We value the views and suggestions of our readers very highly. Please write to: Publisher, DK Eyewitness Travel Guides, Dorling Kindersley, 80 Strand, London, WC2R 0RL, UK, or email: travelguides@dk.com

Penguin Random House

Main Contributers Sarah Lane, Christopher Catling, Anthony Brierley, Kerry Fisher, Tim Jepson, Carolyn Pyrah
Senior Editor Ankita Awasthi Tröger
Senior Designer Owen Bennett
Project Editor Elspeth Beidas
Project Art Editors Dan Bailey, Stuti Tiwari Bhatia, Vinita Venugopal, Hansa Babra, Ankita Sharma, Priyanka Thakur
Design Assistant William Robinson
Factchecker Marcella Simoni
Editors Louise Abbott, Rachel Thompson, Lauren Whybrow
Proofreader Debra Wolter
Indexer Helen Peters
Senior Picture Researcher Ellen Root
Picture Research Vishal Garvi, Sumita Khatwani, Deepak Negi, Sakshi Saluja
Illustrators Stephen Conlin, Donati Giudici Associati Srl, Richard Draper, Robbie Polley, Gillie Newman, Chris Dorr, Sue Sharples, Ann Winterbottom, John Woodcock, Martin Woodward
Cartographic Editor James Macdonald
Cartography Zafar-ul-Islam Khan
Jacket Designers Maxine Pedliham, Bess Daly
Jacket Picture Research Susie Peachey
Senior DTP Designer Jason Little
DTP Coordinator George Nimmo
Senior Producer Stephanie McConnell
Managing Editor Hollie Teague
Art Director Maxine Pedliham
Publishing Director Georgina Dee

First edition 1994

Published in Great Britain by Dorling Kindersley Limited, 80 Strand, London, WC2R 0RL

Published in the United States by DK Publishing, 345 Hudson Street, New York, New York 10014

19 20 21 22 10 9 8 7 6 5 4 3 2 1

A CIP catalogue record for this book is available from the British Library.

A catalog record for this book is available from the Library of Congress.

ISSN: 1542 1554
ISBN: 978 0 2413 5835 1

Printed and bound in China.

www.dk.com